THE JOURNAL OF THE ASSOCIATION OF MOVING IMAGE ARCHIVISTS

OVINGIMAGETHE MOVINGIMAGETHE MOVINGIMAGETHE MOV

SPRING 2010

The Moving Image (ISSN 1532-3978) is published twice a year in spring and fall by the University of Minnesota Press, 111 Third Avenue South, Suite 290, Minneapolis, MN 55401-2520. http://www.upress.umn.edu

Published in cooperation with the Association of Moving Image Archivists (AMIA). Members of AMIA receive the journal as one of the benefits of membership. For further information about membership, contact Janice Simpson, Association of Moving Image Archivists, 1313 North Vine Street, Hollywood, CA 90028 (or e-mail amia@amianet.org or visit www.amianet. org).

Postmaster: Send address changes to *The Moving Image*, University of Minnesota Press, 111 Third Avenue South, Suite 290, Minneapolis, MN 55401-2520.

Inquiries and information about manuscript submissions should be sent to the editors, Marsha Orgeron and Devin Orgeron (marsha_orgeron@ncsu. edu and devin_orgeron@ncsu.edu). All manuscripts should be submitted as a Microsoft Word e-mail attachment, double-spaced throughout, using 12-point type, with one-inch margins, using the *Chicago Manual of Style*, 15th edition.

Please allow a minimum of four months for editorial consideration.

Address subscription orders, changes of address, and business correspondence (including requests for permission and advertising orders) to *The Moving Image*, University of Minnesota Press, 111 Third Avenue South, Suite 290, Minneapolis, MN 55401-2520.

Subscriptions: Regular rates, U.S.A.: individuals, 1 year (2 issues) $30; libraries, 1 year $75. Other countries add $5 for each year's subscription. Checks should be made payable to the University of Minnesota Press. Back issues are $22.50 for individuals and $56.25 for institutions (plus $5 shipping for the first copy, $1 for each additional copy). *The Moving Image* is a benefit of membership in the Association of Moving Image Archivists.

The Moving Image is available online through *Project* MUSE, http://muse. jhu.edu.

Founded in 1991, the **Association of Moving Image Archivists** is the world's largest professional association devoted to film, television, video, and digital image preservation. Dedicated to issues surrounding the safekeeping of visual history, this journal covers topics such as the role of moving image archives and collection in the writing of history, technical and practical articles on research and development in the field, in-depth examinations of specific preservation and restoration projects, and behind-the-scenes looks at the techniques used to preserve and restore our moving image heritage.

REVIEWS

APPENDIX

Editors' Foreword

MARSHA ORGERON AND DEVIN ORGERON

What we have been calling "The Itinerant Issue" of *The Moving Image* was conceived at the Marriott hotel lobby bar during the 2008 Association of Moving Image Archivists (AMIA) conference in Savannah, Georgia. After a long day of sessions, Caroline Frick and Dwight Swanson pitched the idea for an issue of the journal dedicated to the underexplored phenomenon of itinerant filmmaking and exhibition practices. They had both been working for many years on the subject and had already established a network of scholars and archivists doing pioneering work that, with the publication of this issue, will pave the way for future research in, and attention to, this rich area of film history. *The Moving Image* seemed to them to be an ideal venue for disseminating this work to their archival and academic colleagues.

Perhaps needless to say, we agreed. What immediately appealed to us about the subject was that it had such clear relevance for both archivists and scholars and for the many in our field who wear both hats. It is, in fact, a kind of dream topic for a journal like *The Moving Image*, which exists at the intersection of a number of different communities whose work revolves around an interconnected (though perhaps not always seamlessly) archival universe. As new journal editors, we were keenly aware that Frick and Swanson were handing us a strong conceptualization for a thematically focused inaugural issue as well as an opportunity to work closely with a group of top-notch scholars and archivists, many of them longtime AMIA members.

As these pages make abundantly clear, the authors assembled in this issue are dedicated to their sometimes elusive subject and to sharing its importance with members of the AMIA community and beyond. Their considerations of itinerant filmmaking practices—including attempts to define, contextualize, and evaluate itinerant films—set the stage for what will, it is hoped, become an ongoing discussion about this important practice. Convenient as it is, however, the very term *itinerant* competes (even in these pages) with several others for naming rights on the subject. Though it usefully conveys a sense of the mobility that governs the filmmaking and exhibition practices explored here, *itinerant* has its own problematic associational baggage, with which some of our authors grapple. As the articles collected here indicate, there were many filmmakers who traveled from town to town making so-called local films (a term preferred by some to discuss this phenomenon), which they then exhibited to the communities in which they were shot.

These films were often variations on the same script or scenario, tailored to fit the local community and business culture. Once the films were shot and screened in the town in which they were made, the filmmakers moved on, usually—though not always—never to return again. The fate of the films themselves often rested in the hands of the theater owners or projectionists who exhibited them. Fortunately some held on to them, since they typically had the one and only copy ever made. Some of these surviving reels are now scattered in archives, many of them regional, across the country. We think it is fair to say that regional archives, in particular, have rescued this kind of film from what might have been total erasure from our cultural memory, although there have also been many individuals who, alongside and in tandem with regional film archives, have assisted in rescuing lost prints of this material. It is the sincere hope of our contributors that the publication of this issue of *The Moving Image* will further the cause of finding, saving, and studying these films, which—for reasons discussed throughout the issue—might be more likely than other films to suffer from neglect or incomprehension.

As many of the authors argue in this issue, local films produced by itinerant filmmakers offer valuable insights into the communities in which they were made. Their intimacy is often not unlike the home movie, though lurking in the immediate background of each frame is the (often false) allure of Hollywood cinema and its promises of, if not stardom and glamour, at least recognition. But because itinerant films existed in such a truly local sense, they are also a unique challenge for anyone trying to contextualize their historical value. They were not exhibited outside the communities in which they were made, and beyond local newspaper reports, they left virtually no record of their existence in their wake. How, then, can we reconstruct histories of such seemingly ephemeral media, and what place do these films have in archival and film historical hierarchies?

These questions constitute the core inquiries with which all the contributors to this issue contend. Clearly one of the things that draws researchers to this cinematic phenomenon is the allure of an elusive subject that requires rigorous and imaginative investigation. The scarcity and intangibility of many of these productions also explains the paucity of work in this area and, perhaps more critically, the difficulty of ascribing to it a definitive history. As the manuscripts for this issue were being prepared, for example, we received regular e-mails from our contributors alerting us to new discoveries—of extant films, of participants willing to share their memories of a particular film production, of a just-found newspaper reference confirming what had hitherto been an educated speculation. So though "The Itinerant Issue" is certainly the first sustained examination of this subject, it is far from definitive or static. That is, at least partly, what makes the phenomenon such an exciting and promising subject for future exploration.

No matter how they are named or what form they take—itinerant, local, traveling, town, hometown, chamber of commerce, and so on—these films and the ways in which they were exhibited possess commonalities that readers will encounter throughout these pages. Most of the essays and Forum pieces in this issue examine American filmmakers or filmmaking companies that worked regionally—though sometimes between regions—in the 1910s through the 1950s. As our authors collectively demonstrate, itinerant filmmaking should not be relegated to the margins of film history. What we might call the *itinerant impulse*, in fact, seems to form the very foundation of film history, and we might indeed have cause to rethink this history through the lens of itinerant producers and exhibitors. From Eadweard Muybridge's mobile photography studio to the Lumière brothers' roving cameramen, the cinema's prehistory and early years remind us repeatedly that the idea of mobile production and exhibition was there, as it were, from the get-go.

As **Caroline Frick** and **Martin L. Johnson**'s separate essays begin to demonstrate, there may well have been something particular in the combination of America's national character, the draw of its film industry, and its constantly shifting economy that resulted in what now appears to have been a concerted movement of journeying filmmakers who possessed a desire to capitalize on (largely small-town) America's desire to see and recognize itself. Focused on the work of filmmaker Melton Barker, Frick's "Jackrabbit Genius: Melton Barker, Itinerant Films, and Creating Locality" offers a thoughtful introduction to the history of the itinerant phenomenon and to the current state of scholarship within this emerging field. Her exhaustive research into Barker's career offers a valuable portrait of one itinerant producer at work, providing a concrete sense of how at least one such filmmaker went about his business over the course of an extraordinary career that spanned over forty years. With attention to Barker's knack for marketing and publicity—capacities shared by many an itinerant producer—Frick demonstrates the way these productions brought the patina of Hollywood to small-town America.

Frick's focus on a single filmmaker is interestingly contrasted by Martin L. Johnson's attention in "The Places You'll Know: From Self-Recognition to Place Recognition in the Local Film," not just to the filmmaking personalities behind this widespread phenomenon or to the allure of "seeing yourself" on screen, but to the importance of location. Johnson's strategy, which is girded by a carefully constructed theoretical logic, is to examine the value of location and the tangible impact itinerant films had on what he refers to as the "production of place" and "place recognition." His essay suggests a different critical framework that goes beyond the presumed fascination with self-recognition that motivated these productions and the prevailing scholarly emphasis on investigating individual itinerant filmmakers. Examining a home-talent film, a civic film, and a series of different local films shot in one city, Johnson asks us to think about this kind of film as being driven by the desire to document and recognize place.

Vanessa Toulmin's article, "Cuckoo in the Nest: Edwardian Itinerant Exhibition Practices and the Transition to Cinema in the United Kingdom from 1901 to 1906," is the only essay in this issue to focus on itinerant practices outside the United States, and this journey away from the American context is instructive. In this paradigm-shifting article, Toulmin argues that the role of the itinerant exhibitor has been overlooked and underestimated in current histories of film's transitional period in the United Kingdom. Guided by extensive archival work, Toulmin provides us with a new way to view film's exhibition history in the United Kingdom by illustrating the central role itinerant exhibitors played in the cinema's development into an entertainment institution during the Edwardian era. The success of the cinematograph and the cultivation of the habit of going to see moving pictures in particular, Toulmin argues, is a direct result of the practices of itinerant exhibitors who cultivated an interest in the new medium in an array of roving contexts. In fact, Toulmin explains, itinerant exhibitors would ultimately put themselves out of business because they succeeded in developing a desire for cinema through their marketing and exhibition strategies that would result in the permanent theatrical exhibition of moving pictures.

These three groundbreaking articles are complemented by a supersized Forum section, boasting contributions from archivists on the front lines of this emerging subfield. This is where the work of *The Moving Image* as a bridge between archival and scholarly worlds comes into focus. More than a periodic collection of essays, this journal represents the work of a large and diverse community whose relevance, influence, and survival depend on the flow of ideas, and this Forum section aims to promote awareness of itinerant materials in collections far and wide.

The Forum section's breadth, in fact, returns us to the issue of mobility with which we began this introduction. The itinerant phenomenon has been slippery, in part because it appears to have lacked a center or at least an interconnected web. Regional archives, personal collectors, old movie theaters, family members, and chambers of commerce possess itinerant films, but their fit within a larger constellation of films, collections, and scholars has been difficult to ascertain or establish. As a result, the films have often fallen through the cracks of collections large and small. So whereas Martin Johnson's essay reminds us not to lose sight of the films' individual locales, this issue's Forum gives some insight into the broader community that is forming around itinerant motion pictures and the need for interconnectedness and communication between archival collections and researchers.

Karan Sheldon's "Meeting the Movie Queen: An Itinerant Film Anchored in Place" is focused on regional film activism and on the Movie Queen films more specifically. The history Sheldon narrates shares with Martin Johnson's essay a call to archivists and scholars alike to tend to the details and importance of place. The interconnectedness of this Forum piece with Johnson's essay sets the stage for the remainder of the Forum pieces, many of which intersect with or supplement aspects of the scholarly arguments developed in the articles by Johnson, Frick, and Toulmin. **Margaret A. Compton**'s "Collecting Georgia's Hometown Movies: Acquisition, Ownership, Preservation, and Access" offers a fascinating chronology of one Georgia institution's relationship with local films. It is also—like Sheldon's piece—a working template for other archival institutions struggling over what to do with these films and facing similarly difficult decisions with regard to their preservation and dissemination.

Both Sheldon and Compton's emphasis on the specificity of place makes **Dwight Swanson**'s "'Wasn't That a Funny Thing That We Did?' Oral Histories of Itinerant Filmmaking" all the more relevant. Recognizing the value of firsthand accounts of the itinerant phenomenon and that this human resource is in diminishing supply, Swanson offers here a selective compilation of oral histories with participants in a number of itinerant productions. Making a case for the value of such testimony when conducting research in a field as devoid of primary evidence as itinerant productions often are, Swanson contends that the *personal*—an even more deeply localized iteration of *local*—aspect of these productions is essential to our understanding of the films' historic and contemporary value. **Albert Steg**'s "The Itinerant Films of Arthur J. Higgins" also pivots on first-person testimony, though here it is Steg's account of his own experiences as a collector and archivist trying to unite and understand the work of a particular itinerant filmmaker whose work surfaced in the eBay marketplace. Steg's essay articulates many of the competing desires associated with these materials, which include the challenges of discerning the proper home for films that were made in and of particular places. In addition to discussing the politics of collecting such films, Steg offers a case study of Higgins as an itinerant producer and shares one film from his collection that has been uploaded to the Internet Archive (http://www.archive.org/), thanks to the generosity of upstanding AMIA citizen Skip Elsheimer.

Our final two Forum pieces convey more stories from the trenches of itinerant film research. In "Itinerant Filmmaking in Knoxville in the 1920s: A Story Told through Unseen Movies," **Bradley Reeves** and **Louisa Trott** tackle films they have not seen and likely never will: a pair of lost itinerant films made in Knoxville, Tennessee. Reeves and Trott navigate the story of these films' productions in a fashion that reads like a good detective story, replete with twists and turns that seem the particular province of itinerant film research. They make a strong case for why itinerant films matter, especially for regional archives—repeating a refrain established by Compton and Sheldon. **Nathan Wagoner** shares his own harrowing tale of finding—and almost losing—a locally legendary itinerant production in "The *Huntingdon's Hero* Story." Wagoner, who is not an archivist but who took the time and energy to save a film that might have been lost had it not ended up in such determined hands, reminds us that one of the roles AMIA can play is that of an awareness-raising organization, with a set of best practices and resources that can guide those whose interest in saving films leads them to its doors.

All told, these essays and Forum pieces raise critical questions about the work of and in archives. Like the itinerants who made them, these films have a remarkable way of turning up in the strangest places. As archive budgets become increasingly fragile, efforts to take these materials seriously, to preserve them, to make them widely accessible, to research and publish information about them, and to persevere in finding ways to connect the dots of their production and exhibition are all the more crucial. "The Itinerant Issue" begins to work toward these goals. Our hope is that the ideas and issues presented here will spark continued discussion and debate to help focus attention on this important and scarcely understood phenomenon and its place in film history.

To this end, the issue ends with an ambitious document. With the aid of contributions from archivists and scholars working on itinerant producers, **Caroline Frick** has compiled a detailed, though admittedly in-progress, filmography of itinerant film productions and their whereabouts, whenever this information is available. Organized by company, individual filmmaker, and location, this filmography is designed to expand and evolve, and Frick hopes that its publication will inspire archivists to peer into their holdings to see if they might add to its breadth. We are certain that the essays contained here and the filmography will prove to be valuable resources for a wave of scholarship that is beginning to swell.

Finally, we would like to say a few words of thanks as we finish off our first issue as coeditors of *The Moving Image*. We are immensely grateful to the Department of English and the College of the Humanities and Social Sciences at North Carolina State University and feel especially fortunate that our dean, Jeffery Braden, and our department head, Antony Harrison, recognize the value of the work we are doing for the journal.

The process of transitioning into our positions has been quite a community effort. Luckily, we have had lots of help getting into the swing of things from the AMIA community, and we would like especially to single out assistance from the tireless and dedicated Dan Streible; former editors Chris Horak and Karen Gracey; former AMIA president Janice Simpson; our infinitely patient managing editor, Teri Tynes; and the indispensable Laura Rooney; as well as our colleagues at the University of Minnesota Press. We want formally and graciously to thank all our outgoing and continuing editorial board members and to welcome our new board members. We could not do the work of running this journal were it not for their dedication as solicitors and reviewers. Too often, all-but-behind-the-scenes work goes on with little more than a quick electronic "thanks" in return. We also want to acknowledge our ongoing review editors, Michael Baskett and Alison Trope.

Last but not least, we are indebted to Caroline Frick and Dwight Swanson for taking the initiative to bring the subject of itinerant filmmaking to us and for their unyielding commitment to, and enthusiasm for, the issue. We hope that they are the first of many AMIA members who will come to us with ideas for themed issues, articles, or Forum pieces. Our e-mail inboxes are open to the membership, and we hope that we will hear from you.

JACKRABBIT GENIUS

CAROLINE FRICK

Melton Barker, Itinerant Films,
and Creating Locality

It took Hal Roach about 10 days to shoot what I do in a day.
—Filmmaker Melton Barker, 1972

In mid-October 1975, a small announcement appeared at the bottom of page fourteen

in the Blytheville, Arkansas, *Courier-News*. With a headline alerting readers to a "Movie

Producer Arriving Next Week," the article quoted the manager of Blytheville's Ritz Theatre

describing the visiting producer, Melton Barker, as a true "veteran in the field."[1] Barker

would be traveling to Blytheville to shoot a short film featuring children from the com-

munity, talent not required: "The children do not have to be able to sing or dance to get

a part, all they have to do is talk over a mike to see if their voice will record."[2]

Enthusiastic advertisements promoting participation in the film production

proclaimed that Barker had made over a thousand such kids' movies and urged parents

to "get [their children] down there for this tryout and see what they can do . . . [as]

rehearsals and filming of the picture [would] not interfere with school work."[3] What the press material surrounding the 1975 film production neglected to mention, however, was that producer Melton Barker had collaborated with the Ritz Theatre several times before, journeying to Blytheville to shoot the very same children's short subject, the *Kidnappers Foil*, utilizing the exact same method and script in 1936, 1951, and 1969. In fact, in 1951, the Ritz Theatre owners had, with great fanfare, screened the most recent production alongside the 1936 version.

From the inception of cinema, so-called itinerant filmmakers like Melton Barker traveled throughout North America, Europe, Australia, and New Zealand—quite possibly the entire world. Motion picture exhibitors would enter into contracts with traveling producers to create community-based short subjects, then would market and promote the films' premieres, screening them alongside theatrical features. A large percentage of the material produced by traveling filmmakers did not utilize a narrative structure; rather the camera panned groups of schoolchildren, factory workers, and others in a style not altogether different from the early Lumière *actualités*. Other itinerant films either concocted some sort of limited narrative or mimicked popular Hollywood films and genres as a method to encourage community participation and amuse audiences. Itinerant films can be seen as a subgenre of what has become known within media history as the *local film*—movies with targeted geographical appeal featuring community landmarks, businesses, and most important, local men, women, and children.

Over the last thirty years, significant research on film exhibition and movie-going practice has proliferated within North American and European media studies, successfully challenging earlier academic emphasis on textual analysis or assumptions surrounding audience reception. The itinerant or traveling showman has played an important role in the histories of film exhibition, particularly those concerning the first half of the twentieth century. The work of itinerant film producers, including Melton Barker, among many others, adds much to locally oriented media research and historiography by exemplifying an understudied but intriguing and widely prolific mode of production and exhibition. Barker's long career, spanning the 1930s through the latter part of the 1970s, additionally challenges traditional film histories that often associate the traveling filmmaker with the pre–World War II period.

In 1906, a short *Billboard* article detailed the difficulty in compiling accurate statistical data for the burgeoning trade of film exhibition. The article noted that the entrepreneurial (and relatively undocumented) nature of early cinematic presentation could aptly be known as the "jack-rabbit . . . of the business of public entertaining. No one is in a position to even estimate the number . . . [of organizations] now in operation;

for an estimate covering today would be worthless tomorrow."[4] Unwittingly, *Billboard*'s frustration in tracking cinema industry growth in the early 1900s foreshadowed the difficulties faced by those researching the closely related phenomenon of itinerant film production in the first decade of the twenty-first century.

Jackrabbits—jumping or hopping from one place on a vast prairie to the next, leaving little to no evidence of their trail—provide an excellent metaphor for the traveling film producer. Substantive research into Barker's career, or that of any itinerant film-maker, for that matter, proves difficult because of the ephemeral nature of local films themselves. In as early as 1909, the motion picture trade press noted that films with local appeal, whether produced by itinerant filmmakers or regionally based cameramen, bore a close resemblance to short-term "topical subjects" that would "put to sleep an audience fifteen or twenty miles away."[5]

Very few of these local films still survive, and access to the extant materials remains hampered by the materials' disparate locations in abandoned warehouses, crowded domestic closets, or even on shelves in local or regional archival repositories around the globe. Indeed, film historian Stephen Bottomore's research on the topic sadly indicates that the early decades of the film industry viewed local films "like newspapers . . . looked over and then thrown upon the scrap heap."[6] Itinerant-produced films provide an exciting challenge and opportunity to both archivists and scholars for discovery, preservation, and study.

DEFINITIONAL CHALLENGES

Over the last several years, film historians have begun grappling with the value and sociocultural implications of local films, including those created by itinerant producers. Such interest has been driven in part by ongoing discoveries of key archival material; the growing validity of, and attention paid to, so-called orphan films; and significantly, the steady increase in availability of regional and local newspapers via archival collections on the Web. A number of articles have been published related to the itinerant film phe-nomenon, largely in reference to traveling film exhibition, that elucidate the significant potential for future research on local films. Such work also illustrates the frustrations inherent in attempting to study and create preliminary hypotheses for historical ephemera about which reliable information fluctuates daily, depending on what new material has been discovered and made accessible.

As one example, online searches about Melton Barker's production company and/or filming locations constantly change, whether via scholarly or more general search engines. Like other historical research, contradictory data emerge from a variety of sources, including newsprint, archival collections, and the films themselves. In the twenty-first century, researching Barker and the itinerant phenomenon involves a constant barrage of new, equally complicated reference material via the dozens on dozens of Kidnappers Foil participants who send e-mails with questions and reminiscences to the researcher in their own pursuit of knowledge. Without exception, all those who played a role in Barker's films (or those who knew that relatives and loved ones had) desperately hope to find the copy of the movie in which they appeared and wonder how to describe this kind of film to others.

The itinerant or traveling filmmaking phenomenon spanned from the inception of cinema to the 1980s. The modes of practice employed by, and motivations behind, such endeavor by individuals associated with itinerant production fell into a variety of broad categories. In some cases, professional newsreel cameramen began producing local films as side projects for additional money, while others served as truly independent filmmaking entrepreneurs. The well-documented work of H. Lee Waters, the owner and operator of a North Carolina photography studio, exemplifies those who, out of Depression-era necessity and/or interest, branched out into a new form of familiar commercial practice.[7]

Many traveling filmmakers, particularly in North America during the 1920s through the 1940s, claimed some professional experience with "Hollywood," including feature and/or newsreel production. Some of the movies produced by itinerant filmmakers showcased communities and citizens in what can be seen as buy-local campaigns paid for by individual businesses or chambers of commerce. Other films created by traveling producers depicted as many men, women, and children in the film as possible to increase the likely number of future audience members willing to pay to "see themselves on the screen." Itinerant producers who created films featuring a quasinarrative structure—in the United States, for example, the Kidnappers Foil, Movie Queen, or Man Haters series of films—commonly held some form of audition or competition to obtain their local casts and generate additional press and community interest.

Both narrative and nonnarrative itinerant films were promoted in community newspapers, advertised around town, and of course, publicly screened. In the late nineteenth century and into the twentieth, traveling showmen often exhibited the films. Beginning in the 1910s and into the 1920s, local theater owners screened the films alongside Hollywood movies or other industry-produced feature films. One aspect common to the traveling film phenomenon, as opposed to a one-off local or amateur production, was the repetitive, methodical nature of the production process. More specifically, traveling producers would journey to a variety of locations—rural and urban, small, medium, and large cities—and make the same film over and over, differentiated only by geography, population, and location. Melton Barker's career, a fascinating example of this itinerant mode of production, featured hundreds of Kidnappers Foil titles produced in different locations across the United States according to the same script for over forty years.

Today, many who hear about itinerant filmmaking find the phenomenon quaint and nostalgic. For others, however, the work of itinerant film producers embodies a different kind of romanticized past: one more malevolent, with the filmmaker appearing as more of a Professor Harold Hill type of character—a conniving city slicker who waltzes into small towns to swindle and steal. This injurious view, aptly described by Dan Streible as seeing itinerant filmmakers as "bamboozlers, small-time producers trying to outfox small-town exhibitors by trying to claim Hollywood credentials," has proven popular, particularly with twenty-first-century news reporters and documentary filmmakers interested in the historical trend.[8]

This pejorative conceptualization can be seen as linguistically connected to the use of the word *itinerant*, a term that has undergone an historical transition throughout the nineteenth and twentieth centuries. Negative connotations surround so-called itinerant people, particularly in certain regions around the globe, such as the United Kingdom and North America, for whom nomadic cultures tended to have been seen as more primitive than domesticated, agricultural societies. Gypsies, hobos, and carnies convey the core ambivalence and distrust with which particular social hierarchies have viewed the rootless or homeless. Within the United States, as just one example among many, the federal government treated the more domesticated or settled Native American tribes, such as the Hopis, Zunis, or Rio Grande Pueblos, with less force than those even just partly nomadic in the nineteenth century.[9]

The academic use of the term *itinerant*—seen in articles referencing early film exhibition from Kentucky and rural Arizona to Belgium, Luxembourg, and Québec—appears to have grown organically from research done by film historians using exhibitor trade press from the early twentieth century. Jackrabbit movie exhibitors received harsh criticism by local theater owners who felt frustrated that the traveling showmen were taking money from local pockets.[10] According to *National Geographic,* the term *jackrabbit* derived from the breed's long ears, reminding many of the proverbial jackass, now perhaps better known as an American colloquial insult.[11] The industry trade press utilized *jackrabbit* to describe and imbue the work of the traveling or itinerant showman with equally pejorative connotations. According to scholar Kathryn Fuller-Seeley, the term *itinerant* has evolved to be used, if somewhat casually, by film historians to "refer . . .

to anybody back in the day who traveled with a projector and/or film . . . [and] who was not tied to a local theater fulltime."[12]

Stephen Bottomore's essay "From the Factory Gate to the 'Home Talent' Drama: An International Overview of Local Films in the Silent Era," however, focuses less on the local within the context of film exhibition and more on the value of local films, some of which were produced by motion picture exhibitors themselves. In attempting to define the local film, Bottomore notes that this material's import lies less in the production context and more in the films' economic and cultural value to specific communities. Though many films can be seen as produced within local communities (i.e., on location), for Bottomore, local films specifically connote "considerable overlap between the people appearing in the film and those who watch it or are intended to watch it."[13] Bottomore's work significantly shifts the value of the film text—or the film's generic classification— from how it was produced and by whom to the more significant status of the spectator as active participant and active consumer. The itinerant film, therefore, occupies a unique subgenre beneath that of the local film, that is, local films made by traveling producers for consumption within very specific communities.

Literature investigating the history of moviegoing practice utilizes the term *local* in different ways and, as mentioned previously, has proven influential in the early interpretations of itinerant film production. Rarely, however, does conventional film or media history look outside its own area to interrogate the commonly held assumptions surrounding who participates when in determining what constitutes and/or defines the local. Contemporary globalization theory, arguably an outgrowth of critical debate surrounding claims of cultural, and more specifically, media imperialism in the 1970s and 1980s, provides relevant language and insight to assist with better understanding the value and importance of the itinerant-produced local film.

Kathryn Fuller-Seeley's introduction to her recent edited work, *Hollywood in the Neighborhood: Historical Case Studies of Local Moviegoing*, acknowledges that recent studies of global media distribution and reception point to important trends in how the local continues to be reinvented and adapted. Global identities, whether rural or urban, remain interconnected with the local and, for Fuller-Seeley and writing partner George Potamianos, underscore the importance of local "moviegoing histories . . . [in better understanding] the intersections, conflicts, refashionings, and adoption of the mass, the national, the modern, and the urban."[14] Many film historians have investigated relationships between the advent of the motion picture and societal changes wrought by the modern era. Such research, grounded within an historical prism, often approaches cinema as a so-called modernizing force that affected both urban and rural communities.[15] Globalization theory, too, focuses on the role of the media industries as a modernizing force, but within a more contemporary context, and offers assistance to the film historian grappling with similar questions and concerns.

Local films, particularly those imbued with the romance of the nomadic producer behind them, are too often nostalgically viewed as a more organic or real artifact of community positioned against Hollywood's corporate product, providing cultural opposition to the homogenizing force of transnational corporations. Indeed, when local films incorporate aspects of Hollywood, whether through imitation of stars or generic forms, they are often seen as capitulation. Dan Streible's analysis of a 1926 itinerant film from rural South Carolina notes that "in the end, what makes *Anderson on Parade* and similar films disappointingly conventional is their surrender to Hollywood, their abandoning the potential for a distinct alternative."[16] Such "disappointment" echoes globalization theory's concern over the tendency to view modern culture as that of "local assertions against globalizing trends . . . in which the assertion of 'locality' or Gemeinschaft is seen as the pitting of subaltern 'universals' against the 'hegemonic universal' of dominant cultures and/or classes."[17]

With its emphasis on cultural hybridity and complex media interdependence, globalization scholarship challenges the tendency to position local films in a binary opposition with transnational corporate product. Professor Roland Robertson's work in contextualizing the historical trajectory of global theory offers an important intervention for media historians and archivists interested in better understanding local films and their value for contemporary audiences:

> Much of the talk about globalization has tended to assume that it is a process which overrides locality. . . . This interpretation neglects . . . the extent to which what is called local is in large degree constructed on a trans- or super-local basis. In other words, much of the promotion of locality is in fact done from above or outside. Much of what is often declared to be local is in fact the local expressed in terms of generalized recipes of locality.[18]

Robertson, among other globalization theorists, looks closely at the evolution of so-called *glocalization* as a corporate approach. Though the derivation of the term stems from the efforts of Japanese farmers to adapt macrofarming techniques to more local conditions, Japanese businesses in the 1980s increasingly utilized the term to describe tailoring global strategies to local environs. Glocalization, seen by some as pure "micromarketing," importantly and transparently articulates the calculated manufacturing of what is seen (and sold) as community as well as the individuals and cultures that embody this particular form of local.[19] Anthropologists, sociologists, and others join globalization scholars in looking at tourism, an increasingly vital component to the world economy, as the epitome of how marketing the local equates to profit.

Throughout the twentieth century, itinerant filmmakers shrewdly made a business by championing the value of seeing local communities on the big screen, even decades before globalization theorists debated the relative merits and impacts of such endeavors. By partnering with chambers of commerce or theater owners, itinerant film-makers actively participated in, and capitalized on, the construction of the local.

ITINERANT CASE STUDY: MELTON BARKER

In the early 1930s, Melton Barker launched his career as a traveling filmmaker, marketing himself as "Producer and Originator of the Local Gang Comedy idea."[20] In his publicity material, Barker utilized the term *local* repeatedly, reinforcing the unique opportunity offered through his service—giving children a chance to appear on the silver screen right there at home. Whether consciously or not, Barker's sales pitch echoed the discourse espoused by early folklorists, intellectuals, and artists involved with the American regionalist movement of the early twentieth century, who strove to help keep and indeed create distinct differences in local communities across the country.[21]

Despite such comparisons, however, Barker's work, like that of other itinerant filmmakers, inspires more curiosity, amusement, and outright derision than awe. Although Barker did not spend his entire professional career on the road, he spent a great deal of his life traveling from town to town, encouraging locals to become a community, if only temporarily via the medium of celluloid. A good portion of e-mails received in response to news stories about Barker, or via the Texas Archive of the Moving Image Web site, which streams a number of Kidnappers Foil versions, convey amusement over Barker's enterprise and request information on how to obtain copies of his films. Other correspondence registers disbelief that the traveling Texas filmmaker could have been anything other than a charlatan, evoking wariness toward more peripatetic, nomadic lifestyles. Exacerbating the tendency to suspect Barker's true intent remains the frustrating fact that outside the most basic and often cryptic information sources (census records, newspaper clippings, or fading memories), data surrounding Melton (aka Mel) Barker's career remain elusive. For twenty-first-century researchers, tracking the Texan filmmaker's trajectory is not unlike that of tracking the path of his fellow prairie dweller, the jackrabbit.

Born Ennis Melton Barker in 1903 and raised in a number of communities across the Lone Star State, Barker claimed to have begun his professional life by working with a number of major Hollywood studios in Los Angeles during the 1920s.[22] No corroborative evidence has emerged thus far either to prove or disprove Barker's claim of Hollywood affiliations. In early 1931, however, the *Dallas Morning News* covered a variety of local theater productions in which a young Melton Barker appeared as a bit player. By the end of that year, the paper reported that a "talking motion picture" would be incorporated as a critical component to the play, *Spread Eagle*, opening at the Dallas Little Theater.[23] Originally

Melton Barker, circa 1930s. Author's collection.

staged on Broadway and described as a "melodrama of the flag-waving type . . . at once a comedy and an expose of jingoism," *Spread Eagle* told the story of a wealthy man who sponsors a revolution in Mexico to see a greater return on his mining properties there.[24] The short sound film portion purportedly depicted the characters embroiled in heated battle in Mexico.

Although no one has discovered any information to tie Barker to the production of the film used in the play, the *Dallas Morning News* only a few months later referred to a local "All-Dallas Talky" directed by Melton Barker, which supports the hypothesis that Barker had already begun working not only with film but with sound-on-film technologies as part of that theatrical production.[25] Most important, the newspaper reported that Barker's work making local Dallas films in 1932 was particularly noteworthy because of his reputed discovery of Spanky McFarland, one of the most popular child stars of Hal Roach's Our Gang series, who had begun working with Roach that same year.

Throughout his decadeslong film career, Barker claimed to have been the one responsible for Spanky's stardom, having worked with the child in Dallas advertising campaigns for local bread and ice cream companies in early 1930. Although the veracity of Barker's assertion might never be proven definitively, publicity photographs circulated to the press by the filmmaker of himself with Spanky in front of a Hal Roach production truck support the Texan's claimed celebrity connection.

KID MOVIE TO BE MADE IN GALVESTON

Melton Barker of Hollywood who will come to Galveston soon to screen a local two-reel kid comedy with a cast of 100 Galveston boys and girls, is shown here with Spanky McFarland, one of his child discoveries who is now starring in Hal Roach comed'es in the film city. The local movie is being sponsored by the Martini Theater.

> Melton Barker and Spanky
> McFarland. *Galveston Daily
> News,* September 16, 1937.

Barker, throughout his career, referred to his work with Spanky McFarland as sparking his idea to create local gang comedies. However, many entrepreneurial filmmakers in the late 1920s shared Barker's shrewd assessment that producing community short subjects with local children mimicking Hal Roach's popular films would prove successful. Newspaper records and motion pictures deposited in regional collections indicate that numerous local Our Gang films were produced all over North America during this period, from Manitoba to South Carolina, from Massachusetts to New Mexico.[26]

The proliferation of these kinds of local narratives should be unsurprising. The mid-1920s through the mid-1930s has often been called the child star era because of the unquestionable power and popularity of performers like Shirley Temple, Jackie Coogan, and Mickey Rooney, alongside the sheer numbers of child star vehicles produced at this time. Moreover, the majority of these child actors started their careers in short subjects before moving into features. For those involved in motion picture production, as well as for movie patrons, the "kiddie comedy short" was closely associated with Hal Roach and his enormously popular Our Gang series, but Roach was only one of many to capitalize on the market for short films featuring children as lead players.

In as early as the mid-teens, Twentieth-Century-Fox had produced and distributed one of the earliest children-oriented featurette series, the Sunshine Kiddies. Similar series by companies and filmmakers, such as Mack Sennett, with his Hollywood Kid shorts; Educational Pictures, with the Baby Burlesks and Juvenile Comedies series; and Larry Darmour's Mickey McGuire series, further illustrate the proliferation of the child gang comedy genre that dominated screens during the 1920s and 1930s.[27] In Mexico, independent filmmaker Adela Sequeyro produced her own iteration, albeit one more dramatic than most gang comedies of the period. *Diablillos de arrabal (Suburban Devils)* was released in 1938 with a title more titillating than its earlier working designation, *Los héroes del barrio (The Heroes of the Neighborhood).*[28]

But Hal Roach's success with the Our Gang series proved the most enduring and popular, even outside North America. In the 1920s, British Screen Productions created a series titled Hoo-Ray Kids that was a blatant copy of Roach's film troupe starring an overweight kid, a black child, and even a freckled youth modeled after the most popular Our Gang actor of the silent era, Mickey Daniels.[29] Barker's link to Spanky and thus to the quintessential rags-to-riches Hollywood star narrative played a key role in his success as an itinerant—or at the very least, independent—filmmaker. His purported experience with Hollywood films, producers, and celebrity unquestionably lent greater credence to his local endeavors in north central Texas, particularly in the earliest stages of his career.[30] By the end of 1932, Barker had completed two local productions in the Dallas area, one in particular called *Carnival Days*, which starred fifty "Dallas Rascals" selected and trained by Barker himself.[31] Newspaper coverage of the films' production schedules and premieres at the local theaters noted that the audiences would have the opportunity to vote regarding who appeared to be the "best performer" in the films. The winner would receive one hundred dollars and a trip to Hollywood's "film colony."[32]

Americans across the country were well aware of the celebrity and wealth of Roach's child stars. The child star era, arguably ushered in by Roach and his peers, witnessed thousands of stage parents pouring into Los Angeles to find fame and fortune through their children, again echoing the contemporary publicity surrounding the effortless rise from obscurity by the Hollywood film star. The reality of overnight movie celebrity, however, remained more elusive: "Of the 140,000 children to interview for parts in the Our Gang series over a period of seventeen years, only 176 appeared on the screen, and a scant forty-one were put under contract; that put the chances for any remuneration at all at 3,400 to one."[33]

Thus, though the lure of Hollywood success and potential stardom certainly played a key role for many participants in Barker's films, most parents would have realized that the odds of such success remained quite low. Instead, what appears to be a more common trait shared by the child (and the few adult) actors who participated in Barker's films is that which Barker himself felt: passion for Hollywood movies and film culture generally. Interviews with Barker's family members as well as viewings of Barker's own home movies indicate that the Dallas native entertained a lifelong love of Hollywood.³⁴ He often traveled to Los Angeles, and he owned and operated a number of movie theaters in different regions of Texas throughout the forty years he spent in the film business. Despite that the hardworking entrepreneur's life on the road included a lifelong struggle with alcoholism and contributed to three divorces, Barker strove to blend his love of Hollywood product with a shrewd ability to market and create his own local version of filmed entertainment. Barker's Kidnappers Foil films present an excellent example of American moviemaking, a truly hybrid form that acknowledged both the popularity of Hollywood features and its attendant consumer culture in tandem with the entrepreneurial opportunities and sheer enjoyment afforded by making movies.

Barker's own marketing materials bear out this complicated negotiation. His promotional brochure (ca. late 1940s to early 1950s) titled "The Kid Movie: The Inside Story by Melton Barker Productions" begins with a sobering take on the reality of the average American's chance at stardom: "Most every one [sic], young and old alike, have at one time or another, felt that they would like to be a famous movie star, and to have a career in the movies. But it is only a dream—that very few ever realize, because as the old proverb says, 'Many are called but few are chosen.'"³⁵ Barker's brochure continues by promoting the value of Barker's work in allowing children's dreams to come true by appearing on the big screen locally. Furthermore, Barker's stated "pride and satisfaction" as well as his niche micromarketing approach stemmed from giving children the "opportunity to see themselves in the movies without the necessity of having to go to Hollywood."³⁶ Barker's work, alongside that of other itinerant filmmakers, must be seen as a unique component of efforts by individuals, businesses, and community leaders (including theater owners) to define and cultivate an active local culture and economic base.

From his earliest kid films in Dallas in 1932, Barker initiated an itinerant filmmaking career that continued until his death in a Mississippi hotel room in 1977, only two years following his fourth and last trip to Blytheville, Arkansas. Although the itinerant filmmaking phenomenon appears to have peaked during the 1930s and 1940s and is certainly most identified with the Depression era, Barker not only worked successfully throughout the latter part of the twentieth century but also continued to experiment with new technologies. A 1975 advertisement for his film work in Paris, Texas, depicts Barker with a large camera displaying the phrase "Mel Barker TV Shows" painted on its side,

IMPERSONATIONS

MARX BROTHERS — MAE WEST — LAUREL & HARDY

CAN YOU IMPERSONATE YOUR FAVORITE MOVIE,
RADIO OR VIDEO STAR?

possibly indicating Barker's attempt to launch his own version of kids programs to complement, or even compete with, the popular global franchise *Romper Room*.

From Melton Barker's 1950s brochure. Courtesy of Jack Duncan, McKinney, Texas.

Like other independent filmmakers even today, Barker appeared to have worked on a variety of media projects, not just children's short subjects. Other genres included early advertising films, like those he shot with young Spanky McFarland, and chamber of commerce or buy-local campaign titles like *The Cape Girardeau Story*, filmed in Missouri. Undoubtedly, however, Barker's real success was his work with children, specifically in two different series: Last Straw and Kidnappers Foil. With a nod to Hal Roach as well as to the many producers of early serial narratives familiar to moviegoers across the United States, both of Barker's series featured local gangs of children battling either kidnappers (in the case of Kidnappers Foil) or bank robbers (in the case of Last Straw).[37]

The most successful film series for Barker was the Kidnappers Foil, which he shot in over 150 locations found thus far. Barker sometimes filmed three versions with three different cinemas during one visit (as he did in San Antonio in the early 1930s) and returned to a number of cities three or four times throughout his career. With a large portion of his work in Texas and across the Southwest, Barker advertised in both English- and Spanish-language newspapers to encourage as much participation (and profit) as possible. Featuring a basic plot of kidnapping, rescue, and a celebratory talent show, each Kidnappers Foil film shares virtually the exact same dialogue, camera shots, and characters. The talent show material, even from such disparate locations as

McAllen, Texas, on the U.S.–Mexico border, to Brainerd, Minnesota, features similar acts and routines, albeit with different accents and performance styles. Importantly, both the Kidnappers Foil and Last Straw series showcased characters with names like "Betty Davis" and impersonations of other notable Hollywood film stars.

Barker's reference and appeal to familiar cinematic narratives and stars under-score the value and success of putting local citizens in "the movies"—certainly a step beyond the turn-of-the-twentieth-century novelty of "seeing oneself on the screen" to the pleasure and fun of playing "Hollywood."

Barker's mode of production, including substantive preplanning and rehearsal, served pragmatic purposes (i.e., so that the children's voices could be audible on the microphones operated by Barker himself or one of his two-man crew) and, at the same time, capitalized on the Hollywood "dream factory" myth of rags-to-riches fame. Barker required auditions for his local talent or stars as well as three to four days of training before one to two days of shooting. Although interviews with Kidnappers Foil participants suggest that the vast majority of parents saw the filming as a bit of fun, several bemusedly reference the success of Barker's claim that his narratives would showcase whether local children could really make it as Hollywood stars.[38] Noting in the press that filmmaking was an expensive undertaking, and not one that allowed him to become wealthy, Barker charged fees for the special training necessitated to be in the film—fees that appeared to vary from town to town, from four dollars to rumors of twenty dollars.[39]

A Chattanooga, Tennessee, local theater owner received strong feedback in 1949 from patrons who felt "embarrassed" that they needed to pay a fee for children to participate after the kids had auditioned with over a thousand others in the community.[40] In a rare interview about his production process with the Greenville, Mississippi, *Delta Democrat-Times*, Barker expressed frustration when he was asked about critics who castigated him for his work being a "money-making gimmick."[41] Barker said that he grew tired of such complaints from "ignorant" people, hoping instead that community members would continue to support his work so that they would "see it's legitimate. The kids get a big kick out of being in a movie, and besides, I work too hard for this to be a fake."[42]

CONTEMPORARY VALUE

Barker's irritation with being called a fake indicates his acute awareness of the many criticisms leveled at his work, his identity as a seemingly rootless itinerant filmmaker. However, as Dwight Swanson points out in his contribution in the Forum section of this issue, the vast majority of individuals who participated in Barker's films remembered the experience with little animosity and even reminisced with some fondness. The images of people smiling, laughing, or even ducking from the camera in itinerant films testify to general human curiosity about, interest in, and/or discomfort with seeing oneself or one's family and community on the big screen.

A variety of hypotheses can be formulated to attempt to explain the significance of the itinerant film experience and, perhaps more important for the archival and academic communities, the value of the local film artifact today. Moving image archives, often pressured by bureaucratic demands and assumptions, largely tout their collections' worth to university communities. However, itinerant or local films, along with other orphan works, may present more profound data and appeal to less professional but far more numerous organizations, including genealogical and historical societies, chambers of commerce, civic interest groups, and even K–12 educational levels.

From the inception of cinema, the lure of "seeing yourself on film" proved an effective promotional strategy for recreational entertainment, as in the case of the turn-of-the-century Mitchell and Kenyon films as well as in an array of other contexts.[43] For example, in his article "'Watch the Picture Carefully, and See If You Can Identify Anyone': Recognition in Factual Film of the First World War," the Imperial War Museum's Roger Smither details how many British citizens were interested in and encouraged to look for friends and family filmed on European battlefields. Furthermore, U.K. troops' acknowledgment of being filmed by waving or smiling at the camera complemented diary entries and letters indicating their hopes of perhaps being recognized by people at home.[44] Tracking the history of pleasure through cinematic recognition in all kinds of media—from the earliest days of movies to contemporary reality television—provides clues that lead us toward a better understanding of the enduring popularity of the image as well as media's role in the creation of imagined communities from the local to the national and global.

Perhaps the most important contemporary use for itinerant-produced films is to enable one's relations, whether by blood or simply from the community, to see their past in moving images, thus evoking Stephen Bottomore's assessment that the most significant audience for these films is the local community itself. Citing the early trade press from 1912, Bottomore's assertion confirms that human interest in locally produced media remains the same, even in the first decades of the twenty-first century: "There can be no two opinions as to the value of the local topical film. . . . Everyone loves to see himself, or herself, or friends or children . . . and the local topical is the best means of gratifying this desire."[45]

Indeed, many individuals who had participated in itinerant films have searched for years for copies, which indicates the value of these films as quasifamily and community records. When faced with the reality that the Tupelo version of the Kidnappers Foil appeared to have been lost, one Mississippi resident wrote up everything she could remember about her experience with the Barker production and gave the memoir to her brother as a gift in 2005 because he, too, had performed in the film and desired a copy.[46] Clearly personal nostalgia for times past—particularly memories from childhood—contributes to the desire to see and thus preserve local films. Nostalgia, derived from the Greek words *nostos*, meaning "return home," and *algia*, meaning "a painful condition," implies, in its most basic sense, a "painful yearning to return home."[47] Although the term has developed to become most commonly identified with a general longing for the past, nostalgia has always included a sense of homesickness—of locality.

The historical relationship between nostalgia and home/community merits attention, particularly in reference to the itinerant filmmaking phenomenon: an independent, entrepreneurial mode of production capitalizing on, and indeed creating, a unique, shared community experience. In the town of Childress, a small community in the Texas Panhandle visited twice by Melton Barker in the 1930s and 1940s, the discovery of two extant prints of Kidnappers Foil galvanized local civic leaders who had been striving to obtain historical landmark status for their abandoned movie theater downtown.[48] Barker's films, and their subsequent preservation, created new pathways to communicate with those who had moved away and those who remained committed to reversing the difficult economic trends facing them.[49]

The ongoing fascination with the production background of Barker's films and the tale of local rediscovery, combined with the sheer entertainment factor provided by the Childress versions of Kidnappers Foil for all members of the community today, young and old, continues to rally community support for local preservation efforts. Copies now proliferate within the community, across the state, and across the country, which are used by many to identify family and friends.

An additional example of the community value of the local film lies in the work of another Texas itinerant filmmaker by the name of Shad Graham. A former studio newsreel cameraman during the 1930s, Graham launched a "Texas Newsreel" company in the post–World War II period that shot buy-local campaign films commissioned largely by chambers of commerce across the country. One film from a popular Graham series, *Our Home Town: San Marcos*, became a viral video of sorts for the Texas Archive of the Moving Image (TAMI) in spring 2009. A news reporter for the *San Marcos Record*, on hearing how residents in the community had been telling one another about the film streaming online

Frame from *The Kidnapper's Foil,* San Marcos, Texas (circa 1930s). Texas Archive of the Moving Image.

via the TAMI video library, wrote a small piece for the paper about the number of emotional reactions to seeing the 1949 Graham film. The article, quoting one of the members of the San Marcos Heritage Association, articulates the value of itinerant film productions to contemporary audiences, stating that whereas "photographs [were] one thing . . . seeing live videos of . . . meetings and . . . buildings, it's simply amazing. . . . It increases your sense of community."[50] By the end of the weekend following the article's publication, the film had been viewed over six thousand times and continues to climb toward being one of the most watched films in the TAMI collection. As of summer 2010, the film had been viewed nearly twelve thousand times.

Like many orphan film genres, local films and the accompanying subgenre of the itinerant film prove an important addition to the traditional motion picture canon, but only if adequately contextualized and questioned—and not just merely presented as an oppositional form to the Hollywood corporate product. Local films reflect film historian Gregory Waller's description of "small-town theatres as discursive construct, managerial strategy, motion picture industry component, and orphaned 'little fellow'; further, they [provide a] site of social interaction."[51]

New modes of access to archival film provided by the Web are, in turn, increasing the value of local films as sites of such social interaction or exchange. Web 2.0 technologies further enlivened the viral appeal of *Our Home Town: San Marcos* by offering tagging opportunities by members of the community. For example, the film depicts a bank building in downtown San Marcos about which little was noted in the film's audio track. The TAMI library's tagging capability allowed members of the public to note that "the State Bank and Trust Building was robbed by the Newton Gang in 1924, and probably by Machine Gun Kelly in 1933. The building was featured in the 1972 film *The Getaway* starring Steve McQueen and Ali McGraw."[52]

Synched to the point in the film that features the footage of the bank, the information then moves to another tag added by a different member of the public and perhaps of interest to another community or family group: the name of the "longtime bank teller," Will Goforth.[53] Thus the public actively participates in offering information heretofore unknown and valuable to an already understaffed heritage organization and provides concrete benefits to archive, participant, collection, and community. A genealogist might be interested in tracking descendents of Will Goforth, but the local San Marcos Chamber of Commerce might want to capitalize on the bank's notoriety in Hollywood history to increase regional tourism. Itinerant films, with a new life online, have encouraged local communities to "see themselves" on a multiplicity of screens— both large and small—and are once again taking part in the ever-changing conception of local identity.

CONCLUSION

Heretofore lost and neglected itinerant films produced in varying countries around the globe reveal new perspectives that should be included in media histories of twentieth-century production, distribution, and exhibition practice—a particularly acute addition in the context of the United States, where Hollywood continues to cast the longest shadow. A contemporary scholar interested in researching film-related history in Blytheville, Arkansas, would discover quickly that the small city was once home to Hollywood actor George Hamilton, aka the "Tanned One," during his youth but would be far less likely to find mention of the four Kidnappers Foil films produced there over the last century.

Whether called local views, itinerant films, community films, or local films, the information available about such films remains sparse and disparate, causing them frequently to be perceived as one-off titles rather than archival materials worthy of substantive research. In the case of Melton Barker, separate Kidnappers Foil film prints have been donated or collected in historical societies, regional archives, and national repositories across the United States over the last several decades. Connections between a print at the Nebraska State Historical Society, two prints at the George Eastman House in Rochester, New York, and a couple of prints in a personal collection in the Texas Panhandle remained unknown and certainly unconnected until fairly recently. Itinerant-produced material evidences the ongoing need for and value of a more substantive subnational network of media collections—not just national repositories devoted to varying genres but a true federal system of media archives and preservation consortia. In fact, the Imperial War Museum's Roger Smither pointedly acknowledges the vital role of the United Kingdom's "highly developed network of national and regional film archives" to the research undertaken thus far on the local film genre generally.[54]

With their regional and locally specific content, itinerant films provide archivists and scholars intriguing and certainly entertaining artifacts with which to examine communities traditionally underrepresented in images produced by national or transnational production companies. Melton Barker, with his long-lasting career that spanned from the heyday of the Hollywood studio era well into the broadcasting age, might serve as a harbinger of future research to come that will further challenge traditional notions of the relationship between all areas of media production. Itinerant producers like Barker complicate easy assumptions related to our current twenty-first-century era of media convergence, copyright challenges, and the role of the amateur in social media sites.

Globalization theory's interrogation of the local complements and enhances traditional film history practice to caution the contemporary viewer against oversimplifying—or aggrandizing—the intent of community participants as well as those of the itinerant producer in the creation of local films. The media produced by itinerant filmmakers help complicate binary oppositions constructed between amateur and professional, corporate and independent. Furthermore, local communities, armed with copies of such material, can again utilize the films to create opportunities to re-create their local identities. But this can only happen if the films survive, are discovered, and access to them is created and cultivated.

Melton Barker's marketing materials indicated his own belief in the long-term value of his films: "The picture will be made here in the city, using the parks or other scenic spots for location, and upon it's [sic] completion, becomes the property of the theatre. They can, of course, show it, whenever and as often as they desire. The picture is a permanent record of the children, and will remain a memento of their childhood in the years to come."[55] As nomadic as he was, even at times inspiring distrust on the part of parents suspect of his motives, Barker had real foresight in envisioning the value of preservation and access to the films he produced for the benefit of the communities involved.

As remembered by former relatives as well as many of his films' participants, Melton Barker's often gruff manner—which included threatening competitors with jail, barking orders at the hundreds (if not thousands) of children with whom he worked (and purportedly detested), and a penchant for too much drink—makes for a wonderful analogy with the fast-moving, independent prairie hares historically associated with the itinerant cinema showmen, a breed commonly spotted boxing at one another on those same Texas plains driven time and again by Melton Barker Productions. Like other itinerant filmmakers, Melton Barker's hard work, clever entrepreneurial efforts, and, indeed, reputation deserve to be resurrected. But somehow, I like to think that Mel Barker would shrug off academic accolades of artistic auteur and prefer instead to be associated with the peripatetic and decidedly scrappy nature of the Texas jackrabbit.

NOTES

1. "Movie Producer Arriving Next Week," *Courier-News*, October 15, 1975, 14.

2. "Tryouts for Movie Set for Wednesday," *Courier-News*, October 21, 1975, 7.

3. Ibid.

4. "The Jack-Rabbits of the Movie Business," originally published in *Billboard*, October 1906, and quoted in George Pratt, "Images," *Image: The Bulletin of the George Eastman House of Photography* 10, no. 3 (1961): 10.

5. Stephen Bottomore, "From the Factory Gate to the 'Home Talent' Drama: An International Overview of Local Films in the Silent Era," in *The Lost World of Mitchell and Kenyon: Edwardian Britain on Film*, ed. Vanessa Toulmin, Simon Popple, and Patrick Russell (London: BFI, 2004), 37.

6. Ibid.

7. In addition to articles on his work by Martin Johnson and Stephanie Stewart, H. Lee Waters has served as the subject of a 1989 documentary by Tom Whiteside, *The Cameraman Has Visited Our Town,* and in 2005, Waters's film of Kannopolis, North Carolina, was named to the National Film Registry of the Library of Congress.

8. Dan Streible, "Itinerant Filmmakers and Amateur Casts: A Homemade 'Our Gang,' 1926," *Film History: An International Journal* 15, no. 2 (2003): 179.

9. Many books and articles have been written referencing this subject, but see, e.g., Leah Dilworth, *Imagining Indians in the Southwest: Persistent Visions of a Primitive Past* (Washington, D.C.: Smithsonian Press, 1996), 10–11.

10. See Calvin Pryluck's "Bibliography on Traveling Exhibition" in his article "The Itinerant Movie Show and the Development of the Film Industry," in *Hollywood in the Neighborhood: Historical Case Studies of Local Moviegoing*, ed. Kathryn Fuller-Seeley (Berkeley: University of California Press, 2008), 37–52.

11. "Jackrabbit," http://animals.nationalgeographic.com/animals/mammals/jackrabbit.html.

12. Kathryn Fuller-Seeley, e-mail correspondence with the author, July 27, 2009.

13. Bottomore, "From the Factory Gate," 32.

14. Fuller-Seeley, *Hollywood in the Neighborhood*, 9.

15. Ibid., 5.

16. Streible, "Itinerant Filmmakers," 189.

17. Roland Robertson, "Glocalization: Time-Space and Homogeneity–Heterogeneity," in *Global Modernities*, ed. Mike Featherstone (London: Sage, 1995), 29.

18. Ibid., 26.

19. See ibid. as well as John Tomlinson, *Globalization and Culture* (Chicago: University of Chicago Press, 1999) for a more in-depth analysis of glocalization theory and its relevance for globalization critique.

20. Melton Barker Productions brochure, courtesy of Jack Duncan, McKinney, Texas.

21. For more information, see Robert L. Dorman, *Revolt of the Provinces: The Regionalist Movement in America, 1920–1945* (Chapel Hill: University of North Carolina Press, 1993).

22. Conflicting data, including census information, report that Barker was born in either Mississippi or Texas. Numerous newspaper articles as well as Barker's own marketing materials attest to his Hollywood connections.

23. "Stage Actors Making Talky on Location," *Dallas Morning News*, November 15, 1931, 6.

24. "*Spread Eagle* Opens Monday on Maple Ave.," *Dallas Morning News*, November 22, 1931.

25. Ibid.

26. See the filmography published in the appendix to this issue for examples.

27. Leonard Maltin and Richard W. Bann, *Our Gang: The Life and Times of the Little Rascals* (New York: Crown, 1977), 15–16.

28. Eduardo de la Vega Alfaro and Patricia Torres San Martín, *Adela Sequeyro* (Harlingen, Tex.: Archivo Fílmico Agrasánchez, 2000), 86–87. Special thanks to Mr. Rogelio Agrasánchez for alerting me to this particular version.

29. Maltin and Bann, *Our Gang*, 15.

30. *Box Office* trade press from November 1938 documents a plan by retired cowboy star Jack Hoxie to shoot westerns near Hot Springs, Arkansas. Melton Barker was listed as one of the directors involved, although no other report of this endeavor exists. See "Jack Hoxie to Make Western Films on Location Near Hot Springs, Ark.," *Box Office*, November 5, 1938, 82.

31. "Scene from Children's Dallas-Made Picture," *Dallas Morning News*, May 2, 1932, 4.

32. "All-Dallas Talky to Be Produced," *Dallas Morning News*, February 16, 1932, 8.

33. Kathy Merlock Jackson, *Images of Children in American Film: A Sociocultural Analysis* (Metuchen, N.J.: Scarecrow Press, 1986), 57–58.

34. A copy of Barker's home movies has been donated to the Texas Archive of the Moving Image (TAMI).

35. Melton Barker Productions brochure, courtesy of Jack Duncan, McKinney, Texas.

36. Ibid.

37. Only one copy of a Last Straw title has been found as of the publication of this article, so determining the differences between this series and the Kidnappers Foil series proves impossible. This is particularly the case because the extant Last Straw film reels, part of the Minnesota Historical Society film collection in Minneapolis, may in fact be reel 1 of a Last Straw and reel 2 of a Kidnappers Foil.

38. In particular, numerous Childress, Texas, residents have shared with the author local lore of a movie-struck mother from neighboring Quanah, Texas, who took her young son to Los Angeles following his appearance in a Kidnappers Foil production. Although efforts to prove the veracity of this tale have failed, rumor has it that the mother and child returned to Quanah fairly quickly.

39. The money charged by Barker appeared to vary from community to community, as reported by hundreds of newspaper stories as well as anecdotal accounts.

40. "No Money for Theatres in Chattanooga Film," *Box Office,* September 3, 1949, 92.

41. Owen Taylor, "Cleveland's Movie: Quiet on the Set!" *Delta Democrat-Times,* May 15, 1972, 2.

42. Ibid.

43. See Toulmin et al., *The Lost World of Mitchell and Kenyon,* 32–48.

44. Roger Smither, "'Watch the Picture Carefully, and See If You Can Identify Anyone': Recognition in Factual Film of the First World War Period," *Film History: An International Journal* 14 (2002): 396.

45. Bottomore, "From the Factory Gate," 34.

46. "Melton Barker and the Kidnappers Foil," http://www.meltonbarker.com/.

47. Fred Davis, *Yearning for Yesterday: A Sociology of Nostalgia* (London: Macmillan, 1979), 1.

48. The two prints have been preserved thanks to the National Film Preservation Foundation and have been donated to TAMI in Austin.

49. For more information and to see the Childress films, see http://www.texasarchive.org/library/index.php?title=Collection_-_Melton_Barker_Juvenile_Productions.

50. "*Our Home Town:* Online Documentary Shows a Thriving San Marcos in 1949," *San Marcos Daily Record,* March 22, 2009, http://www.sanmarcosrecord.com/features/x1169232272/Our-Home-Town/.

51. Gregory Waller, "Imagining the Small-Town Theater," in Fuller-Seeley, *Hollywood in the Neighborhood,* 181.

52. "*Our Home Town,*" TAMI, http://www.texasarchive.org/library/index.php/Our_Home_Town/.

53. Ibid.

54. Smither, "Watch the Picture Carefully," 393.

55. Melton Barker Productions brochure, courtesy of Jack Duncan, McKinney, Texas.

THE PLACES YOU'LL KNOW

MARTIN L. JOHNSON

From Self-Recognition to

Place Recognition in

in the Local Film

The *local film,* one produced and theatrically exhibited for an audience drawn by the novelty of seeing people and places they know on screen, has primarily been researched as a phenomenon specific to individual filmmakers of the early cinema period. In fact, Tom Gunning goes as far as to call this period (1895–1907) the "era of local cinema" because of the particularity of film exhibition practices as well as evidence of local film production.[1] Using business records and extant films, historians have produced detailed accounts of individual itinerant filmmakers and filmmaker-exhibitors who worked in the first decade of the cinema.[2] In this body of case studies, the conception of the local film has been boiled down to the phenomenon of individual spectatorship. Whether termed *self-recognition,* the *reflected gaze,* or more simply, "seeing yourself in the movies," the brief moment when audience members sees themselves on screen has been defined as the primary attraction, and by extension, meaning, of the local film.[3] Though the local film as a historical phenomenon continues until at least the 1950s, scholars have addressed it primarily as a residue of early cinema practices such as itinerant film exhibition and the incorporation of local entertainments, like amateur vaudeville, into an evening's entertainment.[4]

Though self-recognition is indeed an important, even defining, characteristic of the local film, seeing oneself on screen is not the only attraction of the local film and, in fact, becomes less important after the early cinema era ends and the transitional era begins in 1908.[5] Instead, place has equal, if not greater, importance to the analysis of local film, particularly once permanent movie theaters are established in towns and neighborhoods. The concept of *place recognition*—the moment when audiences see places they know on film—that I use in this article allows us to consider local film as being defined as much by audience perception of local places as by their recognition of themselves and others. Whereas the idea of self-recognition assumes that the subjects of a film are watching themselves on screen, filmmakers also create place through the combination of temporally and spatially disconnected images. Film audiences in some towns saw multiple local films over a period of years or decades, each of which presented local people and places in different ways. The diversity of local film productions makes place a more mutable category than it may first appear. By considering the importance of place recognition and creation for the production and exhibition of local films, I hope to offer a new research agenda for this emerging field of study that uses exhibition sites rather than individual filmmakers or spectators as the locus of meaning of the local film.

This article uses three case studies of local film production and exhibition in the United States in the transitional era (1908–1917) and the classical Hollywood era (1918–1948) to argue that the local film is more productively analyzed in the context of its immediate production and exhibition than as the practice of one or several itinerant filmmakers.[6] These studies offer rich details about practices that were described in trade newspapers such as *Moving Picture World* and *Motion Picture Herald*.[7] First, using an example of a home-talent film produced in 1916 by C. D. Tinsley, a movie theater owner and studio photographer in Corning, Iowa, I show how a filmmaker could use place recognition to attract film audiences even if his films did not feature many local people. In the second case, I consider a civic film, a type of film intended to portray a community (often a town or city) as a governmental entity, commissioned by Alvin Sloan, a theater owner in Washington, New Jersey, who used the film to depict the town as he imagined it. Last, I consider Burlington, North Carolina, which was visited by at least three itinerant filmmakers—Marilyn B. Lundy of the Boston Amateur Theatre Guild, H. Lee Waters, and Melton Barker—between 1937 and 1942, as an example of how local filmmakers multiplied the possibilities for recognizing place by recasting the town as a Hollywood set or a place where anyone could be caught on camera.[8] Local films not only documented people and places but also helped produce, to use cultural geographer Doreen Massey's term, the "event of place" in their production and exhibition. I argue that the local film is the distillation of the event of place, created by the intersection of the times and spaces that exist at the moment of the film's production and exhibition.

MICROHISTORIES AND THE SPATIAL TURN IN FILM HISTORIOGRAPHY

The recent emphasis on empirical, archive-based research for studies of moviegoing has brought phenomena like the local film to the fore. Articles on film historiography have emphasized the *spatial turn*—so called by geographer Edward W. Soja because it privileges the geography of cultural experiences—in film history.[9] The spatial turn began when scholars shifted from generalized cultural histories of moviegoing that relied on textual analysis of representative films toward studies of specific sites of film exhibition, using more detailed but narrower sources, especially newspapers intended for a geographically or demographically defined community.[10] As a result of this shift, scholars have made more nuanced arguments about race, ethnicity, nationality, regional identity, gender, and sexuality in the history of the cinema.[11] Jürgen Habermas's notion of the *public sphere* took on particular significance as it allowed historians to emphasize political and social meanings of moviegoing that were often left out of studies dominated by textual analysis.[12] Though this microhistorical approach has its limits—notably, the difficulty of making generalizable claims from one's findings—Carlos Ginzburg has suggested that microhistory is uniquely helpful in the production of "clues" that can be followed up with additional research.[13] In the case of the local film, individual case studies have been enriched by the use of trade publications and general interest magazines that discuss local film production as a widespread and commercially viable practice.[14]

In this historical turn, which began in the mid-1990s with publications such as Gregory A. Waller's *Main Street Amusements: Movies and Commercial Entertainment in a Southern City, 1896–1930,* emphasis slowly shifted from normative concepts, such as the public sphere, to more descriptive and contingent ones that brought to light the complex and often contradictory events that took place at the cinema. In this vein, Robert C. Allen proposed applying Massey's work on place to studies of film exhibition.[15] For Massey, the salient quality of place is its very "throwntogetherness" or the combination of the many pasts of a particular space with its contingent present.[16] The "event of place" is, for Massey, "the coming together of the previously unrelated, a constellation of processes rather than a thing."[17] In short, place can be used to describe macroprocesses, such as the melting of glaciers and the moving of mountains, and microprocesses, such as the building of a new tourist attraction or the dedication of a building, at the same time, without letting go of place as a material thing.

An emphasis on place allows us to consider moviegoing not just as the individual and collective experiences of moviegoers but also as an activity that helps form the place of the theater and other sites. Thus any study of film exhibition derives its significance in part from the production of multiple geographies and temporalities necessary to re-create the place of the movie theater and the moment(s) of film exhibition. The exhibition of a Hollywood film at a theater in a small town in North Carolina, for instance, could be read as a local *place-event* that relies on such extratextual cues as newspapers, magazines, and posters, which are available to audiences seeing the film and might influence their experience. But this place-event is also affected by local social systems—the ethnic, racial, or gender composition of the audience, where they are seated, and how they interact with one another—that help produce its meaning.

This approach to place and to moviegoing is even more apt for work on the local film, precisely because these practices were significant enough to leave behind historical traces in and of the locality. Not only did local newspapers describe these films and their reception in more detail than they described nonlocal films but the images themselves often produced a map of the place of exhibition that can be measured against city directories and maps from the same period. The different modes of local film production also allow consideration of national, social, political, and cultural discourses in relation to a specific filmmaker or local film. In this way, local films are about both the locality in which they were produced and the institutions (both physical and imaginary) that made such works possible for audiences and participants. Place is a useful concept because it accounts for the singularity of an individual film and for the general spatial and temporal experience to which that film implicitly or explicitly refers.

HOME-TALENT FILMS AND PLACE RECOGNITION: CORNING, IOWA

If early cinema scholarship has focused on the emergence of the medium, scholarship on the transitional period in film history has been primarily concerned with debates about the social, political, and cultural meanings of the cinema as it became a mass medium.[18] As a result, many local film production practices have been either overlooked or subsumed into these larger developments. Although little has been published on local film production and exhibition in the 1910s, place recognition becomes particularly significant for film audiences during this period.[19]

For instance, the term *home talent,* previously used to describe amateur play productions, began to be used in local newspapers in the early 1910s to identify narrative fiction films that featured local actors. These films were not primarily produced for general audiences who wished to see themselves in the movies. In fact, with the exception of crowd scenes, only a handful of local people were cast in such films. Filmmakers selected actors through auditions or contests or simply by choosing prominent members of local society to appear in their films. In some cases, the same people appeared again and again in home-talent films of the period. In addition, these films turned the site of production—the built environment of the hometown—into a fictional movie set, with staged special effects, such as automobile accidents and rescues from burning buildings, as the primary attractions of the film. Filmmakers often used popular genre tropes to suggest their connection with the film industry. Given the dominance of the one-reel film in the mid-1910s, audiences could make a reel-to-reel comparison between the home-talent film and films produced by a studio.[20] Few of these films survive, making it difficult to come to definite conclusions about the formal techniques used in home-talent films; however, newspaper accounts of the productions discuss their reliance on local places to draw audiences.

Charlie David Tinsley's *The Mexican Raid,* a home-talent film made in Corning, Iowa, in spring 1916, is a particularly compelling example of this kind of local film. Like other home-talent films, this film relied on audience recognition of local people and places. But *The Mexican Raid* also depended on a politically sophisticated audience that could understand the implications of the depicted event—actually a reenactment of Mexican revolutionary Francisco "Pancho" Villa's attack on the small border town of Columbus, New Mexico, on March 9, 1916—for the town's volunteer militia. Though the film itself is not known to survive, it is described in detail in Corning's two weekly newspapers. My analysis here will focus on the production of *The Mexican Raid* and Tinsley's use of both self- and place recognition to promote and situate the film in its fictional and real contexts.

By the time Tinsley made *The Mexican Raid,* he was already well known in Corning for his film productions. Newspaper articles from 1914 to 1916 describe several home-talent films he made in town on topics that ranged from house fires to wolf hunts to Civil War reenactments. The event depicted in *The Mexican Raid* precipitated President Woodrow Wilson's decision to send U.S. troops into Mexico to capture Villa. In early May, two months after the raid, an article ran in one of Corning's two local newspapers describing the plot of Tinsley's film and his production plans:

> The title of the picture is *The Mexican Raid* and will be up-to-the-minute stuff, since it will picture Mexicans making a raid on Americans. The principal scenes of the film will be taken on the above date at the Mose Straughan farm, south of town. Co. K will take a leading part in the battle scene and the management of the picture wants the services of 150 men and boys on horse back to act as Mexicans and make the raid. The log cabin, a landmark on the Straughan farm, will be used in the picture and the cabin will be burned.[21]

Tinsley's use of the Corning-based Company K of the Third Infantry of the Iowa National Guard to participate in the reenactment is interesting for three reasons. First, Wilson's commitment of troops to the conflict led many to suspect that the National Guard would be called into action for the first time since the Spanish-American War of 1898, meaning that the actions of Company K soldiers in the film anticipated prospective real-life military service. Second, by casting other Corning residents as Mexicans, Tinsley was asking his audiences to imagine those not in the local militia, which was made up of volunteers, as a potential enemy force, one marked as an "ethnic" other. And third, by planning to burn a log cabin that the newspaper considered a "landmark" in the community, Tinsley was calling attention to the importance of the events depicted in the film by destroying something that was part of local history. In this way, *The Mexican Raid* asks audiences to recognize the place of the film—the Mose Straughan farm—as both a familiar site and a landscape that could be reimagined as a battlefield on the U.S.–Mexico border. In *The Mexican Raid,* which was first shown in Corning on June

WANTED

150 MEN AND BOYS

On horseback, with guns, blank cartridges and large straw hats, to volunteer to take part in a home talent moving picture play entitled

"THE MEXICAN RAID"

Company K will play an important part in the chase of the Mexican Raiders.

MEET AT LYRIC THEATRE, FRIDAY, MAY 12

AT 1:00 O'CLOCK P. M.

The picture will be staged at the Mose Straughan log cabin, 1 mile south of Corning

REMEMBER THE DATE, FRIDAY, MAY 12, 1916

Advertisement in the *Adams County Union-Republican* for participation in *The Mexican Raid,* May 10, 1916. NewspaperArchive.com.

9 and 10, real soldiers reenacted a real military conflict on a real farm that had been reimagined by Tinsley as a battlefield.[22]

On June 18, Wilson called all members of the National Guard into service to protect the U.S.–Mexico border, including forty-five hundred troops from Iowa, seventy-eight of which were from Corning.[23] Tinsley went to Camp Dodge, a training base twelve miles northwest of Des Moines, to film another thousand feet of film to add to *The Mexican Raid*. In an advertisement published on July 13, 1916, Tinsley listed the new scenes in

Advertisement in the *Adams County Free Press* for *The Mexican Raid,* June 3, 1916. NewspaperArchive.com.

Advertisement in the *Adams County Union-Republican* for an added reel of *The Mexican Raid,* July 12, 1916. NewspaperArchive.com.

the film: "Gov. Clarke signing call for National Guard, pathetic scenes at station as Company K leaves for Mexican war. Company K in service at Camp Dodge, aeroplane scouts dropping bombs, sharp shooters bringing down air craft."[24] In Tinsley's description of this added reel, which appears to feature only actuality footage of training activities, he also adds that the viewer might "see yourself in the crowd at the train station."[25] Whereas the appeal of the first reel of *The Mexican Raid* was seeing a farm near Corning transformed into a battlefield, the second reel attracted audiences because it showed scenes that featured local people training for an actual battle. In the first reel, the soldiers in Company K were merely actors. In the second reel, the soldiers were the subjects of a newsreel assembled by Tinsley to show the real-world military response to the fictional scenes he had filmed a month earlier.

This emphasis on place recognition as well as self-recognition was also critical for itinerant producers of local films who increasingly found their films being compared to other film genres and styles.[26] The home-talent film was an attempt to resolve the tension between making a film about a particular community that relied on the attraction of "seeing yourself" and making a film that looked like the ones those audiences had become accustomed to seeing in their local movie theater. Filmmakers accomplished this by using a small cast composed of amateur actors or prominent members of local society for the film narrative and adding an extraneous crowd scene where audiences could still see themselves in the picture. But they also used their ability to transform local places into fictional movie sets to attract audiences. By considering the importance of place recognition, it is possible to see how these films remained local films, even if they did not offer a majority of audience members an opportunity to see themselves on the screen.

CIVIC FILMS AND THE PRODUCTION OF PLACE: WASHINGTON, NEW JERSEY

In addition to appealing to audiences who wished to see themselves and the people and places where they lived, some local films also played a role in creating place by editing together images of local institutions, fraternal and civic organizations, and businesses to form a portrait of a town. These narrative nonfiction films, which I will call civic films, are distinct from both the local films of the early cinema period and the home-talent films of the transitional period because they did not emphasize the spectacle of film production and exhibition; rather, producers of civic films advertised the potential of their films to produce a film portrait of a town that could be used to promote the town to residents and nonresidents alike and simultaneously create a film record of that town for future generations to view.[27] This place creation by civic filmmakers was possible because theater managers and business organizations like the chamber of commerce commissioned the production of local films to foster the development of small-town institutions, from schools to service clubs to local industries. The 1932 film of a school dedication ceremony in Washington, New Jersey, a town sixty miles west of New York City, is an example of how civic films created place.

In September 1932, Alvin Sloan, manager of the St. Cloud Theater, the smaller of two theaters in Washington, a town of just under five thousand people, commissioned a twelve-reel film to commemorate the opening of the new high school. As an article published at the time noted, the film included more than just images from the high school dedication, as scenes were added to show "the congregations at the churches and Sunday schools, a baseball game, scenes in the business district, audiences in the theatre, the fire and police departments and many others."[28] These scenes were selected in advance, most likely by Sloan himself. Before the school dedication ceremony, an advertisement for the production of the film listed several places where one could go to be filmed, including the town square, the baseball field at the town park, the Catholic and Protestant churches, and the St. Cloud Theater.[29] Unlike directors of home-talent films, producers of civic films often worked at the behest of the film sponsor, shooting only those institutions and people considered by the sponsor to be critical for a portrait of the town. As a result, civic films often include shots of prominent buildings, organizations, and people but may not include working-class people, ethnic and racial minorities, and other groups excluded from the sponsor's image of how the town should appear in the film. Civic films were often commissioned to commemorate local events such as the school dedication ceremony discussed here. Others were produced by itinerants who specialized in making town portraits, such as Shad E. Graham, who worked in the Northeast and then, after World War II, in the Southwest, and H. C. Kunkelman, who was based in Ohio.[30]

On the first of September, the *Washington Star* ran an article detailing the schedule of the school dedication ceremony. The list of participants in the ceremony included "clergy, fraternal leaders, the president of the Board of Education, a military squadron from the American Legion, the Washington-High Bridge band, representatives from the Sons and Daughters of Liberty and the Daughters of the American Revolution, the High School chorus, the building's architect and many other leaders."[31] By including political, educational, civic, religious, and fraternal groups in the ceremony and, by extension, the film, Sloan was able to suggest that the film fully accounted for the town of

Washington. The production was thoroughly documented in the newspaper, and one reel, the one that the article mentioned, was given to the school board as a "permanent motion picture record of the occasion" of the school dedication. This reel was recently rediscovered in an antique shop in Tennessee.[32]

The lone surviving fifteen-minute reel opens with a shot of the newspaper story announcing the school dedication, which helps date a film that might have been otherwise difficult for future audiences to identify. The silent film is structured like a newsreel, with brief, single-take shots interspersed with title cards announcing the significance of the events in the subsequent shots. The people who appear in the film do not look directly at the camera, even though it is clear from their brief glances in the direction of the camera that they are aware of its presence. After pans of the school building and the audience and shots of the speakers at the ceremony, the film features interior shots of the school. Students demonstrate the activities that might go on in the classroom, from playing musical instruments to working in the wood shop to typing.

The St. Cloud Theatre

Congratulates Washington on its New High School and joins the citizenship in thanking those who contributed to its successful completion for a task well done.

━━✦✦✦✦━━

We take pride in showing the official motion pictures of the dedication of the school together with other interesting items in the Washington Newsreel for one entire week starting today, Thursday, September 8th.

Advertisement in the *Washington Star* for the exhibition of the filmed high school dedication ceremony at the St. Cloud Theater, September 8, 1932. New Jersey State Archives.

Though people do come in and out of these shots, the camera is not motivated by the actions of particular individuals; rather, the filmmaker continues to use slow pans across each space, as if the intention is to record what the school interior looked like on the day of its dedication, the moving image equivalent of the architectural floor plan that was published in the local newspaper after the school's dedication.[33] This series of shots is followed by several brief film portraits of particular individuals, whose poses range from serious to comical. The title cards that identify these individuals credit them with making the building of the school possible. The film closes with a shot of the American flag, as if to further connect the dedication of the school and the production of the film with a civic spirit rooted in nationalist or patriotic sentiment.

Instead of just serving as an attraction for the audiences of the present, the film's purpose appears to be to record the dedication for future audiences. As a result, the viewer is reminded that the school building is more than just the physical bricks and mortar that they might still see in town when the film is viewed again at a much later date. The film creates the place of the school by connecting it to a civic ceremony that officially marked its founding as an institution as well as picturing both the first students to occupy the building and the people responsible for gathering resources to build it. Though the 1932 advertisements for the film emphasized self-recognition in the other reels, for this reel it is clear that the filmmaker, who is never named in the newspaper and was likely a professional cinematographer, intended to produce the place of the building as it existed on the day of its dedication.

After the success of the 1932 newsreel, Alvin Sloan, who was elected mayor of Washington in 1935, set up his own system for the production and exhibition of local films in his regional circuit of eleven theaters.[34] The newsreels, which were called "Meet Your Neighbors," featured everything from local sporting events to building dedications. Using 16mm equipment, Sloan was able to produce and exhibit these films on a regular basis. Though the exhibition of these newsreels was only advertised on rare occasions in the newspaper, an article about the practice, published in the national trade publication *Motion Picture Herald* in 1940, suggested that the local newsreels were a regular occurrence in Sloan's theater chain. The article also presented the local film as a familiar concept for its readers, praising the "box office and goodwill value of local pictures" for any theater manager who decided to sponsor such productions.[35] The regular appearance of local films in towns like Washington demonstrates their ability to produce a sense of place rather than just capture moments of everyday life that can be recognized by audiences.

THE MULTIPLICITY OF PLACE: BURLINGTON, NORTH CAROLINA

Defining the local film as an object separate from the newsreel, the home movie, or the sponsored film is a necessary, if difficult, task. In my view, the local film is distinct because it emphasizes and assumes local knowledge held by a public audience. By using place as a way to discuss both individual acts of recognition and the collective event of place that is captured or produced by a local film, it is possible also to consider multiple or constantly shifting places, even if the locale of the film's production appears not to have changed.

In the two case studies considered so far, the place created in local films was produced by a single filmmaker. But itinerant filmmakers often crossed paths, so a single town could see multiple local films over the course of a decade. Potential uses and meanings of local film shifted over time in response to changes in film production and exhibition practices as well as broader changes in political, social, and cultural conditions. Though it might be possible to define the local film of early cinema, as Stephen Bottomore suggests, as a film with "considerable overlap between the people appearing in the film and those who watch it or are intended to watch it," by the end of the transitional era, this definition was no longer adequate.[36] Instead, the local film relies on place recognition, which combines audience recognition of local people and places with interpretative frameworks, such as social, cultural, and political beliefs, to create its meaning. Imagining one's town as a potential Hollywood is very different from imagining it as a model city. Burlington, North Carolina, which was visited by several itinerant filmmakers in the late 1930s and early 1940s, is one such site where the "throwntogetherness" required to produce place in local film is most evident.

Home to almost three dozen hosiery mills and a population of more than twenty thousand, Burlington in the 1930s was a prosperous town, with mill workers able to spend their discretionary income on leisure activities, including movies, live music, and vaudeville acts, which were still popular in the South.[37] The town also proved to be a popular stop for itinerant filmmakers. Marilyn Lundy of the Boston Amateur Theatre Guild, one of a number home-talent theater companies that staged productions in small towns in the 1920s and 1930s, produced the stage and screen show *The Movie Queen* in late 1936.[38] H. Lee Waters, a studio photographer from Lexington, North Carolina, who worked as an itinerant filmmaker in the Mid-Atlantic South between 1936 and 1942, visited Burlington four times between 1939 and 1942, shooting almost five thousand feet of film of the town over the three-year period.[39] And Melton Barker, an itinerant filmmaker from Texas who filmed two-reel sound comedies in small towns from the early 1930s to the 1970s, made *The Kidnapper's Foil* in Burlington in the summer of 1941.[40] What a newspaper in Valdese, North Carolina, called the "Home Town Movie Idea" was a commonplace occurrence in Burlington in the late 1930s, with a film of local people being exhibited theatrically at least once a year.[41]

In December 1936, *The Movie Queen,* described in the local paper as a "combination stage show, style show, and moving picture show," was staged in Burlington by Marilyn B. Lundy of the Boston Amateur Theatre Guild.[42] Using a business model developed by home-talent play directors in the 1920s, Lundy produced a three-act play starring local talent, a sixty-minute film, and a fashion show, all in twelve days.[43] Performed at the Municipal Auditorium rather than the movie theater, *The Movie Queen* was sponsored by the Kiwanis Club, with any proceeds to be put toward the cause of "underprivileged children."[44] Under the auspices of charity, Lundy engaged many of the citizens of Burlington in a variety of stunts. For a parade staged as part of the event and filmed by Lundy, the Kiwanis Club enlisted the participation of the town's mayor, merchants, the Boy Scouts, and the local drum corps. Every step in the production process, from the casting of the actress to play the movie queen to the filming of the parade to the kidnapping and rescue of the queen, was covered in the newspaper, with an event announced one day, taking place on another, and described on a third day. These events were in fact planned out by the Boston Amateur Theatre League, an organization that trained female directors like Lundy to put on *The Movie Queen* all over the country.[45] While these events required local participation to succeed, *The Movie Queen* was not advertised as a portrait of the town where it was made or as a chance for local people to audition to be in the movies. Instead, it was a display of how local resources—human and material—could be deployed in the service of charity and entertainment.

The Movie Queen has been primarily researched by a handful of archivists and scholars as an itinerant-produced local film.[46] But for the film's audience, this 16mm black-and-white film, which served as the fourth and final act of a play by the same name, was only one part of a much larger program. Despite the fact that Lundy was identified as being from Boston, the paper announced her visit by writing, "Burlington was entirely too busy to go to Hollywood, so Hollywood came to Burlington."[47] Though the main attraction of *The Movie Queen* was the opportunity to appear in a "real motion picture," there was little evidence that participants felt that such appearances would serve as a screen test suitable for a Hollywood audition.[48] Instead, *The Movie Queen* is a mock homage to the film industry, giving its characters names that referenced well-known actors.[49] Instead of Mary Pickford, the play stars Mary Brown as the simple and sweet hometown actress. Greta Garbo and Marlene Dietrich are mocked as Marlena Slarbo. Erich Von Stroheim becomes Von Vonheim. Other industry stereotypes from the costume designer (Monsieur Flowers) to the fast-talking agent are included in the play as well. Though home-talent plays often emphasize the differences between rural and city life and, on occasion, even satirize Hollywood, the Boston Amateur Theatre Guild took this a step further by including film production as part of their program. Mixing local people and organizations with a play and script that poked fun at Hollywood, and Hollywood's take on small-town life, Lundy was able to create a Burlington that was both in on the joke and the object of it.

In H. Lee Waters's *Movies of Local People,* place took on a different meaning. Waters, echoing the claims of earlier local filmmakers, promised an opportunity to "see yourself as others see you." He filmed local people and places in Burlington for his ongoing

See Yourself In The Movies!

AT THE

STATE THEATRE

BURLINGTON, N. C.

MON. & TUES.   **January 19th & 20th**

MATINEE AND NIGHT

LOCAL MOVIES

FILMED IN BEAUTIFUL TECHNICOLOR

S E E ELON COLLEGE STUDENTS, KIWANIS CLUB MEMBERS, .
LION'S CLUB MEMBERS, ███████████████ MAY-
FLOWER MILL, PLAID MILL, ALAMANCE MILL, Mc-
EWEN HOSIERY MILL, CANDID SHOTS ON STREETS OF
BURLINGTON, MANY INTERESTING CAMERA TRICKS,
INTERESTING SHOTS TAKEN AT BURLINGTON'S OWN
RADIO STATION WBBB, TOUR OF BURLINGTON USED
CAR EXCHANGE, CHURCH STREET GROCERY STORE
AND TILLMAN'S JEWELERS.

SHOWING ALSO

Movies made in Burlington three years ago.

ALSO

**Pictures of Children and Teachers in
Burlington City Schools**

40 Minutes of Thrills--Cast of 4000

ALSO ON THE SCREEN
"ANGEL'S OVER BROADWAY," STARRING DOUGLAS FAIRBANKS,
JR., and RITA HAYWORTH

Don't Miss It---It's Lots of Fun

Flyer from screening of local
films by H. Lee Waters in
Burlington, North Carolina,
January 1942. Personal
collection.

Movies of Local People series four times between 1939 and 1942, shooting both black-and-white and color 16mm film.[50] In 1941 the *Burlington Daily Times-News* praised Waters for having a "whole carload of the latest" camera equipment and because his film "comes right down to everyday life, takes you performing your everyday routine, catches you in candid style."[51] Because Waters filmed with little or no advance notice, he was able to record candid images of a variety of people. Though his films were initially screened a few weeks after they were produced, Waters, who shot on reversal film stock, kept all the films he made and often showed them again on return visits. Waters organized his shooting schedule around particular institutions and locations—visiting schools, factories, and downtown business districts—and as a result, his films became records of local places as well as local people. Whereas the films were initially valued for giving audiences an opportunity to see themselves, their secondary value as historical record became increasingly clear as Waters started to emphasize this aspect of the films in the handbills he prepared for repeat visits. Waters himself returned to many of the towns he filmed twenty years after his first visit, not to make new films, but instead to show his old films once again, telling audiences that the films would "bring back fond memories of people and places that are gone . . . But Not Forgotten!"[52] In 2004, when Waters's films of Kannapolis, North Carolina, were selected for the National Film Registry, they were praised for being the "sole record of these cultural enclaves," particularly African American neighborhoods and white mill workers.[53]

But in 1941, the *Times-News* did not wax about the value of seeing their "cultural enclave" on film; rather Waters was discussed as if he were another producer of Hollywood screen tests. As the paper stated, "whether you are another [Myrna] Loy or [Clark] Gable, or just your plain self, you may be seeing yourself on the silver screen."[54] Another article described Waters as someone "who travels throughout this and surrounding states" producing films that have "helped untold thousands make their first appearance on the silver screen."[55] Though Waters did not associate himself directly with Hollywood in his own advertising materials, newspaper articles often did the job for him, suggesting that the reception of his films may have been influenced by audiences who expected to see themselves as if they were posing for a Hollywood screen test.[56] Although Waters did include so-called screen tests in his films—shots of individuals that run for a few seconds, just long enough for the person to mug for the camera, often in jest—his films were much more than strings of film portraits. He used a variety of in-camera techniques, including speeding up or slowing down the frame rate to create fast or slow motion and holding the camera upside down to create the illusion of reverse motion, that demonstrated his proficiency with his 16mm camera, a Kodak Cine Special. Unlike the producers of civic films, who shot only preselected scenes, Waters was a much more idiosyncratic filmmaker, shooting anything that appealed to him on the day or two he had to produce his film. At the same time, the connection between any film production and Hollywood, particularly in places where very few residents had the inclination or the money to make their own films, was so strong that Waters was inevitably compared to a Hollywood filmmaker, even on return visits, when audiences presumably knew what a Waters film would be like. Even though Waters's films did not share any formal traits with Hollywood films, they nonetheless were associated with the Hollywood star system when they were first exhibited.

In the two examples so far, I have suggested that itinerant-produced local films made in Burlington in the late 1930s and early 1940s are associated with Hollywood film practices, making the place of Burlington as seen in these films inseparable from the film industry. However, Melton Barker, who made *The Kidnapper's Foil* in Burlington

Flyer from screening of local films by H. Lee Waters in Fort Mill, South Carolina, circa 1960. Personal collection.

in August 1941, is the only filmmaker whom the press misdescribed as actually being from Hollywood. The first article that appears in the *Times-News* described how Barker's production would be different from the others:

> Professional Hollywood equipment will be used in making this picture, also the same size film that you see in the theaters every day which is much larger than any pictures made in Burlington in the past. In addition these pictures will be all in sound . . . the children will be heard as well as seen. Burlington has never had the opportunity to make and be in movies as fine as these will be.[57]

That Barker was shooting in 35mm, and making sound films, was given as evidence of his professionalism. But more interestingly, Barker's films are discussed in relation to films made by other itinerants who visited Burlington. This and other evidence I have presented here, such as the discussion of local films in the national trade press, demonstrates that audiences were familiar with local films because they had seen multiple local films. Though the Boston Amateur Theatre League, H. Lee Waters, and Melton Barker are now recognized as significant itinerant producers of local films, focusing on the films they made in one city makes it possible to think about the relationship between their films and place in new ways. When itinerant filmmakers are examined as solo practitioners of their self-defined craft, scholars focus on how they are different from industrial and amateur filmmakers. But comparing them to one another allows us to determine how an individual's film practice differs from the more general, or generic, field of local film production.

More research is needed before drawing definitive conclusions about the impact itinerant filmmakers had on one another or on the production of local film as a whole. When local film was discussed in the trade press, it took the form of small news items in a column targeted for exhibitors looking for new ways to attract audiences; that is, local film has historically been discussed as a phenomenon of exhibition, akin to ballyhoo and theater advertising, rather than as another form of film production. I suggest here that at a single site of exhibition, local film behaves like a genre, with each filmmaker establishing a "horizon of expectations" for film audiences that is met or not met by the next filmmaker.[58] The descriptors used in newspapers to identify films—home talent, "Home Town Movies," screen tests—are not fixed but rather subject to change based on the experience of place in the local community. The Boston Amateur Theatre League updated the home-talent play by including a film as part of the show. H. Lee Waters produced local views and used camera tricks and color footage to attract audiences. Melton Barker made a film based loosely on the popular Our Gang comedies using child actors. For local audiences, the attempt by filmmakers to establish their film practice as unique is offset by the stream of filmmakers who came to town. Considering the multiple places created by itinerant filmmakers is critical to understanding how their work was received in different times and places.

THE CONSEQUENCES OF PLACE RECOGNITION

I have suggested that while audience self-recognition is an important aspect of local film spectatorship, it is not sufficient to describe fully the genre's meaning. Starting in the 1910s, home-talent filmmakers produced one- and two-reel narrative fiction films with local people and places standing in for professional actors and studio sets. Instead of advertising that audiences could see themselves on screen, these filmmakers used the appeal of place recognition and the possibility for audiences to compare their films to those made by national film production companies. Civic filmmakers, who made films intended for political or commercial use, offered film sponsors an opportunity to create the place of their hometown by selecting which institutions, organizations, and individuals would appear in a film that would double as a historical record of the town. Finally, the variety of local film practices allowed audiences who saw multiple local films to respond to any individual film as part of a genre. Rather than only offering audiences their first opportunity to see themselves in the movies, itinerant filmmakers subsequently encouraged audiences to consider new possibilities for the local film production that was already occurring.

Though local film is often described as a historical record of people and places otherwise undocumented, it is also the product of chance encounters between filmmakers and the particular people and places filmed. These fleeting encounters between a person and a camera that appear in a local film make for compelling viewing but are difficult to analyze because so much of the knowledge contained in that moment was only available to the audiences who saw the film at the time of its initial exhibition. Nevertheless, a broader historical view may reveal information that is not obvious from researching the immediate reception of the film.

Revisiting the civic film made in Washington, New Jersey, exemplifies this point. In spring 1933, a special edition of the *Star* was printed to mark the one-year anniversary of Sloan's ownership of the St. Cloud Theater. This article recounted the history of local film production in Washington. The opening three paragraphs of the article are representative of the connections local journalists made between local film production and place:

> Taking motion pictures around town was always met with great popularity here.
>
> The old timers around town remember that years ago John W. Lunge had movies taken of local events including the . . . workers coming out of the Cornish factory and many other interesting local scenes. These pictures were shown periodically at the Opera House and as the years went by were increasingly popular.
>
> The second ambitious picture taking project was at the old St. Cloud Theatre. That time some men came out from New York and made a short feature picture with an all local cast. This film was a big hit. One of the highlights of that attraction was a thrilling rescue from a "burning" Washington Avenue building.[59]

Though this history of local film production might be specific to Washington, New Jersey, many towns could produce similar histories in their communities in the first several decades of film exhibition. The article went on to suggest that the value of the local film is not in its immediate production and reception but rather in its capacity to record life in Washington as "events making history take place, and in this way accumulat[ing] some real entertainment for the future."[60] The pleasure of the local film is not, then, just seeing yourself on screen but also witnessing the event of place as something that resonates in its "throwntogetherness" and that has the potential for historical meaning.

By focusing on place rather than individual filmmakers, I have attempted to ground the experience of local film production and exhibition in particular sites without letting go of broader social and cultural events that shaped the development of the local film from a practice that was simply a local view to one that incorporated many genres and forms. Though it is not surprising that local filmmakers changed their film practices as the film industry changed, the reasons for these developments have not been thoroughly explored by scholars, in part because it has been difficult to map the extent and variety of local practices. Close readings of individual sites of production and exhibition, of which I have offered only a slice here, may identify, as Carlos Ginzburg has suggested, clues about the potential meanings of the local film in the transitional and classical Hollywood eras. In addition, thinking of these films as documentation of the event of place rather than just of local people and places may allow us to consider these films in local and nonlocal contexts that are crystallized because a film happened to be produced in that particular time and space. In short, what we should look for in the local film is not only a series of reflected gazes, people looking at themselves on screen, but also evidence of what it meant to make or be in that particular film at that particular point in time in that particular space. By studying local film in the context of specific exhibition sites rather than as the product of an individual filmmaker, it will be possible to explore meanings and attractions of the local film that go beyond the long-standing, but limited, appeal of seeing yourself in the movies.

NOTES

1. Tom Gunning carries contemporary discussions of the relationship between the global and the local into a reconsideration of early film history after the 1994 discovery of local films made by James Mitchell and Sagar Kenyon in the United Kingdom between 1897 and 1913. The Mitchell and Kenyon collection of itinerant-produced local films is the third largest collection of films made by any single company that worked in the early cinema period, coming only after those of Auguste and Louis Lumière and Thomas Edison. As Gunning writes, "the lure of virtual world tours and glimpses of distant, exotic places marked the global aspect of early cinema, while the gasp of recognition and the naming of familiar faces or places characterized its local identity." See "Pictures of Crowd Splendour: The Mitchell and Kenyon Factory Gate Film," in *The Lost World of Mitchell and Kenyon*, ed. Vanessa Toulmin, Simon Popple, and Patrick Russell (London: BFI, 2004), 52.
2. In the conventionally defined early cinema period (1895–1907), itinerant exhibitors often produced local films to distinguish themselves from competitors and attract audiences. The most thorough studies of such filmmaker-exhibitors are in Charles Musser and Carol Nelson, *High-Class Moving Pictures: Lyman H. Howe and the Forgotten Era of Traveling Exhibition, 1880–1920* (Princeton, N.J.: Princeton University Press, 1991), and Vanessa Toulmin, *Electric Edwardians: The Films of Mitchell and Kenyon* (London: BFI, 2006). For an overview of the scholarship on local film production and exhibition from the early cinema period through the 1920s, see Stephen Bottomore, "From the Factory Gate to the 'Home Talent' Drama: An International Overview of Local Films in the Silent Era," in Toulmin et al., *The Lost World of Mitchell and Kenyon*. Bottomore also makes

reference to "silent" local films made after 1927, which were almost always accompanied by music or narration. Dan Streible discusses several itinerant filmmakers from the 1920s and 1930s in his article "Itinerant Filmmakers and Amateur Casts: A Homemade 'Our Gang,' 1926," *Film History* 15, no. 2 (2003): 177–192.

3. This argument is best summarized by Vanessa Toulmin and Martin Loiperdinger, "Is It You? Recognition, Representation, and Response in Relation to the Local Film," *Film History* 17, no. 1 (2005): 7–18. However, more recent scholarship, including Toulmin's 2006 book on Mitchell and Kenyon and the work presented in this issue, has added nuance to this argument, as scholars account for the volume and variety of local film production. In addition, Uli Jung considers the importance of place to the local film in "Local Views: A Blind Spot in the Historiography of Early German Cinema," *Historical Journal of Film, Radio, and Television* 22, no. 3 (2002): 253–273. However, his argument focuses on a single producer of local films, Peter Marzen of Trier, Germany, who made local views between 1902 and 1914.

4. Because the local film has been analyzed through the lens of particular filmmakers, it is difficult to determine an end date for this phenomenon. Though local film production appears to fall off sharply in the 1950s, when many single-screen theaters in small towns and neighborhoods closed because of the popularity of television, there are isolated examples of local film production occurring today. For instance, My Town Pictures, based in Mondovi, Wisconsin, produces "original, feature-length films in any-sized community using that community's people as actors, crew, and musicians!" On their Web site, one can purchase films produced in small towns in the Midwest in the past decade. See "My Town Pictures," http://www.mytownpictures.com/.

5. Musser has argued that the formation of the Motion Picture Patents Company in late 1908 restricted the sales of film stock necessary to produce local films; see Charles Musser, *Before the Nickelodeon: Edwin S. Porter and the Edison Manufacturing Company* (Berkeley: University of California Press, 1991), 378–79.

6. Much of this research has an auterist bent, as scholars attempt to position studies of local filmmakers in the context of early cinema historiography that emphasizes a handful of prominent film production companies and individual filmmakers. As Streible, "Itinerant Filmmakers and Amateur Casts," shows, expanding the historical scope of research into local filmmaking beyond the early cinema period produces discoveries of new local filmmakers and genres, such as local versions of popular comedies, which did not exist in the early cinema period.

7. In almost all cases, theater managers and owners commissioned, produced, or sponsored local films. For this article, I have drawn on readings of the "Advertising for Exhibitors" column in *Moving Picture World* and the "Managers' Round Table" column in *Motion Picture Herald*, both of which offered suggestions to help exhibitors promote theater attendance. These columns relied on exhibitor reports of local promotional practices, including the production of local films.

8. Corning, Iowa, was selected after a key word search for "home-talent films" on NewspaperArchive.com, a commercial archive that offers full-text searching of small-town newspapers not indexed by scholarly archives, found several dozen articles about the films produced by C. D. Tinsley. After contacting the state archives in Iowa, I received a clipping file on Tinsley that was assembled by Mary Jones, a historian in Iowa, from Paula Mohr, an architectural historian who now works for the Iowa Historic Preservation Office in Des Moines. When one reel of a twelve-reel film produced in Washington, New Jersey, in 1932 was discovered by Bradley Reeves and Louisa Trott, of the Tennessee Archive of Moving Image and Sound, graduate students in the Moving Image and Archiving Preservation program at New York University, then directed by Dan Streible, worked on the preservation of the film. Lisa Fehsenfeld, Yvonne Ng, and Jude Kiernan did the research on the production of the film, and I examined articles from the *Washington Star* to establish further context for the production of the film. Using key word searches on NewspaperArchive.com, I was able to find documentation of visits to Burlington, North Carolina, by three established itinerant filmmakers in the late 1930s and early 1940s.

9. Edward W. Soja, "Taking Space Personally," in *The Spatial Turn*, ed. Barney Warf and Santa Arias (New York: Routledge, 2008), 11–35. Robert C. Allen accounts, and argues, for this shift in "Relocating American Film History," *Cultural Studies* 20, no. 1 (2006): 48–88. Allen casts this transition in film studies specifically as one from a more theoretical model of spectatorship to the empirical one that he prefers. But privileging historical evidence over psychoanalysis does not exclude theoretical questions; rather, Allen argues, an empirical approach allows the film historian to ask different kinds of questions, particularly those concerning the place of the movie theater in everyday life.

10. Robert Sklar's cultural history of the movies, *Movie-Made America* (New York: Random House, 1975), is an example of a study that relies heavily on cultural and textual analysis to make an argument about the role of movies and moviegoing in everyday life.

11. Though it is impossible to list all the contributions made to the history of film exhibition since 1985, representative texts include Miriam Hansen, *Babel and Babylon: Spectatorship in American Silent Film* (Cambridge, Mass.: Harvard University Press, 1990); Jacqueline Stewart, *Migrating to the Movies: Cinema and Black Urban Modernity* (Berkeley: University of California Press, 2005); Kathryn H. Fuller-Seeley, *At the Picture Show: Small-Town Audiences and the Creation of Movie Fan Culture* (Charlottesville: University Press of Virginia, 2001); Gregory A. Waller, *Main Street Amusements: Movies and Commercial Entertainment in a Southern City, 1896–1930* (Washington, D.C.: Smithsonian Books, 1995); and Waller's edited volume *Moviegoing in America* (Malden, Mass.: Blackwell, 2002). Two more recent examples of the fruits of this scholarship include Fuller-Seeley's edited volume *Hollywood in the Neighborhood: Historical Case Studies of Local Moviegoing* (Berkeley: University of California Press, 2008), and Richard Maltby, Melvyn Stokes, and Robert C. Allen's edited volume *Going to the*

Movies: Hollywood and the Social Experience of Cinema (Exeter, U.K.: Exeter University Press, 2007).

12. Hansen, *Babel and Babylon*, makes this argument most forcefully, although it is echoed in more recent and less theoretically dependent scholarship such as Charlene Regester, "From the Buzzard's Roost: Black Movie-going in Durham and Other North Carolina Cities during the Early Period of American Cinema," *Film History* 17, no. 1 (2005): 113–24. Whereas Hansen relies on a revisionist version of the Habermassian "public sphere," which was put forth by Oskar Negt and Alexander Kluge in the 1970s, to argue that the cinema could be an "alternative public sphere," the broader concept of a public sphere has remained important for cinema studies in a variety of historical and cultural contexts.

13. While the books listed in note 11 are rarely identified as microhistories, I identify them as such here to call attention to their use of case studies to make general arguments. The problem of establishing the link between the micro and macro has long vexed sociologists and historians who wish use a micro approach to their research. In "Microhistory: Two or Three Things That I Know about It," *Critical Inquiry* 20, no. 1 (1993): 10–34, Carlos Ginzburg argues that historians should, as film scholar Siegfried Kracauer suggests in a posthumously published book, alternate between the two approaches, giving both a "close-up" and "long-shot" view of history. In *Modern and Postmodern Social Theorizing* (Cambridge: Cambridge University Press, 2008), the sociologist Nicos P. Mouzelis uses a more thorough examination of the relationship between macro- and microsociology and history to argue for the establishment of "bridges" between the "actor essentialism" that dominates microanalysis and the "system essentialism" that dominates macroanalysis. He calls for historians and sociologists to refrain from the essentialization of any one analytical tool or perspective and argues that at "all levels of analysis social phenomena should be regarded in terms of both action/interaction and in terms of institutional structures" (254). This paper answers Mouzelis's call for "bridges" by considering film production and exhibition as a local practice shaped by individual actors and as an institutional practice informed at a macro level by Hollywood, which operates as both an ideology and as a set of film companies that determine what local audiences see.

14. E.g., see Epes Winthrop Sargent, *Picture Theater Advertising* (New York: Chalmers, 1915), 248. Sargent encourages theater managers to make local home-talent films to give audiences an opportunity to see whether they have potential as moving picture actors.

15. Robert C. Allen, "The Place of Space in Film Historiography," *Tijdschrift voor Mediageschiedenis* 2 (2006): 15–27.

16. Doreen B. Massey, *For Space* (Thousand Oaks, Calif.: Sage, 2005), 140.

17. Ibid., 141.

18. Richard Abel's two books, *Americanizing the Movies and "Movie Mad" Audiences, 1910–1914* (Berkeley: University of California Press, 2006) and *The Red Rooster Scare: Making Cinema American, 1900–1910* (Berkeley: University of California Press, 1999), are representative of the kind of work that has been done on the transitional period. See also Shelley Stamp and Charlie Keil, eds., *American Cinema's Transitional Era: Audiences, Institutions, Practices* (Berkeley: University of California Press, 2004).

19. See Michael Aronson, "Charlie Silveus Makes a Quotidian Spectacle: An Exhibitor–Filmmaker and His Local View," *The Moving Image* 5, no. 2 (2005): 1–25, and Matthew Bernstein and Dana F. White, "'Scratching Around' in a 'Fit of Insanity': The Norman Film Manufacturing Company and the Race Film Business in the 1920s," *Griffithiana* 62/63 (1998): 81–127. Bernstein and White discuss Richard E. Norman's production of home-talent films in the 1910s before he turned to the production of race films in the 1920s.

20. Ben Singer has noted that production of one-reel films peaks in 1915, when 3,608 of the 5,973 films, or 60%, produced that year were one reelers. The data are taken from several film indexes, which were unlikely to include local films as they were not made for distribution. Singer also notes that shorts were particularly popular in small towns but leaves open the question of why this was the case. See Singer, "Feature Films, Variety Programs, and the Crisis of the Small Exhibitor," in Stamp and Keil, *American Cinema's Transitional Era*, 76–100.

21. Untitled, *Adams County Free Press*, May 6, 1916, 5.

22. Advertisement, *Adams County Free Press*, June 3, 1916, 4. The attractions of the film are described in this ad as follows: "See train No. 6 hit the Chalmers Six and the hero and heroine buried in the wreck. See the heroine rescued by the rival of the hero. See the Mexicans raid and burn the log cabin. See Company K route the bandits and rescue the American women and children."

23. Dick Dreyer, "Iowa Troops in Mexican Border Service: 1916–1917," Iowa National Guard Museum, http://www.iowanationalguard.com/museum/ia_history/1900%20Mexican%20Border.pdf.

24. Advertisement, *Adams County Union-Republican*, July 12, 1916, 1.

25. Ibid.

26. See "Do Local Pictures Pay?" *Moving Picture World*, July 31, 1915, 847. This article noted that the overproduction of local films, particularly of the home-talent variety, encouraged audiences to become particularly critical of films that did not live up to the standards of local films previously made in their town. For this reason, the author, who is not named, suggested that managers not risk the expense of making local films.

27. In the 1910s, town promotional films were often referred to as industrial romances because they combined a "romance"—usually a fictional narrative of a local couple's marriage—with footage of local industries. The civic films of the 1930s did not incorporate fictional scenes into their narratives.

28. Advertisement, *Adams County Union-Republican*, July 12, 1916, 1.

29. Advertisement, *Washington Star*, September 1, 1932, 1.

30. There is currently no published research on either filmmaker, but I am writing a chapter of my dissertation on their work.

31. "School Dedication Plans Completed for Sunday," *Washington Star*, September 1, 1932, 1.

32. Ibid. As stated in note 8, Reeves and Trott from the Tennessee Archive of Moving Image and Sound discovered the 35mm nitrate film and sent it to the Colorlab film-processing laboratory in Maryland. Colorlab made the film available to students in the Moving Image Archive and Preservation program at New York University, and Fehsenfeld, Ng, and Kiernan did the initial research on the film and prepared it for preservation. At this time, no New Jersey archive has agreed to take the original nitrate, which is currently being held by Colorlab.

33. "New Washington High School Now in Use," *Washington Star,* September 8, 1932, sec. 2, 1.

34. Charles E. Shultz, "A Country Circuit's System for Making and Presenting Local Movies," *Motion Picture Herald,* November 16, 1940, 31.

35. Ibid.

36. Bottomore, "From the Factory Gate," 33.

37. Jacquelyn Dowd Hall, James Leloudis, Robert Korstad, Mary Murphy, Lu Ann Jones, and Chris Daly, *Like a Family: The Making of a Southern Cotton Mill World* (Chapel Hill: University of North Carolina Press, 1987), 255. For population information, see the U.S. Census of 1940, vol. II, part 5, table 28.361.

38. "Kiwanis Sponsored 'Movie Queen' Scores Hit with Capacity Crowd: Premier Performance Last Night," *Burlington (N.C.) Daily Times-News,* December 11, 1936, 12.

39. H. Lee Waters Financial Records, Special Collections Library, Duke University. Waters's footage of Burlington is held at the North Carolina State Archives.

40. "Burlington Children Will Star in Movie," *Burlington (N.C.) Daily Times-News,* August 21, 1941, 13. The film itself is not known to survive.

41. "To Take Pictures of Local People: Cameraman to Visit Community and Take Informal Movies of Local People," *Valdese News,* December 11, 1941, 1.

42. "Kiwanis Sponsored 'Movie Queen' Will Be Presented in Municipal Auditorium December 11–12," *Burlington (N.C.) Daily Times-News,* December 1, 1936, 10. The film itself is not known to survive.

43. Lorelei F. Eckey, Maxine Allen Schoyer, and William T. Schoyer, *1,001 Broadways: Hometown Talent on Stage* (Ames: Iowa State University Press, 1982).

44. "Hollywood Is Coming Direct to Burlington's 'Main Street' in Production of 'Movie Queen,'" *Burlington (N.C.) Daily Times-News,* December 2, 1936, 8.

45. "Description of the Work of a Director," a document produced by the Boston Amateur Theatre League, points out that "in the staging of shows the director follows a highly specialized, tested and tried, successful system." Given the similarity of newspaper articles about *The Movie Queen* in other towns, it is likely that part of the success of the play and film was the use of newspaper publicity. From the Marion Angeline Howlett Collection, 2006-MT-163r, Harvard Theatre Collection in the Houghton Library. Thanks to Karan Sheldon for sharing this document.

46. See Karan Sheldon and Dwight Swanson, "*The Movie Queen:* Northeast Historic Film," in *Mining the Home Movie: Excavations in Histories and Memories,* ed. Karen L. Ishizuka and Patricia R. Zimmerman (Berkeley: University of California Press, 2008), 185–89.

47. "Hollywood Is Coming Direct."

48. Ibid.

49. The play, titled *The Movie Queen*, was copyrighted on August 13, 1934, by Adella Cramer, one of the members of the Boston Amateur Theatre League. The character names are taken from the version of the play submitted to the Library of Congress in 1934. See Catalog of Copyright Entries, part 1 [C], group 3, Dramatic Compositions and Motion Pictures, vol. 7, nos. 1–123, 1934, 4814.

50. H. Lee Waters Financial Records, Special Collections Library, Duke University.

51. "Movie-Taking Man to Visit Burlington Theatre Sponsorer," *Burlington (N.C.) Daily Times-News*, March 8, 1941, 12.

52. Flyer from a screening in Fort Mill, South Carolina, personal collection. Stephanie Stewart takes a somewhat different approach to Waters's films by placing them in the context of other documentary projects of the 1930s, particularly the photographs made by the Farm Security Administration, implicitly suggesting that Waters's films were from the outset historical documents. See Stewart, "*Movies of Local People* and a Usable Past: Mill Town Treasures and Transcendent Views, 1936–1942," *Moving Image* 7, no. 1 (2007): 51–77.

53. "Librarian of Congress Adds 25 Films to the National Film Registry," press release, Library of Congress, December 28, 2004, http://www.loc.gov/today/pr/2004/04-215.html.

54. "Movie-Taking Man to Visit Burlington."

55. "Local Pictures 'Shot' by Lee Waters," *Burlington (N.C.) Daily Times-News*, January 17, 1942, 9.

56. For more on the relationship between Hollywood and film fans, see Anne Morey, *Hollywood Outsiders: The Adaptation of the Film Industry, 1913–1934* (Minneapolis: University of Minnesota Press, 2003). Though Morey's account ends a little before Waters began his itinerant film practice, and her chapter on the Palmer Photoplay Corporation is more focused on what might be called the serious amateur—someone who enters screen contests or writes scripts—than on someone who happens to be in a local film, she does show how ideas about Hollywood were expressed in materials not produced or sanctioned by the film industry. Patricia Zimmermann, *Reel Families: A Social History of Amateur Film* (Bloomington: Indiana University Press, 1995), also addresses the relationship between Hollywood and amateur filmmakers, suggesting that amateurs often rejected the advice offered in film manuals and magazines to make their movies look professional through the use of continuity editing and other techniques common in Hollywood films. Though several of the filmmakers considered here used film equipment that was marketed to amateur filmmakers, I have encountered very little evidence of connections between local and amateur filmmakers. For example, though *Amateur Movie Makers*, a magazine first published by the Amateur Cinema League in 1926, did on occasion discuss making narrative films with local actors, it was rare for the magazine to suggest public exhibition of this work, and making films for profit was frowned on. In fact, a 1928 article defined the amateur as "a person who makes movies but who does not devote the major part of his time to making them for profit." See "Amateur—Typical?" *Amateur Movie Makers* 3, no. 5 (1928): 295.

57. "Burlington Children Will Star in Movie."

58. Hans Robert Jauss, "Literary History as a Challenge to Literary Theory," *New Literary History* 2, no. 1 (1970): 7–37.

59. "St. Cloud Took First Local Movies in Many Years," *Washington Star*, April 14, 1933, sec. 2, 1.

60. Ibid.

CUCKOO IN THE NEST

VANESSA TOULMIN

Edwardian Itinerant Exhibition
Practices and the Transition to
Cinema in the United Kingdom
from 1901 to 1906

When the cinema came, the manager was often a blend of the fairground showman, the travelling theatre proprietor and the panorama lecturer.
                —John H. Bird, *Cinema Parade: Fifty Years of Film Shows*

Rachael Low, in her now-classic study of British film, marks 1906 as the year that witnessed
the widespread realization of permanent purpose-built palaces for the exclusive showing
of "living pictures."[1] This article will examine this belief and argue that development
occurred both regionally and at different rates of acceleration throughout the Edwardian period (1901–1910). The early Edwardian period was when the cinematograph was
the property of the itinerant showmen who commissioned, programmed, and in some
instances produced their own material for a differing and constantly changing audience
in each of the localities they visited. Drawing on material collected during the Mitchell
and Kenyon project, original archives held by the National Fairground Archive at the
University of Sheffield Library, and a close search of U.K. regional newspapers, it will
seek to provide a chronology for the transformation period and suggest reasons for its
development. In addition, it will bring to the forefront the importance of the role played
by itinerant exhibitors who presented the cinematograph in this transitional period and
show how they were ultimately responsible for its success.

INTRODUCTION

The entertainment environment in the United Kingdom in the 1890s was a dynamic and
bewildering mixture of low-class illegitimate venues and practices alongside legitimate
theater, music halls, circuses, operas, lectures, and reading halls and, of course, the
burgeoning cinematograph industry.[2] Leisure time had advanced throughout the nineteenth century as increased wages, improved transportation systems, and a recognized
system of play or nonwork time had enabled a dynamic market to evolve, catering to a
largely urban population.[3] The appearance of the cinematograph in the late Victorian
era has been widely studied in the United Kingdom with perhaps more emphasis placed
on technological developments and film production than its impact on related leisure
industries. The cinematograph's appearance in London in 1895 and its subsequent
impact in the last few years of Queen Victoria's reign have been extensively researched
by scholars such as John Barnes, Richard Brown, and Luke McKernan, among others.[4]
However, its subsequent transformation from a novelty or wonder to a fully fledged part
of twentieth-century exhibition and entertainment culture has never fully been assessed.
Only recently have British scholars begun to examine the first few years of Edward's

reign and the subsequent development of the cinematograph as an exhibition form that evolved into the institution known as the cinema.

The first decade of the twentieth century is often called the long Victorian era by scholars but is, in reality, a very different era. By the time Edward acceded to the throne in 1901, he reigned over a society that enjoyed the benefits of reduced working hours, increased holiday time, and improvements in transportation that enabled citizens to participate in a full range of popular amusements. Free time could be spent on holidays and excursions to seaside and countryside; "rational recreation," in which pursuits were allied to educational activities and the culture of "self-improvement"; or a range of popular entertainments, including music halls, circuses, and the fairground.[5] Many of the forces in industry, commerce, and science that had been instigated in the later Victorian period came to fruition during Edward's reign. Politics, commerce, and the rise of the trade unions; the emancipation of women; and the beginnings of publicly financed education shaped the culture. The Edwardians were essentially living in a fully urbanized society, rising from 77 percent of the population living in cities in 1901 to 80 percent by 1911; working and social conditions were greatly improved and would continue to improve as the decade commenced.[6] The social critic Charles Masterman described the new urban populace as the "City" type of the coming years, the "street bred" people of the twentieth century, the "new generation knocking on our doors."[7] This urbanized multitude became the audience for the emerging developing cinema industry.

The introduction of the cinematograph into the entertainment environment of the late nineteenth and early twentieth centuries has received wide coverage in the United States, ranging from discussions of individual exhibitors to the birth of nickelodeons and the development of the audience to comparative studies of small towns and large cities.[8] In the United Kingdom, the scholarship is more disparate, with greater emphasis placed on the introduction of the cinematograph in the Victorian period rather than on its evolution as an exhibition form and development into a stand-alone entertainment form by the late Edwardian period. As Luke McKernan writes, "the study of early film in Britain still lags behind, fixated upon the screen rather than its consumers," or, I would add, its exhibition practices.[9]

Many factors need to be researched to fully understand the eventual transition of the cinematograph from a touring, itinerant form of entertainment in the Victorian period to the mainstay of the entertainment industry by the First World War. The transition from the cinema of attractions model of film presentation to narrative features, the rise of the film market in business practices, and of course, the structure of the industry itself are all features that are only now starting to be researched in the United Kingdom.[10]

Aspects of this work in relation to the Mitchell and Kenyon collection have been covered in my own work; in particular, *Electric Edwardians* and international conferences in Luxembourg and Exeter have emphasized the role of exhibition in the development of visual and spectacular culture.[11] In addition, London as an entertainment center has recently benefited from the work of the London Project and the research of Jon Burrows and Tony Fletcher on the range of leisure spaces occupied by the cinematograph.[12]

However, it is the leisure environment itself that was the original nest in which the cuckoo first laid its eggs. From its original appearance in the United Kingdom in February 1896, the cinematograph as an attraction became incorporated into a range of existing entertainment forms. It appeared like a cuckoo laying its eggs in a variety of nests. By 1900, a wide range of venues had integrated moving pictures into their existing programs. Venues ranged from shop fronts to music halls to fairgrounds and circus shows, with traveling exhibitors featuring the latest films and novelties to suit the public taste. "Living pictures," as the showmen commonly called them, were included in or formed part of magic shows, magic lantern lectures, waxworks, menageries, or theater shows. Beyond the standard amusement venues and legitimate venues, films were shown in public houses, amusement arcades, educational lectures, department stores, and "penny museums" (alongside waxworks and two-headed animals); the cinematograph, then, occupied most types of social space.[13]

Within this crowded market, distinct types of programs appear to have evolved by the Edwardian period: a turn in a music hall program, a fifteen-minute performance on a fairground bioscope show, a cine-variety performance interspersed with live acts and variety artists, a film showing within a penny gaff, and a two-hour touring stand-alone film show.[14] Catering to middle class, working class, rural, and urban education- and pleasure-seeking audiences, the cinematograph could be found anywhere and everywhere, but it had yet to find a permanent home.

This article will therefore attempt to understand the eventual transition of the cinematograph from a fairground–music hall novelty in the Victorian period to an independent part of the entertainment industry in the following decade by examining the types of exhibitions that took place and providing a context for the range of traveling or itinerant shows that were prevalent at the time. Understanding the theatricality of the entertainment environment within which the cinematograph operated and developed is a major factor in considering the increase in its popularity. Early cinema exhibition and the itinerant showmen who presented it functioned within the entertainment and leisure industry of the late Victorian era. It is only by beginning to comprehend which of the many varying forms of exhibition practices the cinematograph occupied and in which it evolved that can we instigate a model for the cinema industry during its years of expansion from 1906 onward. The resources examined for this article predominantly relate to itinerant entertainment and exhibition practices in north and central England and as such do not necessarily reflect the picture of exhibition in either the south of England or London.[15]

EARLY ADOPTION AND EXHIBITION; OR FINDING A HOME

Although a range of venues presented cinematograph exhibitions throughout the 1900s, including penny museums in Liverpool, Glasgow, and Cardiff; department stores in Manchester; and penny gaffs in London, the fledgling industry from the Midlands upward appears to have developed solely within the three distinct and competing forms of exhibition recalled by the experienced film businessman and then-chairman of Gaumont-British Alfred Bromhead in 1933: the music hall number, the fairground attraction, and the town hall or public hall show.[16] Among this range of contexts, the presentation itself comprised certain features common to the three types of show. This would consist of a lecturer to provide commentary, special effects to heighten their impact, and musical accompaniment ranging from a small orchestra or band to a single musician. The three temporary exhibition types, however, operating within very different venues, were presented within distinct programs and occupied unique spaces within the leisure environment of the time. They also catered to an often overlapping but sometimes dissimilar audience. In what follows, I will present each traveling exhibition type; consider how the different program formats were utilized; examine the composition of the audiences they attracted (if known); and discuss venue location and opening hours, the availability and type of film exhibited, the screen practices adopted, and the social and physical spaces that the venues constituted.

MUSIC HALL SHOWMEN

Music and variety theater halls originally embraced the cinematograph by placing it within its program from 1896 onward. As Rachael Low writes, "the music-hall was the commercial cinema's first home," the shows pioneered by Felicien Trewey (for the Lumières) at the Empire and by Robert Paul at the Alhambra (both in Leicester Square) in March being just a part of the first wave of integrating live theater and animated pictures.[17] These early screenings were in many ways central to the development of the appeal of the cinematograph within large urban populations. The music hall developed from and was influenced by a variety of preexisting performance arenas: backrooms of pubs with sing-songs provided by local entertainers, organized singing saloon concerts, traveling theater companies who would perform in popular theater or on fairground shows, early song and supper rooms, and the entertainment halls in the great pleasure gardens that developed in the north of England in particular from the 1840s onward. The entertainments ranged from middle-class song and dinner evenings to the bawdier affairs of taverns and pleasure gardens.

From the 1850s onward, the format became fixed with purpose-built halls retaining the casual and relaxed ambience of the public house or tavern interspersed with an organized program of entertainment. The event consisted of a chairman or host, with the acts restricted to a particular time limit. The licensing of the halls contrasted with the licenses held by the so-called legitimate theater venues, and they catered to both drinking and dining. The music hall industry rapidly developed throughout the 1860s and 1870s, with over thirty halls listed in London alone and nearly four hundred throughout the United Kingdom in 1870. By the time of the inception of the cinematograph in 1896, the business was largely controlled by a small group of syndicates, with changes to the licensing of these shows making the singing and dancing element of the performance a requirement of the license. The construction of deluxe pavilions from the 1880s onward and the move to a variety performance format employing professional artists, strict fire and licensing regulations, and large audience capacity, created an environment that was fully professional, organized, and in some ways institutionalized.[18]

The entry of the cinematograph into this form of leisure entertainment was at first an immediate success. Certain music halls, such as the Palace Theatre of Varieties in London, provided a regular home for cinematograph exhibition; the Biograph Company's show began a lengthy run there on March 18, 1897, for five years before moving to other venues in London.[19] Film was also part of the program in other music halls in the regions throughout the 1900s, with Robert Paul, for example, associated with venues in Brighton and the Alhambra at Leicester Square.[20]

However, despite the novelty of its appearance in the first few months, film remained just part of the program and not the main show itself. The actual position, importance, and reception of these films among the music hall program in the late 1890s and early 1900s is difficult to gauge. When writing about film and the music hall, Rachael Low states that "the novelty was wearing off, films were good only for the chasers, to be turned on as the audience was filing out."[21] The issue of so-called chasers in the vaudeville theaters in the United States has received greater attention, with scholars such as Charles Musser and Robert C. Allen differing greatly on the notion of chasers and

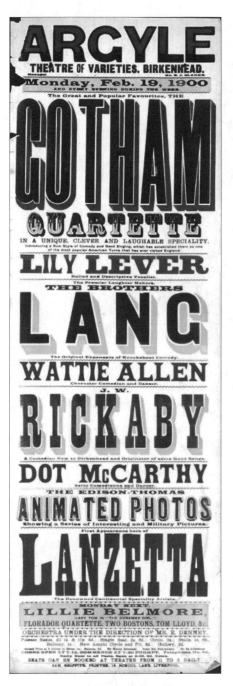

Figure 1. Argyle Theatre of Varieties poster, Birkenhead, showing Edison Thomas Pictures as a turn on the music hall, February 19, 1900. National Fairground Archive, University of Sheffield Library.

the importance of the vaudeville and nickelodeon houses in developing the cinema program.[22] Little comparative work has been done on the relationship between variety halls and film in the United Kingdom either in terms of production of new material or the development of professional and standardized services throughout the circuits. The American model described by Musser suggests a more dynamic and professional relationship between the film companies and the vaudeville houses when relations became widespread and standardized by 1899. Prior to the nickelodeon period, vaudeville houses were the preeminent site in the United States for the exhibition of moving pictures.[23] However, little evidence exists to quantify if films were used as chasers to empty the audience or were an important part of the programming strategy in the United Kingdom.

It has been assumed by scholars, such as Low and Barnes and others, that because of the importance of vaudeville in the United States, the British model must be similar and follow the same pattern. In addition, the prevalence and importance of the nickelodeon business in the United States from 1905 does not appear to have a parallel in the United Kingdom, and because of that, the music hall has been given greater credit than the evidence warrants. Preliminary examination of the archival material in the United Kingdom does not reflect this pattern, and I would suggest that music hall showings in the early 1900s in particular did not advance either the entertainment context or the film program itself. Indeed, contrary to Rachael Low's claim that by "1906 film was no longer regarded as the stop-gap and advertised without enthusiasm, it crept up the bill to be the pride of the evening," film programming in the music hall in that period appears to have remained static.[24]

Although venues like the Palace retained films as part of the overall program, they were rarely the feature presentation. Examination of the Argyle Theatre of Varieties in the Birkenhead Collection in the National Fairground Archive and programs from a number of music halls in Glasgow, Morecambe, and Manchester demonstrates the constant presence of film but also its lack of importance in the program (see Figure 1). For example, in 1900, the Edison-Thomas Animated Pictures was the seventh item on the advertising program, with the individual films not listed but summarized as a series of interesting and military pictures.[25] Topical news events, such as the Boer War, sporting titles, or local films, were often listed. War pictures appeared on the program at the Towergraph in Blackpool's Tower Pavilion and Sheffield United versus Tottenham in 1901 at the Argyle Theatre, with both the Cup Final and the replay at Bolton advertised on the bill (see Figure 2).[26] Throughout the decade, the situation remained constant, with the name of the company, such as the Walturdaw Bioscope in Clacton-on-Sea in 1905 or the Bioscope at the Luna Park and Palace of Amusements at Southend-on-Sea in 1907, constituting the main evidence of their presence in the show[27] (see Figure 3). In fact, examination of over 200 Argyle weekly posters held by the National Fairground Archive for this period up to 1914 shows little change in the position of the films relative to the other entertainment on offer; in fact, the film program is always advertised in the same position on the posters.

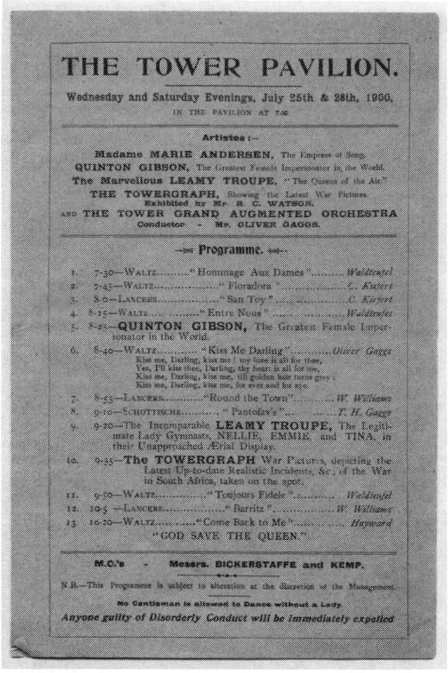
THE TOWER PAVILION.
Wednesday and Saturday Evenings, July 25th & 28th, 1900,
IN THE PAVILION AT 7-30

Artistes :–
Madame MARIE ANDERSEN, The Empress of Song.
QUINTON GIBSON, The Greatest Female Impersonator in the World.
The Marvellous LEAMY TROUPE, "The Queens of the Air."
THE TOWERGRAPH, Showing the Latest War Pictures.
Exhibited by Mr. R. C. WATSON.
AND THE TOWER GRAND AUGMENTED ORCHESTRA
Conductor - Mr. OLIVER GAGGS.

Programme.

1. 7-30—WALTZ......... "Hommage Aux Dames"......... Waldteufel
2. 7-45—WALTZ......... "Floradora"......... C. Kiefert
3. 8-0—LANCERS......... "San Toy"......... C. Kiefert
4. 8-15—WALTZ......... "Entre Nous"......... Waldteufel
5. 8-25—QUINTON GIBSON, The Greatest Female Impersonator in the World.
6. 8-40—WALTZ......... "Kiss Me Darling"......... Oliver Gaggs
Kiss me, Darling, kiss me! my love is all for thee,
Yes, I'll kiss thee, Darling, thy heart is all for me,
Kiss me, Darling, kiss me, till golden hair turns grey;
Kiss me, Darling, kiss me, for ever and for aye.
7. 8-55—LANCERS......... "Round the Town"......... W. Williams
8. 9-10—SCHOTTISCHE......... "Pantofav's"......... T. H. Gaggs
9. 9-20—The Incomparable LEAMY TROUPE, The Legitimate Lady Gymnasts, NELLIE, EMMIE, and TINA, in their Unapproached Ærial Display.
10. 9-35—The TOWERGRAPH War Pictures, depicting the Latest Up-to-date Realistic Incidents, &c., of the War in South Africa, taken on the spot.
11. 9-50—WALTZ......... "Toujours Fidele"......... Waldteufel
12. 10-5—LANCERS......... "Barritz"......... W. Williams
13. 10-20—WALTZ......... "Come Back to Me"......... Hayward
"GOD SAVE THE QUEEN."

M.C.'s - Messrs. BICKERSTAFFE and KEMP.

N.B.—This Programme is subject to alteration at the discretion of the Management.

No Gentleman is allowed to Dance without a Lady.

Anyone guilty of Disorderly Conduct will be immediately expelled

Figure 2. Program for the Tower Pavilion, Blackpool, July 25 and 28, 1900, showing the "Towergraph" cinematograph show. National Fairground Archive, University of Sheffield Library.

The engagement books relating to the Alhambra/Palace venue in Blackpool paint a similar picture. The Alhambra opened in 1899 as a mixed entertainment complex, including a ballroom, variety stage, and menagerie, but by 1903, it was under new management and was renamed the Palace of Varieties. From 1900, the cinematograph occupied a constant if not necessarily important part of the entertainments on offer, and details of the payment received range from the twenty pounds a week paid to Walter Gibbon's Bio-tableaux in 1900 and 1901 to the eight pounds a week to Vernon's Bioscope from 1902 onward. The major change in these economics occurs when the novelty, such as Gaumont's Chronophone, appears on the bill at a weekly rate of twenty-five pounds in 1906 and Urban's Kinemacolour in 1911 for forty pounds. To put these figures in the

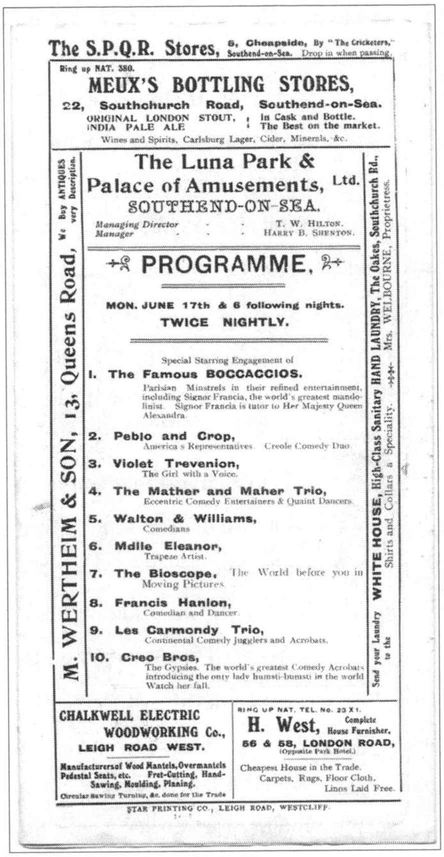

Figure 3. Program for Luna Park and Palace of Amusements, circa 1907, with the Bioscope as one of the turns on the bill, Kinemacolour at the Palace Theatre of Varieties London, December 14, 1909. National Fairground Archive, University of Sheffield Library.

context of the other amounts paid, the cinematograph fee was the lowest paid throughout the period for any act that appeared at the Palace, with the average weekly wage in the region of £25 for a novelty artist and £150 for a headline act such as Little Tich or Harry Lauder. [28]

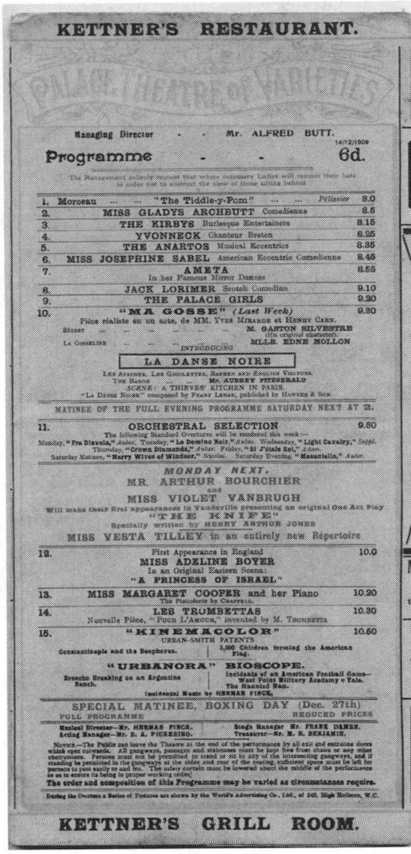

Technological innovations, such as Charles Urban's Kinemacolour show in December 1909, produced greater interest for a limited period with some of the music hall showmen in London, for example; this show moved to Birkenhead for a considerable period in 1911. It was also presented in Blackpool at the Palace of Varieties entertainment complex from December 1911. Interestingly, the Palace by this time incorporated a smaller concert room that showed a separate film program, while Urban's Kinemacolour was on the variety stage. [29] The later Kinemacolour shows were held during a period of rapidly expanding cinema construction and do not herald innovation within the exhibition format, representing instead an attempt to foreground a new technological development (see Figure

3, in which the "Urbanora" Bioscope is placed at 10:50 P.M. in the show—a good billing but not the top attraction).

The music hall is not the model for the later cinema industry because the film element does not appear to have evolved or developed within the venue but remained a static item within the main event itself. Moving pictures may have formed part of the attractions on offer and occasionally were the featured performance, as was the case with the Biograph Company's exhibitions in the late 1890s and later technological variations such as the Chronophone and Kinemacolour in 1906 and 1909, respectively.[30] In addition, later important news features or titles may have occupied top billing occasionally, but on the whole, they failed to create a habit or foster an audience for the films alone. Although the Palace engagement books from Blackpool are only one example, they do provide evidence that as late as 1913, one of the largest and most important music halls in the north of England was paying a fixed fee for film shows as opposed to renting titles individually, whereas in the United States, this transition occurred around 1903.

This brief summary does not have time to examine fully the issue of film as chasers within the performance or in relation to the work of American scholars on the overall importance of the vaudeville theater in American film exhibition. However, the American model of the vaudeville circuit and its importance in early film development should not be applied wholesale to the United Kingdom. Even this limited investigation of the archival material appears to demonstrate that the audience went to see an evening of live entertainment within a standardized, institutionalized, and recognized mode of presentation, which was the music hall and not the films alone. They were not going to the "pictures" but rather to the "halls." The place of the cinematograph in the music hall program in 1914 was the same as it was in 1901: a secondary or novelty attraction and not the main event. The exhibition practice that incorporated or featured the cinematograph during its time in the music hall did not develop into cinema but remained just one of numerous turns on the variety bill.

This does not lessen the importance of the variety circuit as an incubator in the late 1890s for moving pictures, nor does it diminish its influence on later cine-variety shows, which continued until the 1920s. The music hall clearly acted as a stepping-stone for certain exhibitors who moved on from other venues as they sought to develop the exhibition format; it also played a part in introducing the idea of film to large urban populaces. Many of the itinerant exhibitors who started in the music hall moved to other venues to develop the exhibition format and create an audience for the cinematograph as a stand-alone attraction. One such example was A. D. Thomas, who exhibited his Edison Thomas Animated Photos at the Alhambra in Brighton and the Argyle in Birkenhead in

1899 and 1900, respectively. By 1900, Thomas moved to presenting longer, film-centered exhibitions in the St. James Hall in Manchester, where he became part of a more successful group, the town hall showmen (see the following discussion).

FAIRGROUND SHOWS

The second group that Rachael Low credits with both providing a home for the cinematograph and bridging the gap between the music hall and the later, more respectable picture palaces were the fairground showmen.[31] On the British fairground, traveling cinematograph shows catered not only to large urban populations but also to audiences in smaller market towns and villages, which still presented more traditional and less urbanized forms of leisure events such as the local feast or wake fair. In previous work, I have emphasized the importance of the fairground show in developing and marketing this new wonder of the age, and it was the innovative and novelty aspect of the cinematograph that first appealed to the fairground showmen.[32] The fairground has a long history of embracing new forms of technological innovation as well as innovation in exhibition practices, and many entertainment forms found a home on the fairground.[33] Showmen were both innovators and early adopters of the latest wonder of the age.

The fairground was a melting pot of old and new shows where innovation in presentation was the means by which old genres could be repackaged alongside the latest technological wonders of the age. Magicians such as Isaac Hawkes and Professor Anderson presented illusions as part of traveling fairs as well as operating in fixed venues. Pepper's Ghost, one of the most important magic illusions of the era, flourished as a traveling entertainment, and menageries and waxworks shows were first shown on fairgrounds before forming part of the static amusement market. The long-established network of traveling fairs, many of which were founded in the Middle Ages, provided a ready-made circuit for the fairground exhibitor to present a range of new attractions.[34] The introduction of steam-powered roundabouts and merry-go-rounds in the 1860s in England had transformed what was perceived as an antiquated and dying tradition into the exemplar of technological modernity.[35] By the late 1890s, freak shows and menageries functioned alongside steam-powered roundabouts. The insertion of the cinematograph into Randall Williams's former Ghost Show in 1896 was quickly emulated by other showmen, and by 1900, every major fair in the country was presenting living pictures in combination shows, in custom-built booths, or as part of their existing exhibitions.[36] This pattern is also reflected in large parts of Europe, with French, Belgian, and German showmen following a similar pattern of adoption.[37] Fairground showmen were quick to see its commercial possibilities. The necessary equipment for a basic show was cheap, could be purchased in most major cities, and more important, could be incorporated very easily into existing traveling exhibitions. Films could be viewed as part of a menagerie performance with the screen hung over the lion's cage, on the original marionette stage, or as a walk-in entertainment between freak show acts. Local films, showing scenes of the town and locality, quickly became the draw by which showmen kept one step ahead of their competitors at the fair, and business associations with leading cinematograph companies were part of the advertising employed by the showmen to bring in the audience.[38]

THE FAIRGROUND VENUE, PROGRAM, AND AUDIENCE

Within this rapidly expanding arena, certain types of shows—both as architectural forms and as performance genres—were developed, and the fifteen-minute program was created for an audience that was both substantial and transitory. The booths were designed for both optimum audience capacity and fairground flash—that is, the front of the show was as important as the interior, as it needed to compete with the lavish frontages of other types of entertainments on offer. Built as ornate pavilions, with a

Figure 4. Pat Collin's
Wonderland Cinematograph
show, Nottingham Goose
Fair, October 1910. National
Fairground Archive,
University of Sheffield Library.

frontage of eighty feet and capable of holding a thousand people, such attractions would have been featured at all types of fairs.[39] Theater or music hall designs provided the main model for such portable shows, and the interiors of the exhibitions matched the lavish theatrical themes of the exteriors. The shows became bigger and better, and showmen would feature pertinent variety acts on the show's parade to attract audiences. The show was therefore both the acts featured outside and the film programs featured inside. The showmen, as an observer noted in 1907, "vied with each other in the lavishness of their adornments, their show fronts being one mass of gilt"[40] (see Figures 4 and 5).

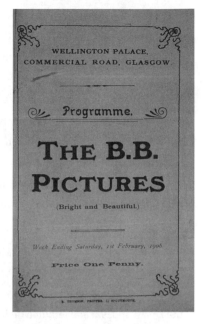

Figure 5. Program for B. B.'s Pictures, Glasgow, February 1, 1908. National Fairground Archive Ephemera Collection.

Unlike the music hall–variety theater, which was a regular part of the weekly fabric of the social and working pattern of the community, the fairground was transitory, occasional, and associated with important traditional holidays.[41] The fairground audience was the holiday crowd, comprising people who were enjoying a break from the everyday and who were similar in composition to the seaside audience, who viewed the cinematograph show as part of their escape from monotonous work routines.[42] To this audience, largely working class but composed of entire communities holidaying together or enjoying the attractions of their local fair, film viewing was not a habit but a one-off occurrence to be enjoyed as part of their trip to the fair or the seaside. Edwardian seaside resorts also provided an opportunity for a mixture of social classes to interact. Edwardian Blackpool, for example, was "a socially mixed resort where the classes and genders could enjoy themselves side by side in harmony."[43]

Therefore the arrival of the cinematograph as an entertainment form placed it alongside long-standing holiday pursuits and did not form part of this community's weekly leisure activities. Films on the fairground occupied the entertainment space of an itinerant and uncanny form of escapism that was part of the holiday–festival calendar. Although the showmen boosted the latest up-to-date films and showcased their products in large and lavish pavilions, this form of entertainment was just one of many fleeting spectacles that the fairgoer would enjoy alongside the roundabouts, sideshows, or games of chance. The fairground was the attraction, not the show itself. It was the appearance of the fair within the local wakes, holidays, or annual feasts that created the audience and not necessarily the individual attractions on offer within the event. Although the fairgoers who watched films during their holidays were essentially the audience who, later in the decade, would go to the first cinemas, it was not in the context of fairground exhibition that their watching habits ultimately came to fruition.[44]

Only a small percentage of traveling fairground showmen made the transition to purpose-built permanent cinemas in towns and cities throughout the United Kingdom.[45] Some showmen, including such notable successes as George Green and George Kemp in Scotland, changed their business model and made the transition to static cinema exhibition from 1909 onward. [46] The introduction of the Cinematograph Act of 1909 was not the killer blow to the fairground as the showmen's trade association had argued and received amendments to the act that granted exemptions for traveling booths. However, the majority of fairground bioscope proprietors (possibly up to 90%) sold, broke up, or replaced their cinematograph booths with the latest fairground sensation by the outbreak of the First World War and retained their base of operations within the fairground industry itself.[47] Some converted their shows to shanty cinemas and played out the remainder of the war years in a temporary but grounded booth, whereas others, such as George Green and George Kemp in Scotland, had already made the transition in 1910 and had successful chains of cinemas by 1914. In many ways, these cinematograph shows were the final expression of a once-great spectacle that had dominated the fairground for over two hundred years and not the creation or benchmark of a new industry.[48] Within the fluctuating and changing fairground landscape, the fairground showmen either had to adapt fully to the new model of permanent cinema buildings or remain on the fairground with a new attraction, the majority choosing the latter course.

TOWN HALL SHOWMEN

> I looked around for a suitable hall which would present a reasonable prospect of success as a temporary or permanent home for the kinematographe [sic] . . . that same building has now run for nearly ten years as a high class picture show to a working class clientele, who for the most part, pay, 2d.[49]

J. J. Bennell, writing here in 1917, falls into the final type of exhibitor, as classified by Alfred Bromhead: the independent traveling showman who presented short-term film shows in public venues and rented spaces. The importance of the exhibition style of these town hall showmen, whose first acknowledgment came from Bromhead in his 1933 address, has been overlooked in favor of fairground and music hall exhibition.[50] Rachael Low, for example, hardly credits them and then appears to mix them up with operators of penny gaffs, who were within a very different tradition and outside the scope of this article. Indeed, although she highlights the importance of traveling exhibition companies, such as New Century Pictures, Ralph Pringle, and A. D. Thomas, she rarely places them, as Bromhead does, within the context of an individual class of exhibition, one that was quite separate from the music hall, the fairground, and the penny gaff, the three main types of venue where, for her, an audience could view the cinematograph in 1906.

With the publication of important work by Richard Brown on New Century Pictures and Jon Burrows and others on Waller Jeffs, coupled with the discovery of the Mitchell and Kenyon collection, it is now possible to evaluate the importance of these independent town hall showmen in the development of Edwardian exhibition.[51] As Charles Musser has demonstrated, in the United States, traveling exhibitors were the principal purveyors of films in towns and small cities where there were no vaudeville houses.[52] Exhibitors, such as Lyman Howe, John Dibble, D. W. Robertson, and Archie L. Shepard, showed films in churches and opera houses for brief periods, often only on one evening or, if the town was big enough, over two or three days. Musser and Nelson's study of Lyman H. Howe's traveling exhibition in America between 1880 and 1920 reveals the fluidity of the exhibition program, which incorporated new innovations such as projected motion pictures.

The years between 1903 and 1906 were the boom years for traveling exhibitions in the United States. Lower film costs, improved projection, and the availability of longer story films made success far easier to achieve. Numerous single-unit companies toured the country playing small-town opera houses, churches, schoolrooms, and vacant storefronts. Howe, like other traveling exhibitors, varied his program according to his audience and survived in the competitive world of early film exhibition because of a number of factors, including showmanship (by his use of the educational program), the knowledge he had built up of the exhibition circuit during his time with the phonograph, and his concern for technical excellence.[53] Despite their importance to American exhibition, no equally comprehensive study has been attempted on town hall showmen overall in the United Kingdom, although significant work has started in Europe and interesting regional studies have appeared in parts of southwest England.[54] Neither has there been any investigation of how the exhibition format they toured and presented could ultimately have created a lasting audience for this new technology and its final and permanent home.

FASHIONING AN AUDIENCE IN BRITAIN

Within the British context, many of the town hall exhibitors had begun their careers in music halls, while others had backgrounds in phonograph or magic lantern exhibitions, which had often played to a wealthier audience than the public of the fairground and music hall.[55] One such town hall exhibitor was A. D. Thomas, who, from 1898 to 1900, appears to have been based in the south of England, hosting regular film shows as part of a music hall program in Brighton and touring an early cine-variety bill throughout London.[56] By 1899 he claimed to have control of twenty-one film shows and ownership of four thousand film titles. However, in 1900, he moved his base of operations to Manchester.[57] His business flourished, with multiple shows touring throughout the north and a parallel show in the southeast named the Edisonograph. Ralph Pringle of the North American Animated Photo Company also offered a similar type of entertainment from his base in Liverpool, as did Sidney Carter of New Century Pictures, operating first from west Yorkshire and expanding throughout the country during the 1900s. Many other exhibitors developed along similar lines in the Edwardian period, forming companies that based their operations at the center of large urban populations such as Liverpool, Manchester, Newcastle, Birmingham, and Leeds.

The stand-alone film or town hall showmen created an audience for their exhibition by combining a policy of mass advertisement with a film program that was tailored to each locality. A fairground show, for example, lasted no more than fifteen minutes, whereas a town hall exhibition lasted up to two hours. The model fashioned by the town hall showmen was originally quite expensive, with an admission price of one to two shillings. This appears prohibitive in comparison with the music hall admission, ranging from two shillings for a good seat in the circle to one shilling in the stalls and balcony to six pence in the circle downstairs and the pit and three pence in the gallery (see Figure 1)—and a penny up front charged for the fairground experience. Richard Brown has argued that New Century Pictures invariably excluded the "factory" film genre from their program because they were performing to a largely middle-class audience.[58] However, Brown's study centers on their operations in 1902; examination of their later shows in Birmingham, Liverpool, and Glasgow shows a shift in their marketing to a cheaper class of ticket price, aimed quite often at women and children.

As the exhibition became more regular in the town or city in which exhibitors were based, a distinct change in pricing and audience development occurred from the 1903 period onward, especially in relation to the shows presented under the management of New Century Pictures by Waller Jeffs in Birmingham and J. J. Bennell in Glasgow. The date at which the early town hall showmen became the later majority in the exhibition class is also far earlier than previously recognized. Whereas Rachael Low cites Balham Palace in 1907 as the first auditorium entirely devoted to films, the creation of an exhibition showing only film occurred as early as 1900 (A. D. Thomas's show in Manchester).[59] In 1916, Sydney Carter, the founder of New Century Pictures, recalled his first stand-alone film show in an interview in the trade journal *Cinegoer:*

> Our first cinema show was in '96; the first full programme of nothing but animated pictures was [in Bradford] in 1901, and soon after that we had frequently audiences of 2,000 to 3,000 in Bradford, Leeds, Hull, Halifax, Manchester and other places, whereas one often reads that the industry was started in this country years later in shops or small places seating about 200 people. And in those days we had good programmes, good prices, (2s, 1s and 6d); we advertised well and generally had a band of twelve or fifteen.[60]

Carter cites 1901 as the date of the creation of a program of nothing but animated pictures, and this appears to be confirmed by the historical record. On close study of early film programs and detailed examination of local newspaper and specialist publications, such as the Glasgow, Dundee, and Manchester *Programme* from 1900 to 1907, a pattern emerges: the showmen often utilized the larger and more aspiring halls for their exhibitions.

Ralph Pringle was based in the St. George Hall, and later Liverpool shows were opened at the Picton Hall, which was also in the Lime Street area. The Lime Street area of Liverpool was a flourishing center of entertainment throughout the Victorian and Edwardian periods, with films appearing in waxworks, theaters, music halls, and penny gaffs.[61] Sydney Carter presented his shows at the St. George's Hall in Bradford, a large and imposing venue capable of holding up to two thousand people, and A. D. Thomas based his center of operations at the St. James Greater and Lesser Halls in Manchester from 1900 to 1902.[62] The Edison Thomas show in Hull continued on the Manchester model and, under the management of Waller Jeffs, provided two shows daily for a period of up to six weeks at a time.[63] Certainly from 1901, they were advertising new films daily in their programs, and the surviving programs, flyers, and handbills in the Sidney Carter Collection in the West Yorkshire Archives in Bradford do imply that this practice continued. From 1903 onward, the town hall showmen's season became longer as their stay within the town extended to periods of up to fourteen weeks or more. Capitalizing on their initial success with the local views, they continued to program the film shows with the aim of capturing an everyday audience.

Capturing this everyday audience was a vital component of the success of these shows, and many of these exhibitors appear to have undertaken a marketing ploy aimed at children. Regional variations do differ, and certainly by 1905, ticket prices for these town hall events had dropped, with only the more impressive stalls and boxes retaining a two-shilling entrance fee. The role of New Century Pictures is very important in this development as it appears to be a company of affiliated traveling film shows with branches throughout the north of England and the Midlands. Thomas, for example, ran the Liverpool branch from the Picton Hall, and the 1905 *Illustrated Programme* advertised that New Century Animated Pictures was running shows from the Coliseum in Leeds, St. George's Hall in Bradford, Curzon Hall in Birmingham, the West End Pier in Morecambe, and the Free Trade Hall in Manchester.[64] Allied to that were other shows at the Olympia in Scarborough and their expansion, from 1906, to Glasgow.[65] The pricing structure of the shows also changed during this period, with seat prices ranging from one shilling, six pence in Leeds and Birmingham (with cheaper seats at three pence) to a shilling at Scarborough and Morecambe (with cheaper seats at three and two pence). Even when the exhibitors expanded beyond New Century, they still followed the model first presented by Thomas and developed by New Century: that of capturing and forming part of the audience's daily experience. For example, J. J. Bennell's program for B. B. Pictures in Glasgow in 1908 was completely aimed at children with a ticket price of one penny and special Saturday matinee performances for children in the Wellington Palace. New Century Picture Hall at the bottom of Mt. Pleasant, again in 1908, produced a special Saturday-only show for children only with admission at two pence from 11:30 A.M. onward (see Figure 6).

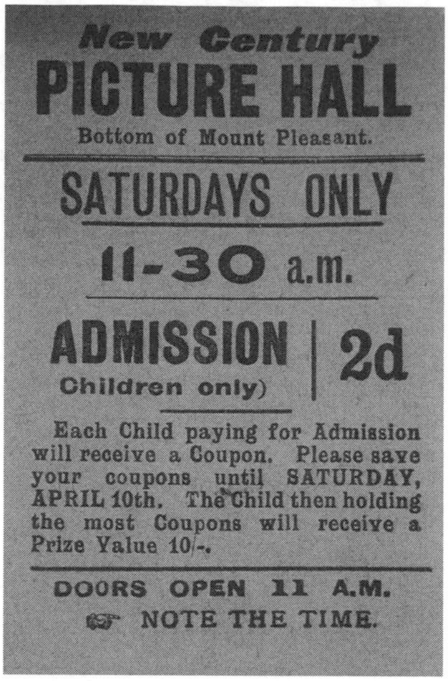
New Century
PICTURE HALL
Bottom of Mount Pleasant.
SATURDAYS ONLY
11-30 a.m.
ADMISSION | 2d
Children only)
Each Child paying for Admission will receive a Coupon. Please save your coupons until SATURDAY, APRIL 10th. The Child then holding the most Coupons will receive a Prize Value 10/-.
DOORS OPEN 11 A.M.
NOTE THE TIME.

Figure 6. Handbill for New Century Pictures show at Mount Pleasant Liverpool, circa 1908. West Yorkshire Archive Service, Bradford, U.K.

Jon Burrows's examination of some of the regional shows presented by Jeffs in Birmingham affirms that "in many respects his [Jeffs's] shows in Birmingham and Carter's [in Bradford] represent the closest equivalent to a permanent fixed site cinema

Table 1. Principal categories of commissioner based on 835 films within the Mitchell and Kenyon Collection from 1900 to 1913

Category	Working definition	Number of commissioners	Number of films
Fairground	Commissioned solely or principally for fairground exhibition	13	139
Proprietor/ variety	Commissioned by owner/manager of exhibition center, whether music hall or theater	9	44
Stand-alone/ town hall	Exhibition practices consisting principally of film, although variety may be a minor component	18	530
Others	Cinemas or part of exhibition	8	54
Total		48	767

Note: The main years of evaluation are the period from 1900 to 1906.

that one can find in Britain during the first half of the 1900s."[66] Further study is needed on the rate of expansion and the entrance price of this type of show. However, within this preliminary investigation, it appears that New Century Pictures, for example, developed throughout the Edwardian period, with each local show reflecting the interests and dynamics of that particular audience. For example, Waller Jeffs's programs were very different from J. J. Bennell's or the Picton Hall shows in Liverpool; Jeffs used the model of the travelogue, whereas the Glasgow and Liverpool shows catered to a young audience. However, they were similar in that film was the motivating and central feature of their programs, and the audience paid for and watched a two- to three-hour film show exhibited twice daily from mid-1901 onward.

An additional set of evidence that can be analyzed alongside this material is the adoption and rate of acceleration of cinematograph consumption by the various categories of exhibitor who commissioned the films in the Mitchell and Kenyon collection, together with the changes in the composition of these categories over the life of Mitchell and Kenyon's productions (see Tables 1 and 2).[67] Of the 835 reels in the Mitchell and Kenyon collection, 767 can now be linked to a particular type of exhibition or commissioner. The remaining fifty-nine consist of titles that were noncommissioned and sold directly by the company, a small percentage of unidentified material, and those used

Table 2. Total films, by year, of the principal categories of commissioner based on titles commissioned in the Mitchell and Kenyon Collection

	1900	1901	1902	1903	1904	1905	1906	1907	1908	1909	1911	1912	1913
Fairs	51	30	26	5	7	3	5	9	3				
Music hall	2	2	11	7	9	7	2	4					
Town hall	7	212	227	23	29	20	7	3	2				
Others		10	5	8						2	11	9	9
Total	60	254	269	43	45	30	14	16	5	2	11	9	9

by all groups of exhibitors. It must be emphasized that these figures are based only on titles commissioned and do not reflect how the changes in the film program and the transition to a more narrative cinema slowed down production of local films from 1903 onward. Also, the survival rate of the later films from 1905 to 1906 are less proportionate than those from the earlier period. However, the collection does demonstrate the growth and spread of the town hall shows from 1901 and indicates that they were the dominant commissioners from the Midlands upward, in particular because of their increasing sole use of film in their programming strategies.[68]

These figures indicate that following an initial concentration on the fairground, local film production was principally exploited by the town hall showmen, in particular in 1902. However, as the role of the latter decreased in local film programming and moved onto features, narrative films, and other types of material from 1906 onward, fairground exhibition and music hall shows continued with local films. The stand-alone showmen no longer utilized them within their shows as the main attraction from 1906 onward. The period from 1909 marks the exclusive production of films for managers and owners of permanent cinemas but also sees Mitchell and Kenyon withdraw from film production. The concentration of stand-alone showmen utilizing local films dropped off in production in the mid-1900s because of the decrease in the popularity of local films as opposed to the reduction in town hall showmen. In addition, the survival rate of the material in the Mitchell and Kenyon collection is greater in the earlier part of the 1900s in comparison to the period from 1906 onward.

CONCLUSION

Of Colonel Bromhead's three major categories of early film exhibitor, it was the itinerant town hall showmen who provided the model for the purpose-built cinema from 1907 to 1908 onward. These traveling exhibitors operated within a large and already vibrant entertainment market but also adapted and expanded their product and thereby created a market for a new form of entertainment. A daily change of film program meant that they were reliant not on other attractions but on the film itself to draw crowds. The two-hour spectacular promised by the showmen, complete with military band, local films, an effective spieler for the commentary, and a high turnover of films, was the start of a new and distinct form of leisure activity—a visit to the cinema.

However, by 1909, they, too, were facing competition from the very market they had created: the permanent cinema owner. The town hall show then had to make a choice either to become supplanted by the local cinema owner or to evolve into the local cinema show by simplifying the program, dropping the middle-class nature of their halls, and emphasizing their local connections. The reporter for the *Ilkeston Pioneer* reporting the opening of the Hippodrome in early 1909 stated that

> Cinematograph entertainments and travelling amusements which return prac-
> tically nothing for the benefit of the rates have had such a continuous run in
> Ilkeston that Mr Rogers, in opening the Ilkeston Hippodrome, is acting partly
> in self-defence, and appeals to the working classes to back him up in this effort
> to provide a permanent place of amusement.[69]

Further research is needed to fully understand the transition to cinema that occurred from 1907 onward, and ongoing research by Richard Brown and Jon Burrows will bring to light this underdeveloped area of research.[70] It is hoped that future research will take into account the role of the town hall showman as opposed to their more glitzy, spectacular contemporaries in the music hall and on the fairgrounds.[71] By the end of Edward's reign, "going to the pictures" had become a habit. From its early days as a section of the program and the evolution of the larger stand-alone events of the early 1900s, from 1909 onward, the building of "picture palaces" occurred throughout the towns and cities of the United Kingdom. Regional variations developed, with Manchester

Figure 7. Illustrated postcard for New Century Pictures, circa 1905. West Yorkshire Archive Service, Bradford, U.K.

ranking second only to London in the number of picture palaces per capita. Indeed, many of the former town hall showmen became part of the first wave of cinema owners. New Century Pictures expanded and moved into the rental market; J. J. Bennell opened his B. B. Pictures in Glasgow in 1907 as well as a branch in Manchester; and Ralph Pringle operated a number of picture halls in the north and southwest of England.

Though further research on this period of transition is needed for a true and complete pattern of the complexity of the situation to emerge fully, there is no doubt that the itinerant town hall showmen, from the early 1900s, had already anticipated the audience that awaited and benefited from these developments. By removing the cinematograph from the constraints of the music hall and the occasional novelty visit of the fairground, the town hall exhibitor created a larger and more adaptable space in which to develop early film. In terms of exhibition practices, the skill of the town hall showman enabled the creation of an audience for the new and emerging context of film exhibition. Using existing and specially commissioned titles, knowledge of the audience, and the culture of filmgoing they created, the stand-alone film exhibitors were predicting the creation of permanent "picture theatres" (see Figure 7).

NOTES

I am indebted to Dr. Jon Burrows, Richard Brown, and Professor Dave Russell for discussions on the varying exhibition forms and the relationship between cinema and the music hall; Andrew Schnail for editorial input on an earlier draft; and the anonymous referees for insightful and informative comments. All images copyright and courtesy of the National Fairground Archive, University of Sheffield Library, and Sydney Carter Collection, West Yorkshire Archive Service.

1. Rachael Low and Roger Manvell, *The History of British Film, 1896–1906* (London: George Allen, 1948).
2. A wide range of material covers the Victorian leisure industry. For shows up to the 1860s, see Richard D. Altick, *The Shows of London* (Cambridge, Mass.: Belknap Press of Harvard University Press, 1978). For circuses, see Brenda Assael, *Circus and Victorian Society* (Charlottesville: Virginia University Press, 2005). For popular music, see Dave Russell, *Popular Music in England, 1840–1914* (Manchester, U.K.: Manchester University Press, 1997). For music halls, see Peter Bailey, *Popular Culture and Performance in the Victorian City* (Cambridge: Cambridge University Press, 1998). For differing forms of exhibition, see Vanessa Toulmin, ed., "Exhibition and Performance," *Early Popular Visual Culture* 4, no. 2 (2006), a special issue on Victorian and Edwardian exhibition practices.

3. For the leisure environment, see Robert W. Malcolmson, *Popular Recreations in English Society, 1700–1850* (Cambridge: Cambridge University Press, 1973); Hugh Cunningham, *Leisure in the Industrial Revolution c. 1780–1880* (London: Croom Helm, 1980); John Walton and John Walvin, eds., *Leisure in Britain, 1780–1939* (Manchester, U.K.: Manchester University Press, 1986); Robert Storch, ed., *Popular Culture and Custom in Nineteenth Century England* (London: Croom Helm, 1982); and Eileen and Stephen Yeo, eds., *Explorations in the History of Labour and Leisure* (Brighton, U.K.: Harvester, 1981).

4. For a full history of Victorian film exhibition, see John Barnes, *The Beginnings of Cinema in England, 1894–1990*, 5 vols. (Exeter, U.K.: Exeter University Press, 1996–98); Richard Brown and Barry Anthony, *A Victorian Film Enterprise: The History of the British Mutoscope and Biograph Company, 1897–1915* (Trowbridge, U.K.: Flicks Books, 1999); Dave Berry, *Cinema and Wales* (Cardiff: University of Wales Press, 1994); Christopher Williams, ed., *Cinema: The Beginnings and the Future* (London: University of Westminster Press, 1996); Andrew Higson, ed., *Young and Innocent? The Cinema in Britain 1896–1930* (Exeter, U.K.: Exeter University Press, 2002); Simon Popple and Joe Kember, *Early Cinema: From Factory Gate to Dream Factory* (London: Wallflower Press, 2004); Harding and Popple, *In the Kingdom of Shadows: A Companion to Early Cinema* (London: Cygnus Arts, 1996); John Fullerton, ed., *Celebrating 1895: The Centenary of Cinema* (London: John Libby, 1998); and Stephen Herbert and Luke McKernan, *Who's Who of Victorian Cinema* (London: BFI, 1997).

5. For further reading, see Assael, *Circus and Victorian Society*; Russell, *Popular Music in England*; Bailey, *Popular Culture and Performance*; Maloney, *Scotland and the Music Hall, 1850–1914* (Manchester, U.K.: Manchester University Press, 2003); and Jackie Bratton, ed., *Music Hall: Performance and Style* (Milton Keynes, U.K.: Open University Press, 1986).

6. Martin Daunton, ed., *Cambridge Urban History of Britain*, vol. 3, *1840–1950* (Cambridge: Cambridge University Press, 2000), and for particular emphasis on the Edwardian period, see Roy Hattersley, *The Edwardians* (London: Little, Brown, 2004); Ronald Pearsal, *Edwardian Life and Leisure* (Newton Abbot, U.K.: David and Charles, 1973); Sidney Pollard, *Britain's Prime and Britain's Decline: The British Economy, 1870–1914* (London: Edward Arnold, 1989); and Paul Thompson, *The Edwardians: The Remaking of British Society*, 2nd ed. (London: Routledge, 1992).

7. C. F. G. Masterman, *The Heart of the Empire: Discussions of Problems of Modern City Life in England, 1901* (London: Harvester, 1973), 7.

8. For just some examples, see Gregory A. Waller, ed., *Moviegoing in America: A Sourcebook in the History of Film Exhibition* (Oxford: Blackwell, 2002); Kevin J. Corbett, "Empty Seats: The Missing History of Movie Watching," *Journal of Film and Video* 50 (Winter 1998–1999): 34–48; Ina Rae Hark, ed., *Exhibition: The Film Reader* (London: Routledge, 2001); and Tom Stempel, *American Audiences on Movies and Moviegoing* (Lexington: University Press of Kentucky, 2001).

9. Luke McKernan, "'A Fury for Seeing': London Cinemas and Their

Audiences, 1906–1914," Working Paper 1 (London: Arts and Humanities Research Council [AHRC] Centre for British Film and Television Studies, 2005), http://www.lukemckernan.com/research.html. This article has been revised and published as Luke McKernan, "A Fury for Seeing: Cinema, Audience, and Leisure in London in 1913," *Early Popular Visual Culture* 6, no. 3 (2008): 271–80.

10. Important work on the growing power of film companies, Pathé in particular, can be found in Jon Burrows, "When Britain Tried to Join Europe: The Significance of the 1909 Paris Congress for the British Film Industry," *Early Popular Visual Culture* 4, no. 1 (2006): 1–19. Further important work by Jon Burrows and Richard Brown on the transition to cinema from 1906 is also under way, including Richard Brown's research in west Yorkshire.

11. Vanessa Toulmin, *Electric Edwardians: The Story of the Mitchell and Kenyon Collection* (London: BFI, 2006). For recent research on exhibition practices, see Travelling Cinema in Europe, a conference organized by Trier University, September 6–8, 2007, and Instruction, Amusement, and Spectacle: Popular Shows and Exhibitions 1800–1914, April 16–18, 2009, University of Exeter.

12. "The London Project: The Birth of the Film Business in London," AHRC Centre for British Film and Television Studies, http://londonfilm.bbk.ac.uk/. Tony Fletcher, "The London County Council and the Cinematograph, 1896–1900," *Living Pictures: The Journal of the Popular and Projected Image before 1914* 1, no. 2 (2001): 69–83, and *Early Popular Visual Culture* 4, no. 2 (2006): 175–221. For details of film exhibition from 1906, see Jon Burrows, "Penny Pleasures: Film Exhibition in London during the Nickelodeon Era," *Film History* 16, no. 1 (2004): 60–91, and "Penny Pleasures II: Indecency, Anarchy, and Junk Film in London's 'Nickelodeons,' 1906–1914," *Film History* 16, no. 2 (2004): 172–97.

13. See Michael Chanan, *The Dream That Kicks: The Prehistory and Early Years of Cinema in Britain* (London: Routledge and Keegan Paul, 1980), for a discussion of the place of the cinematograph at this time.

14. The position of the cinematograph program in penny gaffs has yet to be fully ascertained and is outside the scope of this article, but see Burrows, "Penny Pleasures" and "Penny Pleasures II."

15. As previously mentioned, two large research projects have been funded that cover aspects of exhibition practices and cinema in London and the southwest of England. The London Project is a major study of the film business in London, 1894–1914, organized by the AHRC Centre for British Film and Television Studies. One of the outputs is a fully searchable database, which can be found at http://londonfilm.bbk.ac.uk/. For southwest England, see the AHRC-funded project on the exhibition of moving and projected-image entertainment in the southwest of England from 1820 to 1914.

16. Colonel Bromhead, *Proceedings of the British Cinematography Society* 21 (1933): 4.

17. Rachael Low, *The History of the British Film, 1896–1906* (London: Allen and Unwin, 1948), 36.

18. For general history, see Richard Anthony Baker, *British Music Hall: An*

Illustrated History (Stroud, U.K.: Sutton, 2006), and for music halls and society, see Bailey, *Popular Culture and Performance*, and Maloney, *Scotland and the Music Hall*.

19. Brown and Anthony, *Victorian Film Enterprise*.

20. Frank Gray, "The Sensation of the Century: Robert Paul and Film Exhibition in Brighton in 1896/7," in Vanessa Toulmin and Simon Popple, eds., *Visual Delights Two: Exhibition and Reception* (Eastleigh, U.K.: John Libbey, 2005), 219–35.

21. Low, *History of the British Film*, 37.

22. See Charles Musser, *The Emergence of Cinema: The American Screen to 1907* (New York: Charles Scribner's Sons, 1990); Robert C. Allen, *Vaudeville and Film 1895–1915: A Study in Media Interaction* (New York: Arno Press, 1980); and also Robert C. Allen, "Contra the Chaser Theory," in *Film before Griffith*, ed. John L. Fell (Los Angeles: University of California Press, 1983), 108.

23. For a general overview of both vaudeville and nickelodeon theaters and their importance in cinema development in the United States, see Allen Gevison for vaudeville and Richard Abel for the nickelodeon in Richard Abel, ed., *Encyclopedia of Early Cinema* (Oxford: Routledge, 2005), 672–76 and 478–80.

24. Low, *History of the British Film*, 14.

25. Poster for the Argyle Theatre of Varieties, Birkenhead, February 5, 1900, National Fairground Archive (NFA), University of Sheffield Library.

26. Program for Blackpool Tower and Pavilion, July 25 and 28, 1900; Poster for Argyle Theatre of Varieties, Birkenhead, April 1900, NFA Collection.

27. A handbill for Clacton on Sea, 1905, lists, among others, the Walturdaw Animated Pictures at the bottom of the bill, and a program for Luna Park and Palace of Amusements (undated but c. 1907) also lists a bioscope show (see Figure 3). NFA Collection.

28. Notes on cinematograph at the Alhambra/Palace in Blackpool, 1900–1913, taken from the Admission Books and Books of Artists Engagement, Leisure Parcs Archive Empress Buildings Blackpool.

29. The Artist Engagement Book for the Alhambra/Palace reveals that the cinematograph cost eight pounds a week, with the projectionist being paid around four to six pounds a week.

30. Brown and Anthony, *Victorian Film Enterprise*.

31. Low, *History of the British Film*, 37.

32. See Vanessa Toulmin, "Telling the Tale: The History of the Fairground Bioscope Show and the Showmen Who Operated Them," *Film History* 6, no. 2 (1994): 219–37; Toulmin, "The Fairground Bioscope" and "Bioscope Biographies," in Harding and Popple, *In the Kingdom of Shadows*, 191–207, 219–37; Toulmin, "Women Bioscope Proprietors: The Queens of Showland," in *Celebrating 1895: The Centenary of Cinema*, ed. John Fullerton (London: John Libby, 1998), 55–65.

33. See Vanessa Toulmin, *Pleasurelands: 200 Years of Life on the Fair* (Hastings, U.K.: The Projection Box, 2002), and David Braithwaite, *Fairground Architecture* (London: Hugh Evelyn, 1968).

34. For an overview of fairground technology and art, see Geoff Weedon and Richard Ward, *Fairground Art* (London: White Mouse, 1984).

35. See Hugh Cunningham, "The Metropolitan Fairs: A Case Study in the Social Control of Leisure," in *Social Control in Nineteenth Century Britain*, ed. A. P. Donajgrodzki (London: Croom Helm, 1977), 163–84, and Toulmin, *Pleasurelands*.

36. Vanessa Toulmin, *Randall Williams: King of Showmen* (London: The Projection Box, 1998), 54.

37. See Martin Loiperdinger, ed., *Travelling Cinema in Europe: Sources and Perspectives* (Frankfurt, Germany: Stroemfeld-Roter Sterm, 2008), for a selection of important new research on the importance of traveling exhibitions on German and Belgium fairgrounds and also a range of other types of exhibition forms.

38. Vanessa Toulmin, "Local Films for Local People: Travelling Showmen and the Commissioning of Regional Films, 1900–1902," *Film History* 13, no. 2 (2001): 118–38.

39. Vanessa Toulmin, "The Cinematograph at the Goose Fair," in *The Showman, the Spectacle, and the Two-Minute Silence: Performing British Cinema before 1930*, ed. Alan Burton and Laraine Porter (Trowbridge, U.K.: Flicks Books, 2001), 76–87.

40. *Eastern Morning News*, quoted in *The World's Fair*, October 19, 1907.

41. Fairs in the United Kingdom are granted by charter, prescriptive right or tradition, or act of Parliament linked to an annual holiday, a bank holiday, or a local festivity. This fixes the annual fair on a particular day of the year every year—such is the restriction of the tradition. For one such example, see Vanessa Toulmin, *Hull Fair: Fun for All* (Oldham, U.K.: Oldham World's Fair, 1999), or David Kerr Cameron, *The English Fair* (Stroud, U.K.: Suttton Press, 1998).

42. For a discussion of the playful holiday crowd, see Gary S. Cross and John K. Walton, *The Playful Crowd: Pleasure Places in the 20th Century* (New York: Columbia University Press, 2005).

43. Ibid., 66.

44. Vanessa Toulmin, "We Take Them and Make Them: Mitchell and Kenyon and the Travelling Exhibition Showmen," in *The Lost World of Mitchell and Kenyon: Edwardian Britain on Film*, ed. Vanessa Toulmin, Simon Popple, and Patrick Russell (London: BFI, 2004), 59–69.

45. The original data can be found in Toulmin, "Telling the Tale."

46. For George Green, see Janet McBain, "Mitchell and Kenyon's Legacy in Scotland—The Inspiration for a Forgotten Film-making Genre," in Toulmin et al., *Lost World of Mitchell and Kenyon*, 113–24.

47. This 10% also included the Haggar Family and the Dooners. For examples of fairground showmen who made the transition to cinema, see Kevin Scrivens and Stephen Smith, *The Travelling Cinematograph Show* (Tweedale, U.K.: New Era, 1999).

48. Vanessa Toulmin, "Within the Reach of All: Travelling Cinematograph Shows on British Fairgrounds," in Loiperdinger, *Travelling Cinema in Europe*, 19–35.

49. J. J. Bennell, "In the Days of the Pioneer Showman," *Kinematograph and Lantern Weekly,* March 8, 1917, 19–21.

50. Christopher Dingley, *Waller Jeffs at the Curzon Hall: A Study in Early Film Showmanship* (M.A. thesis, University of Derby, 2000), defines them as public hall showmen, and this term has its merits. In keeping with Bromhead's original description, and although I agree that *public hall* has a wider remit than *town hall,* which appears more formal and civic, I will continue to use Bromhead's original 1933 definition.

51. See Dingley, *Waller Jeffs at the Curzon Hall,* and Jon Burrows, "Waller Jeffs Scrapbooks," *Picture House: Journal of the Cinema Theatre Association* 29 (2004): 44–55. See also Richard Brown, "New Century Pictures: Regional Enterprise in Early British Film Exhibition," in Toulmin et al., *Lost World of Mitchell and Kenyon,* 69–82.

52. Charles Musser and Carol Nelson, *High-Class Moving Pictures: Lyman H. Howe and the Forgotten Era of Traveling Exhibition, 1880–1920* (Princeton, N.J.: Princeton University Press, 1991).

53. Ibid., 53.

54. See Ivo Blom, *Jean Desmet and the Early Dutch Film Trade* (Amsterdam: Amsterdam University Press, 2003). The tenth Domitor conference (2008) also included a range of papers on regional exhibition and distribution, and Travelling Cinema in Europe (Trier, 2007) included papers on local exhibition, fairground exhibition, and traveling shows. There are some British exceptions: see previous notes for work on Waller Jeffs and New Century Pictures and Jon Burrows's keynote presentation on T. J. West titled "West Is Best: or What We Can Learn from Bournemouth," on town hall showmen in Bournemouth, presented at Instruction, Amusement, and Spectacle: Popular Shows and Exhibitions 1800–1914, April 16–18, 2009, University of Exeter.

55. Deac Rossell, "A Slippery Job: Travelling Exhibitors in Early Cinema," in *Visual Delights: Essays on the Popular and Projected Image in the 19th Century,* ed. Simon Pole and Vanessa Toulmin (Trowbridge, U.K.: Flicks, 2000), 50–60.

56. See program for the Brighton Alhambra, Monday, March 5, 1900, Brighton Public Libraries, BB 792/BRI, for details of the Edison-Thomas Royal Vitascope. However, according to reports in *The Encore* (January 11, 1900), Thomas's run at the Alhambra commenced in September 1899. See also Fletcher, "The London County Council."

57. For Thomas in Manchester, see Vanessa Toulmin, "The Importance of the Programme in Early Film Presentation," in *KINtop 11: Kinematographen-Programme,* ed. Frank Kessler, Sabine Lenk, and Martin Loiperdinger (Frankfurt am Main, Germany: Stroemfeld, 2002), 19–33.

58. See Brown, "New Century Pictures."

59. Low, *History of the British Film,* 15.

60. "Great Britain's Leading Cinema Proprietors or Managers. Mr S. H. Carter," *The Cinegoer,* February 26, 1916, 15.

61. Vanessa Toulmin, "Wonders in Nature and Art: Reynold's Museum of Curiosity and the Lime Street Entertainment Industry in Liverpool, 1860–1900," in *Entertainment, Leisure, and Identities,* ed. Roger Spalding and

Alyson Brown (Newcastle, U.K.: Cambridge Scholars, 2007), 83–95.

62. E.g., the *Manchester Programme* from May to October contains a weekly advert for Thomas's shows in Manchester, listing all the films on display, with a pricing structure ranging from three shillings to six pence, showing a two-hour uninterrupted film program twice daily.

63. See *The Searchlight*, April 25, 1901, onward, front page, for details of the show held in the Assembly Rooms in Hull.

64. Illustrated Programme of the New Century Animated Pictures 1, no. 2 (April 22, 1905), Carter Collection, West Yorkshire Archive Service, Bradford.

65. Scrapbooks of Sydney Carter, Carter Collection, West Yorkshire Archive Service, Bradford, 46d 84/4.

66. Burrows, "Waller Jeffs Scrapbooks," 47. This point was also made by Dingley, *Walter Jeffs at the Curzon Hall.*

67. For the story of Mitchell and Kenyon, see a range of articles, including Vanessa Toulmin, Patrick Russell, and Tim Neal, "The Mitchell and Kenyon Collection: Rewriting Film History," in *The Moving Image* 3, no. 2 (2003): 1–18; Vanessa Toulmin, Patrick Russell, and Simon Pole, "Introduction to the Mitchell and Kenyon Collection," in Toulmin et al., *Lost World of Mitchell and Kenyon*, 2–6; and Toulmin, *Electric Edwardians*, 326.

68. For non-U.K. readers, the Midlands are referred to as Birmingham upward and mark the area outside the geographical center of London and the southwest. This article has centered primarily on the north of England and the Midlands, i.e., the large urban areas consisting of Birmingham, Leeds, Liverpool, Manchester, Sheffield, and Newcastle, with a similar pattern in large urban settlements in Scotland such as Glasgow and Edinburgh. Wales, the southeast of England, and the southwest of England are excluded from this study for reasons outlined in the main body of the article.

69. *Ilkeston Pioneer*, March 5, 1909.

70. See, e.g., Richard Brown and Jon Burrows, "Built on Shaky Foundations? The Economics of the Edwardian Cinema Boom," paper presented at the Glow in Their Eyes: Global Perspectives on Film Culture, Film Exhibition, and Cinema-going, Ghent University, December 15, 2007.

71. My own work in early cinema has possibly overemphasized the importance of the fairground showmen in relation to their contemporaries because of the wealth of surviving photographic and source material. Music hall and fairground shows left a visual record through programs, photographs, and handbills that, with the exception of the Carter and Jeffs scrapbooks, present a more interesting visual record from which to work. Local and specialist newspapers are the key to unlocking the true innovators, and this work still needs to be undertaken.

Meeting the Movie Queen

*An Itinerant Film
Anchored in Place*

KARAN SHELDON

Helen Burns of Bailey's Mistake, Maine, signed a Northeast Historic Film deed of gift in 1989 giving the archives the physical film and all rights to *Movie Queen, Lubec* (1936), a silent 16mm black-and-white film shot by itinerant filmmaker Margaret Cram. Burns worked in the town of Lubec (pop. 1,500), about 200 miles northeast of Portland, Maine, and two hours from Northeast Historic Film (NHF), the independent moving image archives I helped create in 1986. The deed of gift formalized our agreement to safeguard the original film. Burns and others in the Lubec area had a series of interactions with NHF that included two public screenings of the newly restored film and oral history sessions gathering information about the making of the film and its reception in the 1930s. The project, which began in 1989 and continues today, is integral to NHF's mission to gather dispersed works into a critical mass, provide opportunities for interaction, and thereby build recognition for previously unknown moving images. In this narrative, I would like to make the case, through an account of activities around films made by an itinerant filmmaker, for the importance of attaching place-based context to original media documents. By layering firsthand production and reception testimonies, documentary research, physical preservation, public presentations, and discussion of accreted meanings, we can enrich our understanding of nonmainstream films as significant cultural records.

Movie Queen, Lubec, like other Movie Queen films that subsequently came to NHF, consists of the arrival of a local girl "returning from Hollywood," a parade through town, a tour of businesses during which the star is presented with various goods, and finally, an attempted kidnapping and comic heroic rescue. The film is rough: shots are often short and the editing is rudimentary.[1] The formula—parade, advertising, and gangster plot—is repeated in the nine surviving Movie Queen films.

We believe that these Movie Queen films were the promotional element of a touring production scheme established by a Boston-based business called the Amateur Theatre Guild, with a revenue model based on remittances from tickets sold by young female traveling directors supervising talent in one small town after another. The director arrived on location to form committees, line up sponsors and advertising, select and train singers and dancers, distribute publicity materials, shoot and edit a film, direct a live show, and collect revenues—aiming for close to universal attendance. Over two or three weeks of work, she reported to the home office of the Amateur Theatre Guild on Boylston Street in Boston. Lauren Kenyon Woods was the guild's proprietor, dispatching young women to direct stage productions he wrote, one called *The Circus,* which did not have a film component, and the other *Movie Queen, A Musical Comedy in Three Acts,* which survives as both the films and a set of documents, including detailed instructions on how to run the production: a sixteen-page *"Movie Queen" Daily Procedure* and *Film Data for Movie Queen Directors.*[2] The latter indicates that Woods intended the film, like the parade, to build ticket sales for the performance; he states on the first of three pink sheets of paper in *Film Data,* "with 'Movie Queen' your primary drawing power is in the film."[3]

Itinerant cinema's relation to local movie houses, to live theater, and to touring theatrical companies will be further revealed as researchers uncover more information on the corps of traveling directors launched by businesses such as Lauren Kenyon Woods's Amateur Theatre Guild. All the Amateur Theatre Guild directors discovered so far have been women.[4] *Movie Queen, Lubec*'s director, Margaret Cram, has so far eluded us. In 1989, a column in the *Boston Globe* printed our query, including a description of Margaret Cram from the memory of the Lubec movie hero: "She was a young lady when she came to town, fairly attractive and well-proportioned. She seemed to know what she was doing. She was very good at getting us on the ball."[5] No leads resulted from the article. John M. R. Bruner of Groton, Massachusetts (1925–2008), who received funding from New York Women in Film and Television to preserve *Movie Queen, Groton,* sought Margaret Cram diligently for years. The records of Marion Howlett, who worked for the Amateur Theatre Guild in 1937–1938 and kept copies of Amateur Theatre Guild scripts, provide insight into the structure of the enterprise, and although she ran only productions of The Circus and no Movie Queens, she did leave a note in her script file from which we can infer the tenor of life on the road for Cram and others: "This is a very hard-sell proposition which definitely will work and successfully IF all the rules are followed exactly. Almost impossible to do in small towns BUT FUN."[6]

There are Movie Queens from three states with 16mm originals or copies in the collections of NHF: from the Maine towns of Bar Harbor, Bath, Lincoln, Lubec, Newport, and Van Buren; from Middlebury, Vermont; and from Groton and Norwood, Massachusetts. They arrived one by one, identified by libraries, historical societies, service clubs, and individuals. Maine Movie Queens that were made but are lost include those from Bucksport, Dexter, Camden, Eastport, and Madison. Individual acquisitions were noted with stories and pictures in NHF's twice yearly *Moving Image Review*.[7] More recently, Dwight Swanson has identified Movie Queen productions in other parts of the United States: Indiana, Montana, North Carolina, Tennessee, and New York. These were likely directed by more women under contract to the Amateur Theatre Guild.

CREATED AND SHOWN IN 1936

The Lubec film was first shown with the live three-act musical comedy *Movie Queen* performance on Saturday, August 8, 1936, sponsored by the Lubec Woman's Club, in the Eagle Theatre on Water Street in Lubec. Throughout the 1930s, the population of the town was more than twice what it is now. A harbor town alive with fisheries and waterfront canneries, Lubec was a tight-knit and active community. Though the film contained only local people, the participants who shared their recollections with NHF in 1989 recalled that the stage show included players from Boston along with Lubec amateurs who sang and danced. Evangeline Morrison (née O'Brien), who played the movie queen, had a double role: in the first part of the film, she tours her hometown and receives gifts from business owners. In the second part of the film, she is captured by kidnappers played by town luminaries before being rescued by a young man. One of the movie bad guys was Reverend Cleveland, pastor of the Ridge Baptist Church. Lubec resident Lois Pike recalled, "He was really a frustrated actor. He had aspirations of going to Hollywood, which he never did do, but he did go on. He left here and went to Vermont, then New Hampshire, and he ended up being a professor at New England College."[8]

DONOR AND ARCHIVES

Fifty-three years after the film was made, NHF engaged with Helen Burns to contact people around Lubec who had an interest in the film, who had participated in its being made, and who would help arrange screenings and distribution of copies once the original had been duplicated. The names offered by Burns suggest the breadth of connection to *Movie Queen:* Norma Small McFadden might have pictures relating to the film, Ruth Pike and Walter Berry appear in the film "with washing machine," Evangeline O'Brien Morrison starred in the film as the movie queen, Gerry Ashby was president of the Lubec public schools alumni association, Tom Brennan was teaching local history, Muriel Whitney and Merle Higgins were in the chorus line, Glen Greenhalgh and Kay Parker might sing if we had a public screening with live music.[9]

In donating the film to the archives, Burns was ensuring that it would be available to researchers and to her community. A responsibility of NHF is to ensure that the work is made known and that related scholarship continues to be accessible as the interests and approaches of academia and the public change—and as technological methods and resources shift. The rootedness of a regional repository is of great significance: the staff members strive to remain open to the donors and to people from the community where the work emerged, together creating a rich record that may be shared more widely. With the cooperation of researchers, our study center collects and maintains further materials related to the original work, including scholarly articles and media projects.

What is the meaning of *Movie Queen* as the product of an itinerant director in a rural location in the 1930s? There is, of course, no fixed meaning. But the starting place is the work itself, to which we then attach widening circles of context. We believe that regional moving image archives can be among the strongest possible structures for media preservation: we intend to safeguard the moving image near its point of generation, contextualize and connect it to related work, and collaborate with others to add value to further interaction with the original material. Such activities are often funded by

grants sought for individual projects. We submitted a grant request for forty-four hundred dollars to support "The Movie Queen: The Arts of Community Expression in Film" in July 1988. We set out to preserve and study *Movie Queen, Lubec* and *Movie Queen, Bar Harbor* and to interview participants in the films, to investigate how the productions promoted community involvement and pride. The proposal narrative stated, "The artistic significance of both versions of *The Movie Queen* is intimately tied to participation in the films by a large portion of the community. . . . *The Movie Queens* are dramas with a sketchy plot and a great deal of actuality footage. In the national context there is a genre of film commonly called Our Town pictures, in which these would fit."[10] We planned to hold two public exhibitions of new 16mm prints, arrange for copies to be made available to community groups in the future, conduct outreach about the project, publicize the screenings, and report on the project in *Moving Image Review,* NHF's twice yearly newsletter started in 1988. The women who played the movie queens of both Lubec and Bar Harbor were in their late seventies; they could help us determine how the 16mm films fit into their lives and into their hometowns. The proposal listed our areas of inquiry:

> How were community members involved in planning and production of *The Movie Queen?* What was the intended audience? How did the audience respond? How did the response compare with reaction to mass market (Hollywood) films? Regarding the self-referential title, *The Movie Queen,* how—in general—were movies regarded locally, i.e., was there a "film mystique"? What is gained by participation in a creative art like film?[11]

The grant program of the Maine Community Foundation, an Expansion Arts Fund for support of rural activities, paid for film-to-film copying, with the creation of a new 16mm print for projection on Saturday, September 23, 1989. Two shows were accompanied by the local Orange River Jazz Band, with "tickets $2 at the door." We hooked promotion of the event to Coastweek '89, an omnibus celebration of Maine's links to the sea coordinated by the

Evangeline Morrison, *Movie Queen, Lubec*, (1936), in the parade, frame enlargement from 16mm film. Northeast Historic Film.

State Planning Office. NHF's 16mm presentation of *Movie Queen, Lubec* was sponsored by the Lubec Alumni Association in Lubec High School. It was an all-school reunion, open to the public. The two screenings were held in the cafetorium, where we set up a 16mm projector and Fast-Fold portable screen. The event, along with the film's laboratory work, was funded by the Expansion Arts grant and was "dedicated to the amateur performers who, over the years, have shared their talents with their neighbors." Jimmy Simmonds, the hero of *Movie Queen, Lubec* played in the Orange River Jazz Band and was a special guest, along with Evangeline Morrison, the movie queen. This text is from the dot-matrix-printed press release:

> The Movie Queen and the Hero will be reunited . . . as a kickoff event of Coastweek '89. The film, which was made in Lubec in 1936 with many local players, was almost lost. Thanks to Helen Burns of Lubec, one copy of the film survived, and a new print will be shown at correct silent speed as part of a project by Northeast Historic Film to preserve, show and make a record of the entertainment of the time. . . . Evange-

line Morrison who plays the leading role in the 1936 film will be present, along with Jimmy Simmonds, the bicycle-riding hero who on screen rescues her from a rowdy band of kidnappers. Along with this mini-drama of kidnapping and mistaken identity, the half-hour film opens with actuality footage of Lubec's citizens, streets and businesses. Highlights include Reverend Cleveland who also plays a gangster, Don Saunders and Bob Dog, the Peacock Canning Co. and the mill at Whiting.[12]

Reading the release today, I am struck by a sense of continuity and coherence around the backbone of the film. There were strong relationships among the people who acted in the film and on stage more than fifty years before, and these people still cared about what had happened to *Movie Queen*. I am aware, even more now than I was then, of the spirit of inclusion (note the named player, a dog who rode in the kidnappers' car) and of the community's generosity to outsiders. The adventurous spirit and sense of play had been present both in 1936, when the itinerant director, Margaret Cram, came to Maine, and later, when our three-year-old audiovisual archives took an interest in the film and offered to maintain it in perpetuity. In 1989, too, I reflected on the sense of continuity and change brought forward in conversations with the stars. What did a film do to carry that experience across the years? After interviewing Jimmy Simmonds, the hero, and others, I had included the following lines in another short press release:

> One of the interesting parts of the interviewing is the consciousness of passage of time. None of the kidnappers (all local businessmen) is still alive. Simmonds comments, "My goodness, we had quite a town and didn't realize it." On being asked when Lubec changed most radically, there's a silence before Helen Burns responds, "It seems as if after the war things just started to fall down."[13]

Showing a videotape of the film to the movie queen and the hero in May 1989 was an opportunity to elicit details of who and what was on the screen and also to discover and record what they recalled of the original screenings and performances:

> SIMMONDS: I was nerved up all right. I was really nerved up, I'll tell you. We run it a couple of nights as I recall. And we packed that theater two nights in a row. Balcony and all. And that held quite a few people for our little town. Six- or seven-hundred people. And we packed it, there wasn't standing room in that place. It was really quite a show when you come right down to it. Course we had all local talent then, but they were doing a good job, apparently, they pulled a crowd in. I used to do a little singing.
>
> MORRISON: You were good looking. You are.
>
> SIMMONDS: I was no polished actor, that's for sure. It seems like all the locals were in on something, out to the Grange or after school. We were active in that sort

of thing and I guess they kind of figured we had the talent for it. And I owned a bicycle. Oh, dear, that's been fifty or fifty-five years. Imagine it.

> MORRISON: "There's a Little Picture Playhouse in My Heart and the Four Star Feature is a Wonderful Creature Called You" [song title and lyrics].
>
> SIMMONDS: That was one of them. Wasn't there also one that, ah.
>
> MORRISON: "You Ought to Be in Pictures." Yes, you sang to me on stage.
>
> SIMMONDS: I tried to sing to you off stage but you wouldn't listen. . . . That's why we say the good old days, those are good memories. Because as I say, there's some faces in there that's to a lot of people in town it could mean something. To get a chance to see them again, to see them in motion, in action. To see that whole carload of ruffians. Are all gone. They're all gone. And of course most of those merchants are gone. We were chickens then.[14]

The texture of emotion comes forward with Simmonds's persistent traces of stage fright. There is also a strong sense of the communal: "all the locals were in on something"; many citizens were ready to participate in the stage show, having previous experience in local plays or music. And there is the bicycle, which the hero rides to rescue the movie queen at the end of the film, a practical and empowering tool for the time. Private erotic attachments delivered with humor are revealed comfortably to a stranger: "I tried to sing to you off stage." The poignancy of advancing age wraps up this section of the conversation: "we were chickens," meaning we were very young, spring chickens. These elements of human emotion come only from conversation and are not contained within the film; nevertheless they belong with it and underline the power of the film as a catalyzing force in exposing elements of community life and the role of cultural expression—particularly of film as a persistent record—in tracing individual and group identity.

Also only captured from the verbal interchange is evidence of the musical accompaniment, the two song titles "There's a Little Picture Playhouse in My Heart," composed in

From left to right, Evangeline Morrison (the movie queen), Helen Burns, and Jimmy Simmonds (the hero), at a screening of *Movie Queen, Lubec* in 1989. Photo by Karan Sheldon.

1935, and "You Oughta Be in Pictures," from 1934. The layering of these elements in the *Movie Queen* experience as recalled by the participants is emotive and self-aware. The movie queen, Evangeline Morrison, had held those songs in her memory for half a century. As presenters, we were happy to reintroduce these elements to the 1989 performance. At the screening in September, Kay Parker sang "There's a Little Picture Playhouse in My Heart" once we'd located a copy of the sheet music.

MOVIE QUEEN AS PART OF 1930S ENTERTAINMENT

Through inquiring about *Movie Queen,* we found that in Lubec, the intertwining of local amusements and broader popular culture was deep. We could attribute this to three main factors that help situate these moving image documents in our understanding of NHF collections from this period. First, early-twentieth-century transportation integrated geographically dispersed communities. Lubec was served by coastal boats from Boston, the train to nearby Eastport, and a growing number of automobiles. The water routes and cross-border trade with Canada had sustained the town in the previous century. In the 1930s, although Lubec saw effects of the national Depression described by our informants, this was not the back of beyond. There was added visibility and a sense of connection to the world based on Lubec's

adjacency to President Franklin D. Roosevelt's retreat at Campobello Island.[15] Second, motion picture culture moved into well-established leisure environments; each town had at least one hall or opera house for live entertainment and motion pictures. These venues mixed film and live presentation easily, with traveling players, Chautauqua circuit educational and entertainment events, talent shows, concerts, and local theater company productions. Many people went to the multipurpose theater every Saturday night, especially, as described by audience member Leroy Carter, "when there was a vaudeville. [It] came out of Boston. They came down on the Boston boat and would do the tour of the state from one theater to another. While in Lubec they stayed at the American House and did the vaudeville at the Eagle Theatre."[16] Third, radio stirred together popular music and marketing, integrating professional and amateur performance aspirations. Lubec people told us they listened to Major Bowes Amateur Hour and that the radio nurtured a sense of being "with it." Enjoying singing with and to others and being a band member, knowing current music, and experiencing amateur and professional performance was a part of everyday life.

The 16mm Movie Queen films, Lubec and others, captured likenesses of the citizens who were the amateur performers and composed the audiences, showing them along with the stores and other businesses that sustained their material and communal lives. Viewing the moving images with all their capacity to transmit a sense of the texture of 1930s life, and to compare one town with another, adds to the discoveries of scholars tracking the rise and fall of transportation through the incursion of the automobile, the material culture left in Main Street buildings, and the business records of local and circuit entertainment. Finding, preserving, and watching such films closely— with people who are still connected with a particular place—has the potential to deepen understanding of the interactions of commercial entertainment and community leisure. There are many answers to be found about who made entertainment and who received it, much of it quite invisible without ongoing work at a number of levels. Had Helen Burns not connected with NHF, we may not have looked for more Movie Queen films, and had we not gathered a critical mass of the films, we may not have been prompted seek information on how and why they were made.

We were also interested in the Eagle Theatre, which was Lubec's cinema in 1936 and had burned down in 1972. Lubec's first movies were shown in the Crescent in the teens, succeeded by the Eagle, later known as the Lubec Cinema. The Eagle's booker in the late 1920s was Nellie N. Shea, and the hall was later owned by Marjorie Nutt. Cinema management by women became a theme of NHF's social history of moviegoing exploration carried out in two interpretive history projects. In 1989, we received funding from the Maine Humanities Council for "Going to the Movies: A Social History of Motion Pictures in Maine Communities," a public screening and lecture tour with commissioned essays, to pursue documentation of the experiences of audiences and the cinema business. In 1996, "Going to the Movies: A Century of Motion Picture Audiences in Northern New England," built on the previous work, opened as a twenty-four-panel traveling exhibition with live performances and lectures by cinema historians, funded by a National Endowment for the Humanities public programs grant. Before the Maine Humanities Council award, it had been an uphill battle to implement what was originally intended to be a survey of places where movies were seen. When we suggested it might be helpful to canvas the state for cinemas that could still be used for film screenings and other activities, another agency, the Maine Arts Commission, responded that we should already have that information. The state arts agency would only later undertake "discovery research" inventories on a county-by-county basis. Many aspects of the knowledge we sought were either below the radar or thought to be automatically known—whereas we had discovered from many hundreds of miles on the road that the legwork of identifying and assessing surviving halls for contemporary use had not been done and would be arduous. The projects called "Going to the Movies" expanded our work touring preserved films, talking to audiences, researching the exhibition business, and collaborating with local organizations.

ORGANIZATIONAL CONTEXT OF OUR EXPLORATIONS

At the time of the Lubec film preservation and research, NHF was in its third year following a steep learning curve collaborating with the University of Maine's Department of History and the Maine Folklife Center in rural humanities programming activities.[17] We had produced two video programs with Edward D. (Sandy) Ives, founder of the Maine Folklife Center, absorbing Ives's methods and philosophical approach. Our initial board consisted of a historian, David C. Smith (1929–2009), University of Maine; a moving image archivist, Pam Wintle, founder of the Human Studies Film Archives at the Smithsonian Institution; and David S. Weiss, who had a degree in semiotics and film from Brown University and experience in 16mm film production and audiovisual presentation. We had begun community screenings in 1985 with a twenty-two-site tour of *From Stump to Ship: A 1930 Logging Film,* another short 16mm locally created record, an amateur industrial about harvesting the forest and moving timber to a coastal mill and on to schooners bound for market.

You could say we were specializing in as

yet ill-defined genres at a time when funding decisions at federal and state arts agencies were stuck like barnacles to so-called artistic excellence. We had carried out preservation and presentation projects with the Maine Maritime Museum (ice-harvesting footage), the Maine State Museum (a video installation on traditional work in the woods), and Ellsworth Historical Society (footage of the burning of downtown Ellsworth). There was a thread of testimony gathering in all our activities, of preservation fused with community work and presentation. We sold fourteen different VHS *Videos* of *New England Life* to the public. Staying afloat as what we believed to be an activist archives, built on a financial strategy of earned and donated income, was, and has continued to be, a challenge.[18]

THE 1989 FAST REWIND CONFERENCE AND THE ESTABLISHMENT OF VALUE

While we carried out local programs, we tracked developing philosophies and practices of moving image archiving by staying in touch with organizations and individuals in the field. NHF had already participated in gatherings of the Film and Television Archives Advisory Committee, the precursor organization to the Association of Moving Image Archivists. Before founding NHF, we met archivists from the National Center for Film and Video Preservation, the Museum of Modern Art Department of Film, and the University of California, Los Angeles Film and Television Archive. Ernest Dick, Canadian Broadcasting Corporation archivist, wrote in 1989 of the role of technological change and appraisal that "there are shifts in the relative prominence and roles of particular communication technologies, and archivists have to develop a profound understanding of these shifts to do proper appraisal and selection of audio-visual records."[19] Appraisal—recognizing the value of materials—was important to NHF and took work to figure out because there was no handbook for being a regional moving image organization in the United States. We were allocating time and scarce preservation dollars while there was a still a tendency among some North American archives to exclude amateur and home materials. Dick's article in *Archivaria*, from a talk he gave in 1988 at the Association

of Canadian Archivists conference, shone light on conservation implications across the board by looking at amateur film, oral history, and television and pointing to future challenges of the digital era.[20]

Our context as a developing moving image archives was embodied in the May 1989 gathering in Rochester, New York, called Fast Rewind: The Archaeology of Moving Images. The conference, attended by about seventy-five people, was organized by Bruce A. Austin from Rochester Institute of Technology.[21] A panel, Specialized Issues in Moving Image Collections, included the presentation "Movies of Local People: North Carolina," by Tom Whiteside. There were sessions on the Family Film, the Commercial Archive: Its Relationship and Accessibility to the User, Local Television News Archives, and Collecting, Cataloguing, and Values with a paper, "Film and Video Acquisition at the Library of Congress: A Study of Academic and Administrative Values," by Julia G. Mack and Seth Finn, that pitched Robert Saudek, chief of the Motion Picture Division at the Library of Congress, against the members of the Society for Cinema Studies (now SCMS) on the battleground of elite versus popular culture. (Saudek, a Maine summer resident, joined our board in 1988.) In the paper, Mack reviewed acquisition and selection criteria in relation to social values; the pressures of imminent loss through film deterioration pushed her to consider who gets to decide what is preserved, she recalls.[22] The Family Movie panel, organized by Brian Lewis of the Canadian Broadcasting Corporation, lined up Jeffrey Ruoff (then at the University of Iowa), the filmmaker Alan Berliner, Robert Wagner from Ohio State, Lewis, and me to discuss the bona fides of home movies to a friendly crowd. Barry Sherman (1953–2000), director of the University of Georgia's Peabody Awards, curated a screening with Sharon Sandusky's lemmings in *C'mon Babe (Danke Schoen)* and William O'Farrell presented *Remembrance Day* (1968), produced by Crawley Films Ltd., Canada. The gathering helped validate a range of moving image forms, important at a time when there was a lingering hierarchy directing, it seemed, greater resources and notice to theatrical and canonical art films. The meeting provided an opportunity for local television and other regional representatives to talk with each other and for scholars who valued this content, such as Lawrence W. Lichty from Northwestern University, to meet with archivists. As Bruce Austin said in 2009, "the intent of the conference was to pull together those who might not ordinarily find themselves in the same place."[23]

NHF would argue—and the example of the *Movie Queen* would demonstrate—that many media works are best understood when rooted in their *where*. Archives need to preserve films like *Movie Queen,* while also researching how the productions came to be and what they meant to creators and audiences. Though creating digitized versions eases dissemination today, it may also dilute the visual power of the original film; projected film and gathered audiences have persistent power. NHF favors more support for research, leading to creation and attachment of production and reception information, and to greater funding for presentation opportunities, leading to deeper discussion about hidden connections. The movie queen left something that has meaning beyond her town in a moment in the 1930s: she connects places and people over time.

NOTES

1. Copies of Movie Queen films from Bar Harbor, Lincoln, Lubec, Newport, Maine, and Middlebury, Vermont, are available from Northeast Historic Film's (NHF) loan program (http://www.oldfilm.org/borrow/). These and four more Movie Queens may be viewed on site at NHF, Bucksport, Maine.

2. Marion Angeline Howlett Papers, Harvard Theatre Collection, Harvard University. Howlett was under contract to the Amateur Theatre Guild in 1937–1938, directing another production, *The Circus,* which did not have a film component. Her papers, donated in 1972–1973, include the stage play scripts for *The Circus* (1935) and *Movie Queen* (1934), both by Lauren Kenyon Woods, copyright Amateur Theatre Guild, and documents such as *Plot Shots "Gangster Pictures,"* outlining thirty-seven individual shots for the kidnapping drama, and *Film Data for "Movie Queen" Directors,* instructing directors to order film stock from EMF in Cambridge, Massachusetts, and to process it at Agfa Laboratories in New York. *"Movie Queen" Daily*

Procedure is obsessively detailed, a checklist of committee meetings with items such as "Be sure to have a good charitable cause" and "Check ice cream."

3. *Film Data for "Movie Queen" Directors,* Bulletin 1-200-80, pages included in album labeled "Amateur Theatre Guild, 1937–1938," Marion Angeline Howlett Papers, Harvard Theatre Collection, Harvard University.

4. Doris Hamel directed a Movie Queen in Oswego, New York, in 1935 (*Oswego Palladium Times,* June 5, 1935); Marilyn B. Lundy directed a Movie Queen in Burlington, North Carolina, in 1936 (*Burlington NC Daily Times-News,* December 7, 1936); and Agnes Winslow directed Movie Queens in Kokomo, Indiana (*The Kokomo Tribune,* May 19, 1938), and Helena, Montana, in 1938 (*Helena Independent,* August 22, 1938). Citations courtesy Dwight Swanson.

5. "Has Anyone Here Seen Margaret?" quoting Jimmy Simmonds, the hero, in the column Our Towne, Jack Thomas, *Boston Globe,* July 20, 1989.

6. Marion Angeline Howlett Papers, Harvard Theatre Collection, Harvard University.

7. *Moving Image Review* back issues are available through http://www.oldfilm.org/. Images and articles include Bar Harbor and Lubec, Maine, winter 1989 (2); Middlebury, Vermont, summer 1992 (8); Lincoln and Newport, Maine, summer 1998 (4, 16); Groton, Massachusetts, summer 1999 (9); Van Buren, Maine, with a map of located and lost Movie Queens in northern New England, winter 2003 (7).

8. Transcript of screening discussion by Karan Sheldon, NHF, September 23, 1989.

9. Notes from conversation with Helen Burns, NHF, March 22, 1989.

10. Grant proposal to the Maine Community Foundation Expansion Arts fund, NHF, July 12, 1988.

11. Grant proposal to the Maine Community Foundation Expansion Arts fund, NHF, July 12, 1988.

12. "Movie Queen to Be Shown in Lubec," NHF undated press release (1989).

13. "Lubec's *The Movie Queen,*" NHF press release, June 15, 1989.

14. Transcript of interview by Karan Sheldon with Morrison and Simmonds, May 24, 1989.

15. Morrison recalled that the film had portions that did not survive, "and one day we went to

Campobello and President Roosevelt's mother was there. They were having an affair at the church and I remember she came out and I was quite thrilled to have my picture taken with her. But that was part of the film that was lost or broken." Transcript of screening discussion by Karan Sheldon, September 23, 1989.

16. Carter goes on to say that he met a dancer who had been in Lubec who was paid in silver dollars to which fish scales were stuck, traces of the cannery-based economy. There were also annual sardine queens in the town. Transcript of screening discussion by Karan Sheldon, September 23, 1989.

17. The Maine Humanities Council funded NHF's first 16mm film preservation and touring program and provided training in project conceptualization, proposal writing, and evaluation as well as a string of grants for preservation and outreach.

18. The phrase "activist archives" was first used in the summer 1989 *Moving Image Review* (2) in the executive director's report in connection with the expansion of video distribution: "Northeast Historic Film is not a production house. We're not a video store or a circulating film library. Think of us as an 'activist archives.' We provide preservation services, and then make the results of our work available to you— to be seen, enjoyed and used."

19. Ernest J. Dick, "Through the Rearview Mirror: Moving Image and Sound Archives in the 1990s," *Archivaria* 8 (Summer 1989): 68–73.

20. "The consumer and production worlds have caught up to us, and would agree with us more now than they did then. What we did not understand, or foresee, was how digitizing the moving image would change popular access to moving images. We still do not understand how this will evolve and how the new mechanisms, markets, technologies, compensation and further uses will work out." Ernest J. Dick, e-mail correspondence with the author, April 9, 2009.

21. Conference program, "Fast Rewind: The Archaeology of Moving Images," May 4–7, 1989.

22. Julia G. Mack, telephone conversation with the author, March 18, 2009.

23. Bruce Austin, telephone conversation with the author, March 8, 2009.

Collecting Georgia's Hometown Movies
Acquisition, Ownership, Preservation, and Access

MARGARET A. COMPTON

In addition to home movies, there are professionally made movies of various kinds that might have been made in your community in the past. During the mid-1920s, for instance, a number of enterprising young cinematographers went from town to town to create local dramas on film. The scripts were written by local persons, usually someone on the newspaper staff, and were so structured as to include the largest possible number of local persons as actors . . . the philosophy being that whoever was in the film would surely pay to attend the movie showing once the production was completed. . . . There were other, similar, movie-producing groups during those years that went from one town to another to spend a movie-making week in each. Although those movies were presumably dramatic in intent, certainly not historical, they can provide an intriguing look at the town as it was.

—Dorothy Weyer Creigh, "Old Movies: A Source of Local History Programs," *History News* 32 (October 1977)

ACQUIRING HOMETOWN MOVIES

In March 2009, the University of Georgia Libraries' Media Archives acquired in one week two of what I call *hometown movies* made by itinerant filmmakers. Though this is not a record archival acquisition, in the world of itinerant filmmakers' films, it certainly pushes the limits of mere chance, given how astonishing it is that the films survive at all.

I first heard about itinerant filmmakers and the different types of films they made from Caroline Frick and Dwight Swanson, who had been researching Melton Barker's films (see their respective contributions in this issue). Wondering if there were any of these films made in Georgia, in 2005, I obtained from Swanson a list of those itinerant filmmakers, film titles, and town locations that he and Frick had compiled by that time and thought about how I might locate any surviving hometown movies made in Georgia for our archives. Acquisition of such films would fit our mission to preserve the variety of moving images of Georgia, including home movies, educational films made in Georgia and on our campus, documentaries, Southeast Emmy entries from regional broadcasters, videotaped field recordings, and interviews. All these materials have expanded the Media Archives in the last decade, but the itinerants' films were something new to explore. As time went by and the Media Archives workload grew, it seemed unlikely that I would ever have time to do the research and legwork involved in locating these films. As it turned out, they came to us.

Swainsboro, Georgia: *Our Home Town* (1947), Filmmakers Sol Landsman and Arthur Loevin

In November 2005, I got a call from a gentleman historian (Party A) with a friend (Party B) who had a 35mm film depicting 1947 Swainsboro, Georgia. As it was described, this sounded like an itinerant filmmaker's reel, and I wanted to acquire it for the Media Archives. Party A wanted a copy made of the film so he could identify everyone in the film; Party B wanted to sell DVDs of the film online. The only way for us to copy the 35mm film was to have it donated to us and then sent to a lab when our film preservation budget permitted. A newspaper article from 1947 reads,

> Swainsboro's a movie star: This week two ace cameramen from New York are in Swainsboro taking films of the way we live, become educated, go to church and have fun. . . . The picture, at present titled *Our Home Town* is a cooperative venture sponsored by the businessmen of Swainsboro. It will be two full reels when finished and will run for 20 minutes on the screen. Sol Landsman who has made similar reels for many other Georgia communities, is in charge of the camera work, his Associate is Arthur Loevin. . . . Films

like *Our Home Town* have been made at Savannah, Augusta, Waycross, Dublin, Americus, Fitzgerald, Thomasville and other Georgia communities.[1]

That brief article contained some valuable information, chiefly the names of other Georgia towns that had been subjects of itinerants' lenses. The newspaper later announced that the film would be shown at the Dixie Theatre on July 23 and 24 as well as "each Tuesday, Wednesday and Thursday for 4 weeks" and that "there will be no advance in prices" at the theater.[2]

The Media Archives department head, Ruta Abolins, was the main contact person with Party A, who said he would represent Party B. Abolins describes the ups and downs of this particular acquisition:

> Preserving the Swainsboro hometown movie has been an experience in donor relations, or rather a hard lesson learned in donor relations. Negotiations to acquire the film occurred with Party A primarily doing the talking for Party B. Apparently, a transfer of the film to VHS videotape had been done years ago, and Party B had sold copies on VHS to people in the community. He now wanted a better copy on DVD that he could sell to the people of Swainsboro as well as on eBay. I made it clear from the beginning that anything we spend funds on from our preservation account must become part of our collection or there is no need to continue the conversation. I did not rule out Party B being able to sell copies of the film, as I feel the film is in the public domain, so we continued the conversation. The 35mm reel (safety stock) was sent out for full preservation work (new negative, new sound track, new print, master tape, and DVD viewing copy) at a cost to us of approximately eight thousand dollars. We agreed that we would send the donor a new DVD that he could sell copies of but that we would keep the original print and the new preservation elements. We also put in our deed of gift that we would stream the newly preserved print from our Web site, with a burned-in University of Georgia logo,

Figure 1. Frame from
Swainsboro: Our Home Town
(1947). UGA Media Archives.

free to be viewed. This worked for a while, but then I got calls and e-mails from Party A saying Party B was shocked to see the film on our Web site. Party B now claims he owns copyright simply because he purchased the only known print of the film. I explained that the deed of gift allowed this streaming and that Party B had signed it. However, the difference between intellectual control and physical control did not seem to register with Party B. Party A insisted that Party B was not aware enough to know what he had signed in the document. What to do? I did not want to make a legal case out of this and possibly alienate the townsfolk—which is no small consideration for a regional archive in a major state university—so I decided to take the streaming film off our Web site. Party A is still working to identify all people in the film, and we assume Party B is still making copies from the DVD we sent him. Over time, we expect to hear from him again, when he needs another copy of the film.[3]

So who does own copyright of itinerant films? If the films were not registered for copyright when they were made, and the filmmaker left all his original work with the town (whose businesses or chamber of commerce likely paid for the film) and no one there has registered copyright since the film was produced, are the films in the public domain? Should our archives register copyright on the Swainsboro film because we spent thousands of dollars to preserve this slice of Georgia's visual documentation, and more important, would the university's legal office allow one department to do that? According to our deed of gift, materials donated become the property of the Board of Regents of the University of Georgia, and it is highly unlikely that the Board of Regents would want to monitor copyright on our films, especially if and when someone puts a clip of one of our films on YouTube (which has happened). Preserving the film and making it accessible (to students on campus, to documentarians, by streaming clips on our Web site, etc.) is our mission, but spending the money and then putting the film back in the can, so to speak, is not what we would like to be doing.

At this point, we were disappointed that Party B wanted the film removed. Clearly we need to make some further effort to educate him on our mission, what we spent on the film and what that expense means to us, and the burgeoning research and interest in these films and filmmakers, but at this time, because of limited staff and time, we are not pursuing the copyright/

ownership/sales/streaming video topic. This lesson in these sorts of mediated negotiations has made us more careful with acquisitions, determining what donors' expectations or desires for these films are at the time of donation, and making sure they understand our budget constraints.

Hometown movies are an especially odd commodity. Since the town, the chamber of commerce, or local businesses originally paid the filmmaker for his services, the town should have a new copy of the film (whether DVD or print) for local use, historical reference, and possibly as a fund-raising tool. For our own investment in transferring the film, assuming it is not grant funded, we hope to be repaid in word-of-mouth descriptions of our efforts, which may bring future film or monetary donations or funding partnerships on specific donations to continue expanding the archive's holdings and fund more preservation of local scenes.

Our Home Movie Day events, which we have put on several times a year, both on and outside the official Home Movie Day, publicize film preservation efforts by the Media Archives and serve as one way we can do outreach into small towns around Georgia that otherwise do not have a University of Georgia presence. We are finding that these events make people think twice about their films being an important documentation of historic events, daily life, and their towns' histories. Itinerants' films are actually very good documents of pre- and immediately post–World War II life. As noted later, in newspaper reports of the times, itinerants emphasized the way they were preserving images of these towns for future citizens when they were selling their filmmaking services to the community.

As we can see from the Swainsboro film, these were thriving communities made up of dozens of local businesses, large families, schools with hundreds of children pouring from them every day, and active and numerous churches, all of which created a community of neighbors dependent on each other for public harmony and mutual assistance. The towns depicted in these 1930s and 1940s images are not nearly as large or prosperous now; when interstate highways bypassed their downtown corridors, mom-and-pop businesses boarded up their storefronts and Wal-Marts decimated the independent grocer and the appliance dealer. After taking in the Swainsboro film, collecting itinerants' films of small towns is no longer just about my interest in seeing and having some of these films represented in the archives but is more about historical documentation of the changes brought about after World War II in the South, in rural communities, and in a nation where the franchise along the interstate is often all we see of any town during travels around the state.

Cordele, Georgia: Local Movies (1936), Pacific Film Productions

I heard about the second hometown movie we were able to acquire at a brunch in late 2006. I was describing my search for hometown movies made in Georgia, and someone told me that Cordele had such a film and sold it on DVD. I contacted the Cordele-Crisp County Public Library and the Cordele Chamber of Commerce and, in 2007, obtained a DVD that we added to our collection for research study. I could tell from the transfer that the original film was nitrate, already deteriorating when it was transferred. I wanted to know who might still have the original film, discover what kind of shape it was in, and offer my help to ameliorate the hazard of storing it or assist in its proper disposal. During two years of contact with Susan Barge—the person in Cordele responsible for the film's original transfer who was helping me try to locate the film—I found two historical mentions of the film in the 1936 *Crisp County News*. The first brief mention appeared on page one:

> Cameramen of the Pacific Film Company are now working in this city, taking pictures of important scenes in the residential and business districts. Pictures will also be taken of civic and other organizations, together with prominent citizens of the city. When the pictures are completed, they will be converted into a long film and shown at Wood's Theatre in this city.[4]

The other is in the theater's daily block advertisement:

> SPECIAL: Local movies shown here on both days in addition to our regular pro-

gram. Folks here's where the fun starts. See yourself on the screen, and many of your friends who you all recognize. These pictures were taken in Cordele a short time ago including business firms, civic clubs, schools, factories, power dam, public buildings, etc. Be sure and see these local movies. It's a treat for young and old. Something you'll never forget.[5]

In March 2009, Susan Barge located the original nitrate film as well as some other films in the city hall building. The nitrate was in a powdery state, the color of mustard (stage 5 nitrate deterioration), and she removed it from the city hall and put it on her front porch. This was a potentially dangerous level of deterioration, so on March 19, I drove to Cordele to assess the condition of the original and recommend next steps for its disposal as well as to find out what other films she had found with the nitrate.

Susan told me that the city of Cordele had paid for this film to be preserved to new

Figure 2. Deteriorated nitrate reels of Cordele home town movie. Photo by author.

16mm film in 1991, when the original reel was still in transferable condition. An Atlanta lab, no longer in existence, sent the nitrate reel to John E. Allen Inc., which made a 16mm picture negative, two 16mm projection prints, a 16mm sound track negative, a one-inch videotape master, and a VHS videocassette, then returned these new elements and the original 35mm nitrate reels to Cordele. These new preservation elements, along with the nitrate, were what Susan found at the city hall. But an even more exciting discovery was that George W. Cofer, lifelong resident of Cordele, had kept some other pieces of the 35mm film that came to him from the owner of a local drive-in theater, who had possibly gotten them from the filmmaker in 1936. These thirty-eight spools of nitrate had been stored in a wooden box that was

ventilated and stored in a cool, dark location. Mr. Cofer's cache was made up of both negative and positive 35mm segments in very good condition, except for some dirt and evidence that mice had nibbled at the few remaining paper labels on the spools of film. I had not heard of any other archives having outs and trims from an itinerant's film, so I was thrilled to accept the donations of these nitrate spools and the 16mm preservation elements for the Media Archives. I had to leave behind the original deteriorated film (see Figure 2) along with a copy of Kodak's "Cellulose Nitrate Films Material Safety Data Sheet" for Ms. Barge, advising her to contact the fire department immediately for proper disposal.

Cordele's finished town film (thirty-one minutes in duration) focuses heavily on the business community: a bakery; four restaurants and cafés; a bank; two drugstores; three gas stations; the lumberyard; Hudson-Terraplane and Buick car dealerships; two beauty shops (one with a barber shop); a laundry; a shoe repair shop; a florist; a funeral home; a grocery; an ice and coal (appliances) shop; postal service employees; and chamber of commerce, Lion's Club, and Rotary Club members. Only one scene of children appears in the finished film—several panning shots of a group of teens at the junior high school.

At the archives, I examined Mr. Cofer's 35mm outs and trims to see what they depicted. Oddly enough, considering that one of the reasons for making these films was to sell theater seats, the positive trims are all scenes of elementary school children (as shown in Figure 3) and teenagers, precisely the population one would expect to be most likely to buy a movie ticket. But with the emphasis on businesses, perhaps the filmmaker saw more money in catering to local businessmen—especially if they had funded the picture. Whatever the reason, the kiddies wound up on the cutting room floor.

Within the outs and trims, of the thirteen spools of positive print material, five are of elementary school children, six are of teenagers, and two are title and production company segments for Pacific Film Productions. Among the negative film spools, eleven are of elementary or teenaged children who did not make it into the film, and the rest are trims from business scenes that did appear in the film: restaurant interiors, teenagers outside their school, the barber shop, chamber of commerce officials, the movie theater exterior, a gas station attendant, the bank, and so on, which can be matched exactly to the end frames of scenes in the finished film.

Other films known to have been made by Pacific Film Productions were titled *Things You Ought to Know About [town name here].*[6] No title appears on the finished Cordele film, but two rolls of introductory production cards, the second possibly used as a title, are found among the outs and trims.

The opening of the nonsynchronous sound track for Cordele's film is the same as the film that Pacific Film Productions made for other towns:[7]

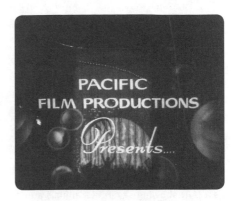

Figure 4. Producer frame cut from Cordele home town movie (1936). UGA Media Archives.

Figure 5. Introduction frame cut from Cordele home town movie (1936). UGA Media Archives.

> Hello, everyone. This is a picture of your city. Did you ever stop to wonder what each and every one of your neighbors and business associates do? How they operate their business? How they carry on? This picture is not designed for advertising purposes only, but also to show you the things you should know about the town in which you live. Perhaps you would like to have seen pictures of your city in the past good old grandfather days. But movies were just in their infancy then. So we trust this picture of your city as it is today will be worth seeing in the years to come.

Music comes and goes during most segments of the Cordele film—the jaunty, 1930s tunes "Happy Days Are Here Again" and "Call to the Post" for horse races are played over early scenes. Narration comes in over sequences at the lumberyard, a restaurant, a car dealership and garage, and a shoe repair shop. Other segments completely lack music or narration. The film ends suddenly after a segment at a florist shop.

Because there is so much previously unseen Cordele footage among the spools of outs and trims, we hope to have them all preserved and to return to Cordele to screen the preserved material. Because we are not licensed to store nitrate film, the unique surviving 35mm footage is being stored for us in a certified nitrate storage facility pending preservation. George W. Cofer, who kept the outs and trims for so long, is now eighty-two years old. Because he was in the film as a child, I hope that other residents of Cordele who have stayed in town since 1936 can also be present at a preservation screening. As with so many historic scenes and events, those who were present at the time are growing old and dying, so documenting their experience with these films is something we would like to accomplish.

Fitzgerald, Georgia: *Our Home Town* (1946), Sol Landsman

In December 2008, Ruta Abolins got a call from Jon Durkovic, the manager of the Grand Theatre in Fitzgerald, Georgia. He had read a newspaper article about our 2008 Home Movie Day event in Hawkinsville, Georgia, and contacted Dwight Swanson through the event's Web site (http://www.homemovieday.com/), who referred Durkovic to us. Durkovic told Ruta he had a film about Fitzgerald that he wanted preserved and sent us a DVD showing several local films and a very poor transfer of an obviously deteriorated nitrate hometown movie about Fitzgerald made in 1947. The DVD showed a film-to-VHS transfer from 1988 with new narration and music added, obliterating the original film's sound track. It also included a hand-lettered title card for the film as *Our Home Town*. The narrator for that 1988 transfer, believed to be Louis Fussell, the longtime projectionist for the Grand Theatre, recounts in his narration that the hometown movie was shown in the Grand annually from 1947 to 1978, when the film became too deteriorated to screen.[8] The DVD also contained 1930s–1940s Kodachrome 16mm local home movies showing people and places around the town. Intrigued by all this footage, I arranged to meet Durkovic at the Grand on March 19, the same day I acquired Cordele's films.

What I expected to find in Fitzgerald was a badly deteriorated 35mm original nitrate reel, precisely what I had seen on the DVD he sent us. What I found instead was a second 35mm, 940-foot nitrate print of the film in excellent condition, which had for the last five years been kept in the theater. Prior to that, it was stored in the police department's safe.[9] Durkovic did not know what had happened to the original print, which had deteriorated decades ago and which appeared on the DVD he sent us. Previous attempts at professional lab preservation on this second reel had been abandoned because of high costs, so Durkovic was hoping that by donating it to the Media Archives, we could partner to preserve the film. Durkovic had already signed our standard deed of gift for donation to the Media Archives, and because the film was in very good condition, I returned to Athens with it and the Cordele footage.

At the archives, comparing the DVD foot-age of Fitzgerald's original deteriorated print (long gone) to the second print I had picked up from Durkovic, it appears to be a very similar but not identical print. The possible explanations for the differences are numerous, but the newly found print is likely a second cut made by the filmmaker, including a full sound track through-out. Because we do not have 35mm equipment in our archives (our holdings are small gauge, primarily 16mm, 8mm, and Super 8mm as well as videotape and audiotape), I could not play the actual film to hear the narration. As to the identity of the filmmaker, because the June 1947 article about the Swainsboro film mentions that similar films had been made in towns including Fitzgerald, I suspected that this film was by Landsman and Loevin, but no credits exist on the film. After many hours of searching microfilm, I found the information I needed in the November 5, 1946, *Fitzgerald Herald-Leader*. Sol Landsman was filming *Our Home Town;* it was to be shown at the Grand and Pine theaters and would be "exchanged with Douglas and Tifton and their movies given here." There is an emphasis on the long-term value of the film.[10]

During my research, I contacted Sherri Butler, a reporter with the Fitzgerald *Herald-Leader,* asking what the newspaper's clippings morgue might contain. She found that this was not Fitzgerald's first time in the movies, inform-ing me that the February 22, 1929, edition of the *Herald-Leader* described

> a two-reel comedy being made which was to be called *Fitzgerald's Hero,* sponsored by the *Herald,* directed by Don O. Newland, and made by a "well-known company from Hollywood, Cal.," Consolidated Film Pro-ducers of Hollywood. The cameraman was to be Bob Williams "former cameraman for Eric von Stroheim at University [sic] City, Cal." . . . "Three thousand feet of film were taken here—*Fitzgerald's Hero* plus scenes in and about the newspaper office and on Central Avenue.". . . The entire picture was to have 168 scenes and the final film was to be shown at the Grand for three days.[11]

According to Ms. Butler, a photo from the making of *Fitzgerald's Hero* in the newspaper

Figure 6. Strand Theatre in 1959. Courtesy Marietta Museum of History, Marietta, Georgia; http://projects.ajc.com/gallery/view/metro/cobb/strand0404/7.whtml.

morgue has information with it indicating that this film was lost when the theater burned.[12] However, knowing that Newland had traveled as far south as Fitzgerald has assisted in Nathan Wagoner's research (see his contribution in this issue) on Newland's travels and filmic output. I hope to find more of Newland's films in Georgia. In the meantime, we are committed to preserving the 1947 Fitzgerald hometown movie and hope to identify its filmmaker. The print donated to us is currently being stored in a certified nitrate storage facility pending preservation. We are already discussing with Durkovic how the city of Fitzgerald might use the film locally and anticipate a gala screening at the Grand during its seventy-fifth anniversary in 2011. A Home Movie Day event held on July 11, 2009, at the Grand brought in a small but enthusiastic crowd of local residents, each bearing home movies to view and enjoy, including the original 16mm compilation print of films of local townsfolk shot in 1940 and 1941, possibly made by the local school principal, which appeared on the DVD Durkovic gave us in 2008. These films have elements of itinerant films about them, especially in the black-and-white segments, which focus primarily on local businesses and the newspaper office, but we do not know if they could be the output of an itinerant. Local interest in footage of the town is high, and we expect to gather more information on Fitzgerald's filmed history through future screenings and publicity.

Marietta, Georgia: *Hometown Movies of Cobb County* (1936), Pacific Film Productions

At this time, we know of one other Georgia hometown movie extant in Marietta, Georgia. By chance, I ran across an article about the history, renovation, and reopening of Marietta's Strand Theatre in the *Atlanta Journal-Constitution* in November 2008.[13] In looking through the newspaper's site for more information about the Strand, I found a photo of the theater showing a banner advertising *Home Town Movies of Cobb County*.

The photo credit listed its source as the

Marietta Museum of History. Amy Reed of the Marietta Museum of History told me that a longtime employee and historian, Dan Cox, said the film being advertised is a Pacific Film Production from 1936 and that he is still looking for information on a 1915 local film.[14] The photo in the newspaper dates from May 1959, and an article in the *Marietta Daily Journal* from that time states that the film showing was shot around town in November 1958 but lists no filmmaker or production company.[15] I have not yet located any article from 1958 that invited townsfolk to be in the film, which may support Mr. Cox's belief that the 1959 screening was of the 1936 film.

Ms. Reed put me in touch with Philip Goldstein, who owns the original 1936 three-reel nitrate film and who also owns, with his father, Herbert Goldstein, and other family members in a limited partnership, the building that houses the 1935 Strand Theatre. The original nitrate film was stored in the projection booth of the Strand and given to Herbert Goldstein when he bought the building in January 1977. The elder Goldstein appears in the film at age twelve. Goldstein stated that the thirty-five-minute nitrate film is still in good condition but can no longer be projected. He had it copied to VHS several years ago and then transferred that to DVD.[16] He confirms that there are "Pacific Film Productions" and "Your Town on Parade in 1936" titles at the beginning of the film and that the film has a nonsynchronous sound track, which I suspect is identical to Cordele's (it was made in the same year).[17] Newspaper research turned up two articles with information about the film, which was made in January 1936 through the cooperation of the Strand Theatre's owner, Clarence Smith, and the *Marietta Daily Journal* newspaper, which would appear prominently in the film.[18] This focus on documenting the workings of the local newspaper office turns up in various itinerant filmmakers' publicity for their films, especially in the numerous articles promulgated by Don O. Newland.[19] The second article dates to April of that year and describes the "shots of local civic, industrial, and fraternal organizations of Marietta" and emphasized the long-term value of the film being "stored and kept as a historical record of the city for the year 1936."[20]

An April 9, 1936, advertisement for the Strand states, "Interesting local movies being shown today and tomorrow! Be sure to see them!"[21] Because the newspaper offices were involved in the making of Pacific Film Productions films, and because we know that Newland also worked directly with local newspapers, this symbiotic relationship of funding and publicity worked to get more people interested in the filming and in buying a ticket and attending the screening. Compared to Don O. Newland's films, Pacific's films are much less intensely publicized, but like Newland, it appears that Pacific had a large output in a vast swath of locales. I hope that research will turn up detailed information about Pacific Film Productions, its filmmaker and crew, their travels, and how many more of their films survive.

Athens, Georgia (1947), Filmmaker Joel A. Wier

Although not a hometown movie in the commercial–itinerant filmmaker sense, our 16mm film of Athens, Georgia, in 1947 fits in to the hometown movie genre. Joel A. Wier, a longtime Athens resident, made the 16mm color film. Wier was then secretary-manager of the Athens Chamber of Commerce and executive director of the Athens Housing Authority.[22] According to Dorothy Weyer Creigh, chambers of commerce had often made films about their towns and ended up keeping them stored in the chamber offices.[23] Wier's forty-five-minute long film incorporates both the housing and chamber aspects of his work as well as aspects of the itinerant filmmaker films he may have seen elsewhere. A portion of the film is streaming on our Web site (http://www.libs.uga.edu/media/collections/homemovies/housing.html).

The film shows Kiwanis Club members going into a downtown restaurant for lunch, bankers in front of their banks, businesses around downtown, Lions Club members, the chamber of commerce building, a hosiery factory, a stockyard/auction barn, firemen, police officers, an aerial view of town from an airplane, buildings on the University of Georgia campus, churches, schools, children at play, and a downtown Shriners parade (including some parade members in blackface) on what appears to be the Fourth of July.

Wier also showcases Athens's grand

Figure 7. On the set of
Americus' Hero (1928). Frank
Sheffield Jr. Home Movie
Collection, UGA Media
Archives.

homes and smaller bungalows along Prince
and Milledge avenues in the spring as well as
various gardens around town. He then turns
his camera to the poorer African American resi-
dential areas, where small, unpainted frame
houses stand in rows on hillsides along the
edges of downtown near the railroad tracks.
These scenes appear to be taken in late autumn
or winter as the trees are bare and some of
the children are wearing coats. It was laundry
day when he filmed the neighborhood, and
he captures mothers working at boiling wash-
tubs alongside small creeks, their children
on makeshift swings and playing in the dirt.
These communities have been identified by a
local minister and historian as Tip-Toe Alley and
Lindentown, both of which were demolished to
make way for several of the university's dormi-
tories and for low-income housing projects in
the 1970s.[24] It is hard not to view this part of the
film as having been made with an eye toward
what might be improved in these neighborhoods; though shooting in 1947, Wier likely
did not envision the massive urban renewal
projects of the 1970s.

Wier also films what were then new groups
of two-story apartment buildings—which still
exist today as low-income housing—with grassy
lawns filled with young schoolchildren, black
and white, playing games. It appears that he
is trying to show how happy everyone could be
if only they could live in new housing, in con-
trast to the muddy yards and unpainted frame

homes of those residents near the railroad
tracks. In this respect, Wier's hometown movie
has a more personal edge than the itinerants'
films. We hold the original 16mm color print as
well as BetaSP masters made during previous
transfers and plan on full film preservation
this fiscal year.

Americus, Georgia: Home
Movie (1928) of *Americus' Hero*,
Filmmaker Frank Sheffield Jr.

In April 2009, we received sixty-two four-hun-
dred-foot cans of 16mm camera original reversal home movies, shot by Americus, Georgia,
resident Frank Sheffield Jr. and donated to us
by his grandson, Sheffield Hale. During my
inspections of the Sheffield films, I noticed
that one scene on a reel from 1928 appeared
to be taken on a movie set, but I was unable
to identify it from other content or from can
markings. However, during the course of researching hometown movies for this article,
I found out that Don O. Newland (see Nathan
Wagoner's contribution in this issue) had made,
besides *Fitzgerald's Hero* (mentioned earlier),
Americus' Hero in 1928.[25] I suddenly realized
that the mysterious movie set home movie
was in fact Frank Sheffield Jr. filming Don O.

Newland filming *Americus' Hero.* A frame from the engagement scene of *Americus' Hero,* shot on the stage of the historic Rylander Theatre, is shown here (see Figure 7).

I double-checked the film's manufacture date code (1928) and confirmed information on the filming from Americus newspapers of November 1928. Newspaper coverage of the film lasted two weeks, from November 23 to December 5, 1928. Indeed, this is home movie footage of Newland's filming—unique documentation of itinerant filmmaking. Perhaps other hometown movies were captured by local amateur filmmakers. I hope that this discovery inspires archivists and film scholars to look closely at early home movie collections in towns known to have had itinerant films made in them for moving images such as Mr. Sheffield's.

As we have found in researching the 1947 Fitzgerald hometown movie, and with our Home Movie Day event there bringing out 16mm local footage of 1941 businesses and townsfolk, there was clearly a common effort in small towns to film local activities in ways similar to itinerants' films, well before what many consider the heyday of home movies—the late 1950s and 1960s. As an archivist, I see how many more donations of home movies from the 1940s and earlier are coming in as donors' parents are aging, going into assisted living facilities, or dying. These donors are usually baby boomers who know they have home movies from *their* childhoods (the 1960s) but never imagined that home movies were made in the 1920s or 1930s and are astonished when I present the evidence. This illustrates the level of education about amateur film history that still needs to be reached.

CONCLUSION

Publicity about our holdings and itinerants' films has slowly brought these films to the Media Archives, but chance has also been a factor. The more intrigued I am by the variety of films itinerant filmmakers created, the more time I want to spend locating extant films or combing microfilmed newspapers for mentions of the films to create a database of Georgia towns that were the subjects of the films. The reality is that with a bad economy and a small and very busy staff with no potential staff growth

on the horizon, it is all we can do to properly preserve and describe the materials we now hold as well as take in normal acquisitions—we simply do not have the time or resources to search for more itinerants' films in an active fashion, despite a desire to do so. Our preservation budget (which funds lab transfers, among other things) was cut recently, so preserving our holdings in the Peabody Awards Archives that are on obsolete media as well as a backlog of home movies and other donations from the past several years are high priorities. Within our newly limited budget, the issue becomes how to continue to fund full film preservation when these hometown movies do survive and come to us.

Though chance can bring hometown movies to us, chance cannot fund their long-term preservation. Obviously, grants and partnerships become more crucial to our efforts, though with the downturn in the economy hitting everyone, it is less likely that small-town governments will have grant funds for such projects. As the de facto film archives for Georgia, we want to continue preserving such films to new negatives and prints in their original format, but what may be most feasible within our own preservation budget is simply to transfer them to a master tape format and a digital file, along with DVD viewing copies. What concerns me most is that taking the easiest path (tape master, digital file) for our holdings may become the new standard, simply because of our economic constraints. Thanks to some National Film Preservation Foundation grants, we have been able to do full film preservation for several of our unique hometown movies. As an archivist trained to work to the highest standard, anything less than full film preservation is difficult to aspire to. And in an age of digital delivery to YouTube and iPhones, do our users really care if the film has been preserved to a 35mm negative, with accompanying sound track master and projection print, backup digital tape, and file? Or do they just want to see it?

These are looming issues currently confronting film archives, especially regional archives and small historical societies, which often depend on individual patrons and donors to fund their efforts. Marketing, publicity, and strong pushes to fund targeted projects are necessary to bring attention to our holdings, our efforts, and how these films are relevant today. Unfortunately, the economic downturn and limited staff time means that we are all wearing multiple hats, and marketing is not necessarily an archivist's strength. Again, this means that partnerships with friends' organizations, board members, and local businesses or experts may be the best way to get the word out, much like the itinerants did. It appears that these filmmakers still have something to tell us, all these decades later.

NOTES

1. "Swainsboro Being Shot by Cameraman," *Swainsboro Forest-Blade,* June 12, 1947, 12.
2. "Our Home Town on Local Screen," *Swainsboro Forest-Blade,* July 17, 1947, 1.
3. Ruta Abolins, e-mail correspondence with the author, May 1, 2009.
4. "Picture Is Made of Crisp County," *Crisp County News,* March 26, 1936, 1.
5. Wood's Theatre advertisement, *Crisp County News,* August 20, 1936, 3.
6. Dwight Swanson, e-mail correspondence with the author, December 15, 2005.
7. Dan Streible, e-mail correspondence with the author, February 8, 2007.
8. Jon Durkovic, e-mail correspondence with the author regarding the narrator's identity, July 6, 2009.
9. Jon Durkovic, interview by the author, July 11, 2009.
10. "Fitz-Hi Students Appear in Local Movie," *Fitzgerald Herald,* November 5, 1946, 2.
11. Sherri Butler, e-mail correspondence with the author, March 25, 2009.
12. Sherri Butler, e-mail correspondence with the author, March 24, 2009.
13. Tucker McQueen, "Milestone in Marietta: Old Theater Lives Again," *Atlanta Journal-Constitution,* November 30, 2008, http://www.ajc.com/news/content/metro/cobb/stories//2008/11/30/strand_theatre_marietta.html.
14. Amy Reed, e-mail correspondence with the author, December 8, 2008.
15. "Cobb Movies to Be Shown in Marietta," *Marietta Daily Journal and Cobb County Times,* May 27, 1959, 12B.
16. Philip Goldstein, e-mail correspondence with the author, December 11, 2008.
17. Philip Goldstein, telephone interview with the author, July 7, 2009.
18. "Marietta Scenes in Movie Planned by Theatre Head," *Marietta Daily Journal,* January 27, 1936, 1.
19. Nathan Wagoner, telephone interview with the author, July 15, 2009.
20. "Scenes of Marietta People, Industries Coming to Strand," *Marietta Daily Journal,* April 7, 1936, 1.
21. Strand Theatre advertisement, *Marietta Daily Journal,* April 9, 1936, 1.
22. *Baldwin's Athens, Georgia, City Directory 1947,* vol. 3, ABCD No. 135 (Charleston, S.C.: Baldwin Directory Company), 364.
23. Dorothy Weyer Creigh, "Old Movies: A Source of Local History Programs," *History News* 32 (October 1977).
24. Rev. Charles Knox, interview with the author, Athens, Georgia, January 18, 2008.
25. "Americus and the Silver Screen," *Americus Times-Recorder,* December 4, 2007, http://www.americustimesrecorder.com/columns/local_story_338000145.html.

"Wasn't That a Funny Thing That We Did?"

Oral Histories of Itinerant Filmmaking

DWIGHT SWANSON

The history of itinerant filmmaking involves hundreds of films and thousands of people, each with his or her own memories of the experience. The films themselves, which were made quickly and often just as swiftly discarded or misplaced, generally exist now only as references in newspaper advertisements or articles hidden in reels of microfilm, to be found again by sharp-eyed researchers. A tiny fraction of the original films have reemerged from theater closets or attics in the homes of the filmmakers' families in the decades since they were last publicly screened. When seen again, these rediscovered movies have prompted sparks of recognition among the original participants and nostalgia or curiosity among those too young to have experienced the making of the films themselves. The memories of itinerant film culture live on, even when the film prints do not.

Most of these films were truly ephemeral because they were often shown publicly just a handful of times, or perhaps only once. They were geographically limited as well because a film may have been a huge success and an important event (however briefly) in one town but would have had no audience and no relevance in a town just a few miles away. Because the primary draw of the films was seeing yourself, your community, and your neighbors on screen, they generally were of no interest to those outside of the town in which they were shot. Even today, when removed from their local contexts, the films largely cease to be meaningful, except as documents of specific times and places or as examples of a type of filmmaking that has long ceased to exist.

Perhaps the most surprising aspect of itinerant filmmaking is just how widespread the practice was. Melton Barker, certainly one of the most prolific itinerant film producers, claimed to have filmed one thousand productions on his own—an exaggeration perhaps, but

well over one hundred of his films have been documented.[1] The life of an itinerant filmmaker was difficult and tedious, resembling the work of a traveling salesman more than a creative artist. Production demands of the genre usually kept the filmmaker in each town for only a few days before he or she packed up the car and headed to a new hotel in a nearby town, ready to start all over again on the production of another nearly identical movie.

The number of people who sat in movie theaters and saw images of themselves projected on the same screens as the starlets and matinee idols of the cinema is almost unimaginable now, especially considering how quickly the itinerant film genre itself was forgotten. Itinerant filmmaking was largely a small-town phenomenon. Perhaps the filmmakers were capitalizing on the sense of community that existed in smaller towns, though this is contradicted by the number of productions in larger cities. Melton Barker, for example, made films in Tucumcari, New Mexico, and Guthrie, Oklahoma, but also in Memphis, Little Rock, and San Antonio.

Both the look and the concept of the locally made small-town film seem to have had little lasting resonance beyond the screenings, except among the people who were directly involved with the productions. The itinerant films that incorporated narratives, scripts, and acting (however unpolished) required the directors to have slightly longer relationships with the townspeople who appeared in their films, though sometimes this only meant that they filmed them for hours instead of seconds. Despite the ballyhoo that many of the filmmakers put into selling themselves as being "from Hollywood" and their local films as stepping-stones to stardom, it appears that few of the local participants really gave much credence to that far-fetched notion. Instead, most participants remember perceiving the films as just "a fun thing to do," as one of the child stars would later put it.[2]

Itinerant filmmaking worked as a business in part because it capitalized on the excitement generated by seeing one's image (or that of one's child, neighbor, or friend) on the screen. Talking to participants today, many decades later, there is a wide range of responses from the "stars" when they are asked to remember the films. Some think back on the films frequently and fondly, proudly pointing out to their children and grandchildren that they had once been in a movie, however small. For most of the local stars, however, the films were generally not remembered as being particularly significant moments in their lives but rather whimsical one-off events.

Because itinerant filmmakers operated at the furthest fringes of industrial filmmaking, they left few records behind and were rarely mentioned in industry literature of the time. Most of the information about these films is found almost entirely in local newspaper articles and the advertisements taken out by the filmmakers themselves. Unfortunately, because itinerant filmmaking peaked in the 1930s, the discovery of a new filmmaker is often followed by a search that ends with the discovery of his or her obituary. The lack of written information about this phenomenon makes oral history one of the more fruitful methodologies for studying local filmmaking because it both unearths facts about the productions and reveals the feelings that the films evoked for participants at the time of their creation and in intervening years.[3]

The pages that follow are excerpts from interviews, both published and unpublished, with the subjects and makers of four narrative itinerant series. These oral histories show the diverse and sometimes contradictory stories to which the productions gave rise. By uniting them here, I hope to provide a new perspective on a genre that has been all but lost to film history.

DAN DORN SR.

One of the few existing interviews with an itinerant filmmaker is an oral history of the late Daniel W. Dorn Sr. of Red Bank, New Jersey, recorded by oral historian Gloria Stravelli of the Monmouth County (New Jersey) Library on September 20, 2000, as part of the "Oral History of Monmouth County" project.[4]

Dorn began making films with his father, Daniel B. Dorn, a projectionist and Fox Movietone News cameraman, and together they started the Supreme Productions Movie Company. Between 1927 and 1935, the Dorns made a series of local films that intertwined a brief romantic plot with scenes of local businesses,

a common technique for itinerant films that allowed producers to increase their revenue through product placement and sponsorships. Of the Dorns' approximately thirty local films, only two are known to survive: *A Romance of Freehold* (1931) and *A Romance of Red Bank* (1933), both filmed in New Jersey.[5] Both films are periodically shown in their hometowns. In a press release for a 2009 screening of *A Romance of Red Bank* at the Red Bank Public Library, Dan Dorn Sr.'s daughter said that "time and nostalgia have turned [the film] into an engaging documentary of life in the 1930s," succinctly capturing much of the appeal of itinerant films for modern audiences and historians alike.[6]

The Dorns never traveled far from home in their eight years making the Romance films. "We made most of them in New Jersey," said Dorn, "but Stroudsburg was in Pennsylvania, just over the river. Greenwich, Connecticut, of course, was the other border. We just kind of did a circle." Dorn added that they also ventured into New York, making films in "three towns in Long Island, and Stapleton, Staten Island."

After decades of neglect, prints of the two known Romance films were rediscovered in the 1990s. Oral historian Gloria Stravelli recalled that a copy of *The Romance of Freehold* had been found in the trunk of a car. "Yes. We have a tape of that, too," confirmed Dorn:

> When they showed it in the American Hotel in Freehold, the boy and the girl who played in it came to the show, the hero and the heroine. That was quite a nice night when they showed it so many years later. After we filmed a movie, we left it there. We usually had a sponsor, like the Chamber of Commerce, or the Rotary Club. They would more or less check on us to make sure we were legitimate, and they were sort of sponsors. After we'd finish, we'd give them the movie because we had no use for it, and Lord knows what has happened to them all.

Although the Romance series did have a minimal narrative, the core of the films, as was common practice among itinerant series, was devoted to giving on-screen time to the local businesses that sponsored the film. "The advertisers paid for the whole thing," described Dorn.

"We would go to a furniture store in Red Bank and get the owner to pay for the advertising. And then they'd go to a jeweler, buy a ring, and go to buy an automobile, whatever they needed. In Red Bank the hero of the story got a job in Wyckoff Feed and Oil, and that tied him in. It showed the boy checking the tanks, and taking the orders, and it showed Wyckoff's facilities." Explaining how the narrative intertwined with the advertising, Dorn said, "The way it was tied in with business, was when they were thinking about getting married, they wanted to go buy furniture and rings and gasoline and cars and whatever the advertiser was selling. They're all tied into the story."

The Dorns also incorporated another standard trick of the nonnarrative itinerant film by including shots of as many townspeople—and therefore potential audience members—in the film as possible. "People coming out of church, high school classes, we'd take everything in Red Bank," recalled Dorn. "I remember we took a fire drill. We set the camera up and got every kid coming out the door." The Dorns also got the municipality involved by incorporating the fire department into the plot:

> We had set up a fake fire, that's how the boy met the girl in one film. We had a smudge pot in the house with smoke coming out the window, and we got the fire trucks coming to the fire—the boy would rescue the girl and it was love at first sight. We set up a ladder, and the hero runs up the ladder and takes the girl out of the window and carts her down the ladder and kisses her when he got her to the bottom. That's how he met her. Then they courted. It was the little story mixed into the film.

Supreme Productions also relied on an established Hollywood promotional ploy to build up excitement for the production—choosing their cast through a popularity contest. To select the cast of *A Romance of Red Bank,* for example, they sponsored a contest to find the most popular couple in the local high school. Yet despite utilizing all the commercial gimmicks of the itinerant film trade, Supreme Productions was not a lucrative business, especially given the economic conditions of the 1930s. "There

wasn't a whole lot of money in it, I'll tell you," said Dorn, who gave up filmmaking in 1936 in favor of the more steady income provided by their photo studio in Red Bank:

> You see, as business went downhill, and got worse and worse, there was less money around. The multitudes are what keeps things going. When people don't have any money, the businesses suffer. So advertising in a town where a lot of people were out of work doesn't do it. Because if they don't have the money or are out of work, they can't spend it. We had to quit making those movies because advertising was out. They tried to pump it up with advertising when it first started going down, but we just went into the Depression, and then, of course, no advertising would help.

THE MOVIE QUEEN OF LUBEC, MAINE

Most itinerant productions are lost films that exist only in the memories of their participants. As Karan Sheldon discusses elsewhere in this issue, itinerant films that still exist can also find new life, once preserved, and again become part of a town's collective memory. As a follow-up to a series of interviews that had been done earlier by Northeast Historic Film, in summer 2003, I accompanied documentary filmmaker Karen Shopsowitz to Lubec, a small town at the easternmost point in Maine, to interview Evangeline Morrison, who had starred in Lubec's 1936 version of *The Movie Queen,* and Helen Burns, a local resident and amateur historian who had been central in the rediscovery and preservation of the film in the 1990s.[7]

The Movie Queen phenomenon was unique in that the film was the culmination of a larger show and was screened as the finale in a four-act theatrical production staged by Boston's Amateur Theatre Guild. The guild sent a troupe of female directors around the United States to direct both the play and the film, and while the films featured solely local talent, the play incorporated a traveling troupe of actors. In the film, the movie queen character, played by a different young woman in every town, returns home following her screen success, where she is given the key to the town and is warmly welcomed by the town's businesses. As sponsors of the production, these businesses were given liberal screen time, thereby subsidizing the costs of the production.

As the star of both the play and the film, Evangeline Morrison spent several days with the director, Margaret Cram, during the filming of the movie but remembered few personal anecdotes about her. Morrison recalled that the director gave off an air of big-city sophistication, and she had assumed that Cram and the outside actors had come from Boston. "They were a group," she said, and left town together as soon as the production finished. "Perhaps when they left here they went to the next town, and so on," speculated Morrison.

When asked if she thought that Cram appeared to be a professional producer, Morrison answered, "I felt that it was nothing new to her. She was very comfortable. . . . She must have had training somewhere . . . but I don't think it required all that much to do what she did. I think she could learn it in a short time."

Since it was preserved by Northeast Historic Film, the film has been widely seen in Lubec and by the families of the participants. Helen Burns recalled that when she saw the film again, she thought,

> Oh, this is great. I knew some of these people. I knew just about everybody in it, and I was just fascinated. . . . I just thought it should be preserved, and this is great, I just loved it, especially because I'm a town kid and I walked those streets, that Front Street, Water Street, you know, when I was a kid, and I knew all those stores and all the people that run 'em, and it kind of just brought back memories of stuff we used to have that we don't have anymore.
>   . . . And of course like Evangeline, the older people they're not around anymore, or they're sick and not able to come out and see, but this kind of brings a little spark to their eyes. "Oh yeah, I remember that, I remember her, I know who that is."

Evangeline Morrison's own recollections of the experience are also fond ones: "What was I, maybe nineteen, after all? It was great, I loved it! And I wasn't that long out of school that it didn't bother me to do it. I enjoyed doing it." The film has become a sort of family heirloom, she said, because her son and her grandchildren also enjoy seeing their grandmother on the screen. "Oh, they think it's wonderful!"

MELTON BARKER AND *THE KIDNAPPERS FOIL*

The plot of *The Movie Queen* specifically reflected the allure of Hollywood, even in the far-flung towns from Maine to Montana where the Amateur Theatre Guild appeared. At the same time, Texan filmmaker Melton Barker attempted to cash in on the popularity of the Our Gang series with his own "kid movie."[8]

Melton Barker was the most widely traveled and long-lasting of the itinerant film producers, returning again and again to his series the Kidnappers Foil for more than four decades. Barker clung to his original 1930s script with amazing tenacity over the years, keeping it virtually unchanged into the 1970s. The barebones plot revolves around the kidnapping and attempted ransoming of "Betty Davis," a local girl who is eventually rescued by a gang of local kids. The script was designed to get as many children on screen as possible, with one spoken line per child, to lure their parents and friends into the theaters as well as to collect the fee that Barker charged for so-called acting lessons.

As he crisscrossed America, Barker frequently returned to the same towns to film different versions of *The Kidnappers Foil*. He traveled to the Texas Panhandle town of Childress twice, once in 1936 and again twelve years later. Childress's two Betty Davises were Dory Dugan, who starred in the 1936 version, and Eugenia "Genie" Houseman, featured in the 1948 film. Dugan, who was interviewed by Caroline Frick and American Public Radio's Michael May in 2006, said that her memories revolved largely around going to "a big house on the other side of town" for the filming. "That was a big treat for me," she said. "It was very expensive, since we had nothing. We were very poor people." When asked about the screening of the film, she responded, "Oh yes, I remembered it because I was so horrified when I saw myself on the screen. I'll never forget just cringing, you know?" Frick pressed her on why she would have been so embarrassed, to which she responded, "I was a child, I don't know. I don't remember the *why* of any of it; I just remember that I was."[9]

Genie Houseman's recollections of her participation were somewhat hazy at first, but over the course of my 2009 interview with her, she was able to recall many memories of the film.[10] When asked how she came to hear that the film was being made, Houseman stated that her mother had been a music teacher "and so probably would have heard about the film through school." As with all Barker's films, a cursory "audition," which was in fact just the briefest of interviews, was held beforehand to give the illusion that each of the young cast members was specially chosen for his or her role. "Auditions were held at the old Hotel Childress, and it was packed full of mothers and children," remembers Houseman, continuing,

I'm guessing that there was at least two hundred to three hundred people. I played piano, but they didn't ask me to do that for the audition or the movie. I got the lead in the school programs, so I must have been pretty good. We were given numbers and then brought into a room one by one. The audition was in front of several people. I think there was three judges. This man had on a felt hat and he wore that thing the whole time. They called us to the table and asked us to recite a line. I was real nervous and kept asking my mother, "What am I supposed to say?"

I was chosen to be the girl who was tied up and kidnapped. It was very much a surprise. After the audition—I don't remember how many days later—we were taken to the park at Childress. I just remember bits and parts of the filming. There was not that much rehearsal, and then it was time to film it, and all of the filming was done in one day.

Melton Barker Juvenile Productions was well into its second decade of filming *The Kidnappers Foil* by this point, and the filmmaking process had been honed to maximum efficiency. The only impediment to this efficiency was the fact that Barker and his crew worked exclusively with children, many as young as three years old. Genie Houseman recalls her own

acting experience as being particularly confusing and terrifying for her: "I was tied up and was really scared that they wouldn't untie me. They brought me to a shed, and I don't know if they didn't film that or left out that scene, but I screamed and screamed. You can imagine what a seven-year-old girl thought about it."

Asked how much direction Melton Barker had given her during the filming, Houseman replied, "He just told us what to do and how to do it." Barker, never missing an opportunity to play up his fictitious Hollywood connections, occasionally attempted to convince the parents that their children were on the way to stardom. "Later, it must have been when they brought the movie back [for the screening]," remembered Houseman, "he offered my mother eight hundred dollars to bring me to Hollywood. My mother was a schoolteacher, and she said, 'Oh, no, no, no.'"[11]

Although screenings of *The Kidnappers Foil,* as well as most other itinerant film series, were generally held as soon after filming as possible to capitalize on the publicity that had accompanied the production, Houseman's recollection was that

ten years later they showed it at the [Childress] Theater for the first time—I would have been seventeen at the time. I remembered crawling down in my seat because it was a little embarrassing. My mother didn't know that they were showing it, so she never saw it. They said that they were going to show it every ten years, but I guess they just left it in the theater, because that's where they found it later.

The version of *The Kidnappers Foil* in which Mrs. Houseman starred not only exists but has been preserved, screened at an all-school reunion, and posted online by the Texas Archive of the Moving Image, so she has had the opportunity to view the film repeatedly.[12] Looking back at the experience, Mrs. Houseman said that "it was neat for my family to see the movie, and my daughter was really excited. When people saw it later [following recent local screenings of the preserved print] they said [when she appeared on screen] 'that must be Genie, because that looks just like her daughter.' The people at the all-school reunion were really excited and they all laughed. The ones who have seen it have been really happy that it has been preserved."

For those itinerant film actors lucky enough to see themselves on the screen again decades later, the impact of the childhood experience is often multiplied by both the passage of time and the ability to share it with their children and grandchildren. Judy White was five years old when she played the Betty Davis role in the 1947 Odessa, Texas, version of *The Kidnappers Foil*. She spoke with me by phone from her home in Grand Prairie, Texas, more than six decades after her star turn, but her memories of the film were still fresh, and she grew more and more animated as she recalled the story:[13]

> I can really remember only filming one scene. I remember that I was supposed to dress like someone whose parents would be able to ransom her, so I wore my piano recital dress, my pink dotted Swiss dress. We were outdoors, we were in a park . . . and there were lots of kids. I was sitting between two of the kidnappers and they told me to look back and forth between the two, and I didn't know exactly what they meant by that, so I sat perfectly still and just turned my eyes back and forth and everybody thought that was really funny.
>
> It was very exciting, because I really thought that I was a star at that point, so going to the premiere was wonderful. And I don't know if they sold tickets, but I know that those of us who were in the film got in first, and I thought that was pretty special. And they had lots of lights and there was lots of noise and a big crowd outside the theater as we went in. So we really felt "Hollywood." I don't know that they had the big lights that turned around, but it was a well-lighted place for downtown Odessa. It was very special for somebody my age. Whether as an adult I would have thought that was a big commotion or not, I don't know, but I went expecting it to be special, and I thought it was. I don't know if it was like a premiere or not, but that's the way I felt about it.

Mrs. White remembered the crowd's reaction to seeing her sideways glances at the kidnappers:

> Because they laughed that was kind of embarrassing to me, but it was real exciting. There I was on the big screen, imagine that, do I really look like that? So yeah, it was an exciting thing. Everybody thought it was a fun thing to do. I've thought about it through the years, just off and on, thinking, "Wasn't that a funny thing that we did?" I bragged to my grandchildren that I'd been in the movies, you know? They were impressed! It was a fun thing, and a fun thing to remember.

There was virtually no attention given to the filmmakers themselves during their careers, and aside from the occasional mentions in *Box Office Magazine*, filmmakers relied primarily on coverage in the local newspapers, but only to promote the filming and the screenings, not to discuss their films or careers. As a result, the contemporary documentation of them and their films is primarily found in the most hyperbolic self-generated hoopla, which repeats the press releases that the filmmakers used in town after town. The only known interview with Barker about his filmmaking appeared in Greenville, Mississippi's, *Delta Democrat-Times* in May 1972, when, at the tail end of his career, the sixty-nine-year-old Barker returned to Cleveland, Mississippi, for a second time to make yet another Kidnappers Foil film.[14]

In the article, Barker, whose Kidnappers Foil plot and characters relied on references to the Our Gang comedies to an almost litigious degree, compared himself favorably to producer Hal Roach, saying that it took Roach "about 10 days to shoot what I do in a day. You see, he had a lot of help and everyone was getting in the way."[15] Barker claimed to have discovered Our Gang star (and Dallas resident) "Spanky" McFarland and said so at nearly every possible opportunity, even long after most of America had forgotten who McFarland was. In the *Delta Democrat-Times* interview, Barker repeated his story, recalling, "The first gang grew up and Roach dropped the series. I was in Houston in 1933 shooting commercials for local movie houses. Spankey McFarland *[sic]*—I never knew his real name, but his mother called him Sonny—was a little kid I used for bread and ice cream commercials."[16]

The once flourishing genre of itinerant films had long been forgotten by 1972, so reporter Owen Taylor, perhaps anticipating skeptical readers' feelings that the entire operation might be a scam, also interviewed two mothers of children who appeared in the film:

"A lot of people think it's fake or something," says Mrs. Roy Peacock, whose 6-year-old Brain [sic] is in the cast, "but we think it will be a good experience for Brain. He really wants to do it, too." Mrs. Lyndol Ellison says that she told Barker she thought it all sounded like "a money-making" scheme when she registered daughter Penny, 10, and son Scott, 8. "He said that he made money from this, alright, but he said that he also had to pay for his expenses. But if he does what he promises it will be worth it," she says.

Barker, apparently responding to Mrs. Ellison's comment about his movies being merely a money-making gimmick, replied, "I get that sort of thing. It usually comes from ignorant people who don't know what's involved. Actually, I could probably make some money at this sort of thing if I didn't have to buy film and have it processed," which he estimated cost him four hundred to five hundred dollars. Barker continued,

If people follow through on this, I think they'll see it's legitimate. The kids get a big kick out of being in a movie, and besides, I work too hard for this to be fake. There have been other people who have tried making this type of movie, but they usually messed things up. There was one guy I caught . . . who had been making this kind of movie for two years using my name. I told him that if I caught him doing it again, I'd have thrown him in jail. He got out of the business.

Penny Ellison-Battistelli, in a 2009 e-mail about her experience in Cleveland's The Kidnappers Foil, recalls, "There were many kids in it . . . over one hundred, I'd say. . . . We just did

what they told us." The film was sponsored by the local theater owner, and according to Ellison-Battistelli, the theater showed the print annually, always on a Saturday, for three or four years. Her memories of the film (of which no print has yet been found) are that "it was real cheaply made." Her mother, on the other hand, does not remember the film at all.[17]

Two of the other stars of the Cleveland The Kidnappers Foil, Laura Smith Legge and her brother Lance Smith, were eleven and six years old, respectively, at the time of the film's production. Because of their age differences, Laura's memories are clearer than Lance's, who wrote that "my sister was in it, and I am sure I tagged along with her like I always did."[18] Laura recalls that Charles Collier, the owner of the movie theater, advertised that a movie producer was coming to Cleveland to make a film starring local children. "The auditions were held at the theater on the stage," she explains, and "my mother took my brother and me to read for Mr. Barker along with other children in the community."[19] Laura's audition consisted of reading her line—"Come up and see me sometime, boys"—in the style of Mae West, another remnant of Barker's 1930s script.

The core scenes of Kidnappers Foil films were always shot in the towns' parks, and Laura notes that while in Cleveland's Fireman's Park on the day of filming,

I remember Mr. Barker asking where the little red-headed curly haired girl was and someone said, "Here she is, right here," and he asked me to come over to him. So I walked over to where he was standing and he told me that he wanted me to introduce the movie! Well, I was ecstatic! Then he went on to say that he also wanted me to say "That's all folks" at the end of the movie. So I was in the very beginning by myself introducing the movie . . . during the movie I said the Mae West line . . . and I was at the very end closing the movie. Well, I was looking for an Oscar after all that!

Lance Smith remembered, "Many of the kids were there standing around waiting to be told what to do. Each of the kids were given a line to say and then the cameraman would shoot it and stop. This process went on for quite some time that afternoon. I remember thinking it was a lot like having your picture taken." Laura continued,

> Mr. Barker had us to sit on top of a picnic table in a row and also on the bench part of the table. One by one, he told us what he wanted us to say. When he came to me, he told me to say "Come up and see me sometime, boys" and to put my hand behind my head and push my hair up like I was flirting . . . then he told the boys to say "Woo-wooo" after my line. Well, that embarrassed the stuffing out of all of us, as we were at the age that flirting didn't come that easy yet. Then he gave out the rest of the lines and told us to speak up and not to squint our eyes (it was a sunny day). He set his camera up on a tripod and the filming began. He played the part of the robber that day and some kid's father played the Dad. We did several takes and that took the better part of the day. Parents were standing on the edge of the filming area watching intently. I remember everyone having a good time. Mr. Barker was a very nice man and he enjoyed every minute of it.

The film was first shown at Cleveland's Ellis Theater several months after the filming, and Laura recalls that everyone in the film was notified when the screening would be. She saw the film a second time a few years later, when she was in junior high school. "We really got a kick out of it," she wrote, "especially that second time when we had aged a little. I remember lots of laughs and snickers in the audience as we watched." Lance's recollections are primarily of this later screening. "Many of the children and their families were there," he writes. "I remember not hearing the line I actually said as it played on the silver screen because my sister was sitting next to me and yelled out, 'There you are!' and I missed hearing my line. It must have been humorous because I remember everyone in the theater laughing at what I had said. But I missed it."

The Smiths' parents have both passed away, but Lance notes that "I remember them commenting on it, and how impressed they were that we were in a movie," and Laura recalls that they attended both screenings and "enjoyed their children being involved with the project." Both children look back fondly on the experience, and Lance says that he would love to see it again and that he has "thought how easy and fun that was that day and that acting must be rewarding as you get to say things that you would never say, and get away with it too." For Laura, it was "an experience of a lifetime, especially in a sleepy delta town like Cleveland!" "I have thought of it a few times through my life," she reminisces. "I even wondered if I should have pursued acting since [Barker] singled me out to do extra appearances and lines in the movie. I think back now how significant that was, but I was too young to realize, at the time, that it may have been an omen of some sort! Oh well . . . c'est la vie."

GEORGE SANDERSON AND THE GANG COMEDIES

Although the nature of his professional relationship with Melton Barker is not entirely clear, George "Sandy" Sanderson, a longtime Dallas cameraman, directed versions of *The Kidnappers Foil* between 1951 and 1953.[20] Sometimes using the title *Kidnapped,* the films were often advertised simply as a local "gang comedy." Sanderson, a beloved figure in the Dallas film and television communities, was described by a former boss as "a delightful individual whom every person in the newsroom thought very highly of."[21] Many of the children who starred in Sanderson's local gang films, however, had different recollections.

Marvin Kaye, who grew up in the Philadelphia suburb of Upper Darby, acted in one of George Sanderson's films in the early 1950s. According to Kaye,

> the newspaper advertised for "tacky boys" and for a few dollars we were cast and told to dress up "tacky." . . . I remember asking [Sanderson] where the producer, Mr. Barker, was, and the reply I got was, "He's dead." Sanderson was not a kid-friendly person. His tone of voice when he said Barker was dead was nasty. I think Barker's name was in the newspaper ads, which makes it sound suspicious.

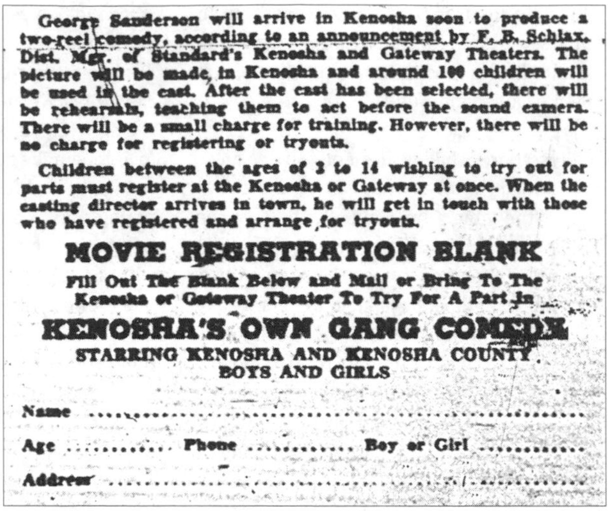

George Sanderson will arrive in Kenosha soon to produce a two-reel comedy, according to an announcement by F. B. Schlax, Dist. Mgr. of Standard's Kenosha and Gateway Theaters. The picture will be made in Kenosha and around 100 children will be used in the cast. After the cast has been selected, there will be rehearsals, teaching them to act before the sound camera. There will be a small charge for training. However, there will be no charge for registering or tryouts.

Children between the ages of 3 to 14 wishing to try out for parts must register at the Kenosha or Gateway at once. When the casting director arrives in town, he will get in touch with those who have registered and arrange for tryouts.

MOVIE REGISTRATION BLANK

Fill Out The Blank Below and Mail or Bring To The Kenosha or Gateway Theater To Try For A Part In

KENOSHA'S OWN GANG COMEDY

STARRING KENOSHA AND KENOSHA COUNTY BOYS AND GIRLS

Name ....

Age .... Phone .... Boy or Girl ....

Address ....

Figure 1. Kenosha Theater advertisement, *Kenosha News,* October 6, 1952.

Continuing, Kaye writes that "the filming was itself tacky. We all stood in a circle and each got one line to say into the camera. The film was eventually shown at the Tower movie theater in the then thriving Sixty-ninth Street shopping district of suburban Philly."[22]

Most of the children who appeared in itinerant films gave the quality of films little consideration. Lou Rugani, now an entertainer and disc jockey at WLIP radio in Kenosha, Wisconsin, went into his film, a 1952 George Sanderson production (titled *Kidnapped* in its newspaper advertisements), with higher expectations than most.[23] As a result, he saw most of those expectations dashed by the realities of low-budget itinerant filmmaking. Rugani is perhaps the only second-generation itinerant film star as his mother Katherine Rugani had acted in *The Belle of Kenosha,* a 1923 comic melodrama filmed by the relatively ambitious Hudris Film Company, led by director Walter Steiner, who simultaneously worked on two itinerant film series, including productions such as *A Romance of Seattle* (1919) and 1917's *The Belle of Biddeford* [Maine].[24]

The Ruganis had seen an ad for "Kenosha's own gang comedy" in the Kenosha newspaper announcing the call for child actors. The advertisement was reused in town after town, with only the name of the city and the theater changing (see Figure 1).

On reading this advertisement, Lou Rugani's parents asked him if he would like to be in a movie. "I remember it made a big impression," he recalls now, "kind of intimidating too." His intimidation, he explained, was the result of his already growing interest in the cinema, saying, "I know some of the other kids would brush off the film as just entertainment for the moment, but me, I kind of took an interest in it, so when the chance came I really had respect for the idea of being in the movies, such as it is," adding "that's kind of a laugh, calling *The Kidnappers Foil* a movie."

On the day of the auditions, Rugani joined dozens of other local children at Kenosha's Polonia Hall. "There were a lot of kids milling around outside on the sidewalk," he remembers. "I felt a little nervous going in because I thought at first this was a big deal, and they had promoted this as a knockoff of an Our Gang comedy."

> And when I went in there . . . they hadn't organized anything yet, and somebody hustled us into the main auditorium, [saying brusquely] "Have a chair" and "What's your name?" I guess my mother was there and I don't remember much . . . I didn't sit with her, I know that. I think they asked the parents to sit separately or wait outside or something, or come back later, perhaps. . . . The kids were milling around

or seated and signing up at the table. I remember that everybody was pretty well behaved. There was no noise. There was a lot of respect, actually, being shown. We were kind of awed and intimidated by the whole process of being in a movie, so we behaved pretty well. When we signed in I remember they took my name and address very methodically and I remember there was a fee being paid later but I don't remember when that happened.

Rugani does not recall precisely what he was asked during the interview, adding, "I'm sure that was just a token audition. I'm sure that everybody was accepted with the ten bucks or whatever it was." Despite the cost, Rugani's parents paid the fee because, in his words, "my parents wanted me in this movie."

The filming followed soon afterward on Simmons Island in Kenosha. "I tried to get as close as I could to the production," says Rugani, "to see what I could see and learn what I could learn."

And I remember him [Sanderson] saying into the microphone, "Kenosha Theater, Kenosha, Wisconsin; Kenosha Theater, Kenosha, Wisconsin," doing that in order to get a handle on what this was and for whom it was, so they didn't give the theater the wrong reel. They propped the camera up, we went through our thing and "Here's your line, you say this. Say it." I don't remember what my line was. It was probably one sentence. And I said my line, I did my best. . . . I was only eleven years old. So we did our thing and then somewhere along the line they asked who could do dancing and instrumentals, who had a talent . . . if you knew any acts or did any dancing. Back then a lot of kids did. . . . So we did our things and it was very static, the production. There wasn't a lot of action, and it was rather boring at times.

In retrospect, Rugani wishes he had been able to get a closer view of the camera, but he had been intimidated by Sanderson's casting assistant, who, on the day of the auditions, had barked at the children, "Sit down, sit down!

No questions!" "I had a question about the whole production," said Rugani, because he was "bubbling with ideas and was pretty impressed by the whole concept." His attitude going into the filming was, "Wow, you know, a film is being done here," but quickly he realized that very little attention was going to be given to the quality of the finished product:

I couldn't believe that anybody would do something that was less than good. And looking back I see how it was so slapdash, and it was disappointing, and had I known that as a parent, I would say, "Come on, kid, never mind that, we'll make our own home movies," you know, get a Brownie [movie camera] or something.

His feeling of being let down by the experience was immediate and palpable. "When it was over I felt pretty unfulfilled, I'll be honest," he said. "I was really looking forward to doing a good job for these people and contributing something to the world of quote-art-unquote. I thought to myself going home, 'There must be more that I'm missing here. Well, I'm sure it will all work out.'"

Two months later, there was an ad in the paper announcing that *Kidnapped* (advertised as "Kenosha's own 'Our Gang' Comedy with 150 Kenosha Children as Its Stars") would be the short opening a "Gala Christmas Show" program with *Horizons West* as the main feature.[25] When the ad appeared in the Kenosha newspaper, Katherine Rugani showed it to her son, and the two of them went to the theater to watch the film, and it was there that Rugani's feelings of disappointment truly sank in:

So we went up there and sat in the balcony of the Kenosha Theater. Sitting up there with all these people, the picture came up and there was no applause. I didn't recognize any overt demonstration—"There's me!"—no, none of that, I didn't see any of that, it was just the picture ran, we saw it, and then they went on to the next picture we left. My mother was not exuberant. There was none of this, "Wow, you were wonderful," none of that. "OK, let's go, Dad's going to pick us up," [she said] and we left, and there was no discussion of

FORUM 112

Figure 2. Kenosha Theater
advertisement, *Kenosha
News,* December 23, 1952.

the film. I didn't say anything, she didn't
say anything, and life went on. And I'm
guessing now, knowing adult mentality,
she was disappointed.

I don't think she was disappointed over
the five or ten bucks. I think she wanted
more for her only kid. I think she was really expecting something. I wish she had
said, "Lou you were wonderful up there."
I just wish they had tried a little harder to
make a better movie.

Looking back as an adult, I realize now
how little we really meant in the whole
scheme of things over there, and as you
grow up you realize some things you didn't
grasp as a kid, although you get an in-
kling, of the value that this production
company had placed upon you, which was
very little value at all. You were a ten dollar
bill to them, and you were a necessary evil,
something they had to film and teach you
to say a dialogue, and I'm sure that some
kids couldn't even do that easily.

Rugani's perspective on both the itiner-

ant filmmaking process and its end results
is in many ways an accurate reflection of the
assembly-line style of the productions, but
because his experience was not tempered
by the amiable personal manner other itinerant filmmakers cultivated, his story is unique
among the interviewees here in that his recollections are largely, if not entirely, negative.
He concludes,

> So am I bitter? No, I'm not bitter, it was just
> another experience. However, I'm disap-
> pointed that people like this, these itiner-
> ant producers, couldn't have valued our
> presence and our memories a little more,
> and to make it something a little more
> than just what it was. I don't remember
> him [the director] being nice to us, saying,
> "Thank you, kids, you were wonderful,"
> none of that. It was very matter of fact,
> like they'd done this before.

CONCLUSION

> KAREN SHOPSOWITZ: It would be really neat to know that your grandmother was the movie queen.
> EVANGELINE MORRISON: It made a good story, if you didn't elaborate.[26]

Listening to the recollections that people have about these itinerant productions, it is striking how little talk there is of the films themselves. Admittedly, this becomes more understandable after watching some of the movies. Itinerant films were quickly and cheaply made, with amateur actors who only had the briefest access—if any—to the scripts. Given these limitations, it is no surprise that the films were, as a rule, not great artistic achievements. Most audience members were satisfied with a film that was merely watchable, but even so, many went home unsatisfied. The sister of one of the stars of Muncie, Indiana's, *The Man Haters* (1915), one of the earliest existing itinerant film series, said that she really wasn't that impressed with her sister's film and that her only memory of it was that "it flickered a lot."[27]

Nevertheless, the films' deficiencies were often overcome by clever jokes, camera tricks, or the sheer charisma of the performers, and though the lack of quality is unfortunate for the impartial, unconnected viewer, these films were not made for impartial viewers; they were made for families, friends, and neighbors. This is why itinerant films, which were commercial products through and through, often have much in common with (and are often mistaken for) home movies: much of the appeal of both home movies and itinerant films comes from the same sense of recognition that the participants felt on seeing their images on screen. The makers of the fictional itinerant films, however, were consciously capitalizing on the aura of Hollywood by screening the films in the same theaters to which the local "stars" went to see their favorite movie stars. For film historians, itinerant films are still largely curiosities of a lost and not fully understood genre, and for local historians or later generations of the performers, the films are often perceived as charming documents of times gone by.

Oral history is a technique that is used occasionally in traditional cinema studies, but historians of itinerant film do not just benefit from interviews with the participants, they *require* them. This is not just because of the historiographic limitations mentioned earlier but rather because itinerant films derive so much of their importance, and perhaps even their primary meaning, from the reactions of the audience. These screenings, which were often literally a single show but at the most a week of shows in the local theater, were designed to be an *event* for the local people in attendance, even if the film itself was just a ten-minute short that played in the program where the cartoon would usually go. Ultimately, it is only through listening to the impressions of the participants that we can begin to understand these films.

NOTES

1. Owen Taylor, "Quiet on the Set," *Delta-Democrat (Greenville, Miss.),* May 15, 1972, 2. A list of known Barker productions appears online (http://www.meltonbarker.com/). As of May 2009, 135 different Melton Barker–directed Kidnappers Foil productions have been documented from between 1936 and 1975.
2. Judy White, telephone interview with the author, February 7, 2009.
3. Though the business models for most itinerant filmmakers appeared to be very similar, actual business records are known to exist for only H. Lee Waters (at the Rare Book, Manuscript, and Special Collections Library at Duke University) and, to a lesser degree, *The Movie Queen* (at Harvard's Houghton Library). Because most of the theater owners and other sponsors who hired the filmmakers are deceased, much of the information about the financial workings of the filmmakers can only be inferred from contemporary newspaper articles about the films.
4. Daniel W. Dorn, interview with Gloria Stravelli, Red Bank, N.J., September 20, 2000 http://www.visitmonmouth.com/oralhistory/bios/DornDaniel.htm.
5. Dorn's daughter Kathy Saverini, along with her husband, George, maintain the Dorns' cinematographic and photographic archive through their business Dorn's Classic Images in Fair Haven, N.J.
6. Jane Eigenrauch, "Dorn's Classic Movie

'Romance and Red Bank' at Library," March 14, 2009, http://www.ahherald.com/index.php/Red-Bank/dorns-classic-movie-romance-and-red-bank-at-library.html. See also Zach Lischer-Katz, "MIAP Students Uncover Origins of Forgotten Film," http://www.nyu.edu/tisch/preservation/newsletter/2007fall/miap_students.shtml, for additional information about the rediscovery and preservation of other Dan Dorn films instigated by students of New York University's Moving Image Archiving and Preservation Program.

7. Evangeline O'Brien Morrison and Helen Burns, interview by Karen Shopsowitz and Dwight Swanson, Lubec, Maine, 2003. This interview is a follow-up to interviews that Karan Sheldon did with Morrison, Burns, and Jimmy Simmonds in Lubec between March and May 1989.

8. See Dan Streible, "Itinerant Filmmakers and Amateur Casts: A Homemade 'Our Gang,'" *Film History: An International Journal* 15, no. 2 (2003): 177–92, for more discussions of other locally made Our Gang–style films.

9. "Melton Barker," *Weekend America,* American Public Media, December 9, 2006, http://weekendamerica.publicradio.org/programs/2006/12/09/melton_barker.html. In this clip, producer Michael May and Caroline Frick interview several participants from the Childress, Texas, Kidnappers Foil productions.

10. Eugenia Houseman, telephone interview with the author, January 10, 2009.

11. It is unclear what would have happened if any parent had taken Barker up on his offer because, despite Barker's claims, there is no evidence that the Hollywood connections he claimed were legitimate.

12. Three versions of *The Kidnappers Foil* are streamed online as part of the Texas Archive of the Moving Image's Melton Barker Juvenile Productions collection at http://www.texas-archive.org/library/index.php/Collection_-_Melton_Barker_Juvenile_Productions.

13. Judy White, telephone interview with the author, February 7, 2009.

14. Taylor, "Quiet on the Set," 2.

15. Ibid.

16. Ibid.

17. Penny Ellison Battistelli, e-mail correspondence with the author, March 8, 2009.

18. Lance Smith, e-mail correspondence with the author, March 23, 2009.

19. Laura Smith Legge, e-mail correspondence with the author, March 21, 2009.

20. It is unclear whether Sanderson was working in conjunction with Barker or if he was the filmmaker "using my name" to whom Barker referred in the 1972 article.

21. Eddie Barker, e-mail correspondence with the author, March 16, 2009.

22. Marvin Kaye, e-mail correspondence with the author, February 9, 2009.

23. Lou Rugani, telephone interview with the author, February 25, 2009.

24. See *The Belle of Kenosha* on IMDb, http://www.imdb.com/title/tt0218040/. Currently the only known Hudris Company production in existence is *A Romance of Butte,* available on DVD from Old Butte Productions.

25. *Kenosha News (Kenosha, Wisc.),* December 23, 1952, 10.

26. Morrison and Burns, interview, 2003.

27. Nancy Turner, *"Having Fun with It": The Man Haters Project* (Muncie, Ind.: Ball State University Press), 31.

The Itinerant Films of Arthur J. Higgins

ALBERT STEG

Just about everything I can tell you about Arthur J. Higgins comes from the films themselves, beginning with his name, which is penned on the "To" line of the Kodak film mailers. I have 114 of these mailers, each with a one-hundred-foot roll of black-and-white 16mm film inside and the name of a small American town on the side, along with film expiration dates ranging from 1936 to 1942. The towns range broadly along the middle swath of the United States, from Texas to Wisconsin. The films are full of pictures of people—mostly children streaming out of their schools and men loafing in front of small shops and gas stations. A woman beating a rug on her lawn, a man unloading canisters from a milk truck, or a boy puffing on a tuba are all we see of work, for the films are primarily interested in faces, not industries, and capture as many as possible in the three or four minutes available on one hundred feet of film.

Winding through the collection, in reel after reel, you see children ushered out of school doors, often from youngest to oldest. The films give the impression of a generational faucet having been opened up in taps all over the land, the progeny flowing out and growing taller until the scenes shift to dusty main streets where their elders go about their business or loaf in front of the hardware store. The teachers are usually youngish and smiling, except for one older man who you'd think must be the principal until it registers that the same suited figure appears in all the films. This, then, must be Arthur J. Higgins—and so the person running the camera, at least in the school shots, must be someone else. It seems likely to have been Mrs. Higgins, and although I have yet to locate any direct corroboration that the man is Higgins and the photographer his wife, I will write under that assumption.

Valders, Wisconsin (1938). Arthur J. Higgins Collection; courtesy of the author.

ITINERANT FILMS ON THE OPEN MARKET

To describe the Higginses' film production and the disposition of the 23,400 feet (100' × 234 reels) of small-town footage I know them to have shot between the years 1936 and 1942, I will recount in some detail how I came to acquire roughly half of that footage in that wonderful and infuriating marketplace, eBay. Archivists often express an antipathy toward the site, where unique cultural and historical artifacts are auctioned off to the highest bidder. Many archives have standing policies against paying for donations, and there is something naked and unsettling about seeing items that "belong in an archive" consigned to the auction block. Cryptic eBay usernames mask deep-pocketed collectors who squirrel away their takings in some unknown trove.[1] Even worse, sellers can seem nefarious in their seemingly bottomless access to precious materials to sell and their willingness to "part out" coherent collections for sale in multiple auctions to gain the greatest profit per item, historical record be damned.

The market for home movies on eBay was the subject of a conference panel, "Ebay: More Than a Four-Letter Word," at the 2007 Association of Moving Image Archivists (AMIA) conference in Rochester, where I shared my experience acquiring the Higgins films along with Bill O'Farrell, whose particular eBay nemesis routinely cut up single *reels* of film into ten- or fifty-foot segments to sell separately, and Snowden Becker, who shared quantitative data she had gathered on the quantity and selling prices of home movies on the site. The upshot of the session was that while, as archivists, we may lament significant moving image materials changing hands in such a market, (1) this is not always necessarily a bad thing in itself insofar as many of the materials that make it to eBay are already orphaned and might otherwise have wound up in a landfill and (2) archivists who care about this sort of material might reconsider their policies prohibiting acquisition through purchase, given that mission-relevant material may after all be available there for prices commensurate with their value to the institution.[2]

I came to the archival profession through my activities as a film collector, discovering 8mm and 16mm films by chance at the Todd

Farm Flea Market in Rowley, Massachusetts, in the late 1990s and finding on eBay a twenty-four-hour venue to indulge my pastime. Making contacts with Boston-area archivists through my *Zampano's Playhouse* microcinema screenings and with the wider circle of AMIA members at Northeast Historic Film and Orphan Film Symposium events induced me to leave a career teaching high school English in favor of archival studies at the Selznick School. Since graduating from the Selznick program, I have pursued archival work rehousing and inventorying the film collection at the National Baseball Hall of Fame in Cooperstown, New York, and providing customized Filemaker Pro solutions for collections management at a number of archives. All the while, though, I have continued my own film collecting in the area of home movies and ephemeral films—and I am one of those mysterious buyers on eBay who squirrels away interesting film materials: in this case, a remarkable collection of itinerant films.

The provenance of the films is this: some time in the 1980s, Arthur Higgins's widow, passing her later years in the Nebraska City, Nebraska, area, was grateful to a friendly man who helped her do some cleaning and gave him a collection of films, which he took with him back to his home in Minnesota. This man kept them for the next few decades, until he asked his son to sell them on eBay. This son,

Arthur J. Higgins leads children before the camera, *Advance, Wisconsin* (1939). Arthur J. Higgins Collection; courtesy of the author.

with whom I corresponded during and after the auctioning of the films, was of a friendly but laconic nature and often cryptically brief in his replies about the films' origins. He did convey to me a minimal confirmation that "it was [Higgins] and his wife only" who made the films, but his father was not familiar enough with the widow to recall her name. He added only that the Higginses had "once lived in our stompin' grounds Staples and Sandstone Minnesota."[3] The films appear to have been a commodity like any other gratuitous oddity around the house, ripe for conversion to cash on eBay's online garage sale.

And so in 2005, there appeared a stream of auctions, one reel apiece, bearing titles and dates evocative of small-town America: Rutersville, Texas; Roxton, Texas; Fulton, Kansas; Millard, Nebraska; Roslie, Nebraska; Xenia, Illinois. There were perhaps twenty or thirty reels for sale in all, with attendant years in the range 1936–1941. Each auction included pictures of an original film box, with the name "Arthur J. Higgins" heading the delivery address. Having attended the presentations on "Itinerants of the 1930s and 40s" at the Orphans IV Film Symposium (2004), I was familiar with the itinerant film phenomenon, and several aspects of these auctions raised a suspicion that these might be of a similar genre: the wide range of locations, the devotion of each reel to a single town, the late Depression-era dates.[4]

I appealed to the seller for more information on the films, especially any sense of their content, condition, or the extent of the collection, but his minimal response was along the lines of, "Quite a few yet to list. No vinegar smell that I can make out." I went ahead and purchased a dozen or so of the films, hoping for the best. Meanwhile, he had posted another dozen of the films at a somewhat higher "Buy It Now" price in the fifteen to twenty dollar range.[5]

Many of the films went to other buyers at the "Buy It Now" prices, whereas some were bid up to forty-four or eighty-five dollars each, evidently by buyers from locales that had engendered two or three enthusiasts willing to invest more in the hopes of finding local footage. One of the more active buyers was a familiar seller of home movies whose auctions I had noticed over the course of the previous year.

Looking more closely into his selling history for the previous thirty days, I could see that he had recently listed multiple reels of a carefully edited and intertitled home movie charting the workings of a small 1930s Rochester, New York, bakery in separate auctions. If the Higgins films turned out to be as interesting as I was imagining, there would be a peculiar range of buyers vying for the remaining reels—some motivated by the historical interest of the footage, others by the prospect of turning a profit on resale. And as it turned out, when the first shipment of films arrived, they turned out to be just what I had hoped.

AN EXEMPLARY FILM: MOORE, TEXAS (1941)

This one-hundred-foot reel of Kodak reversal film bears a 1940 edge code and a postal delivery date stamp of February 22, 1941, on its mailer box (this reel is viewable online at http://www.archive.org/details/MooreTexas1941). Higgins used a general delivery address to himself in San Antonio for the return of the film, and it is possible to group his various town films together by their approximate date and general delivery addresses, which are always larger local towns that Higgins does not appear to have filmed. The Moore film, like the others I have acquired, is a continuous sequence of many brief shots with no editing splices or title cards. At a projection speed of 16 fps, which would yield fairly natural movement and a chance to focus on the brief shots of faces, each film runs about four minutes.

Typical of the Higgins formula, the Moore film begins with sequences of children issuing from the front door of school in entire class groups, mixed with brief portrait shots of two or three children at a time, teachers in close-up and various images of schoolyard play. The graying gentleman whom I take to be Higgins himself appears fleetingly at the head of the lines of children, typically leading the first boy or girl by the hand past the camera. Much of the beauty of the images arises from the tension between the generic quality of the many children passing through the scene, in their haircuts and clothing typical of the period (as has been noted in the H. Lee Waters films, aviation helmets were all the rage with boys in

Moore, Texas (1941). Arthur J.
Higgins Collection; courtesy of
the author.

the 1930s[6]), and the intriguing particularity of each subject. There is something both beautiful and chilling in the way that each portrait, lasting an average of a mere thirty frames, memorializes the shift of a grin, the turning of a face toward some distraction, or a mechanical blinking of eyes. In the Valders, Wisconsin, film, a boy holds up a small skull figurine, a toy memento mori.

Groups of children are captured playing basketball, leapfrog, or various racing games. A few have special skills that are briefly showcased: a girl tap-dances, with a determined expression suggesting that this could be her ticket *out*. Another performs a flip and lands squarely on her backside. Various smaller couplings of two or more pose for miniportraits, some of them quite artfully arranged with faces at contrasting angles and at different depths of field.

About three-quarters of the way through the reel, there is an abrupt shift from the schoolyard to the main street, and a rapid series of individual portraits comprise the remainder of the reel. Again, many of these portraits appear to have been carefully arranged, and, typical of all the Higgins films I have viewed, there is

a deliberate inclusion of commercial signage as a framing device: Dr. Pepper, Shoe Repair, Camel cigarettes, Coca-Cola, Hires root beer. Elsewhere the abstract patterning of venetian blinds or brickwork performs a similar aesthetic function, and in many shots, there is a compositional and focal valuing of the background that makes still frames of the Higgins film particularly compelling. The care taken in preparing each of these portraits is further suggested by the ready expression and stance of each shot: there are no frames wasted getting the subject's attention and no editing out of bad footage.

There are about twenty-five separate portraits in the final quarter of this film. A boy in an aviator cap devours an ice cream cone; a dog reclines on the sidewalk behind a toddler and her mother, whose pleated trousers ripple in the breeze. Though it is at first natural to view these fleeting sequences as candid shots, they are, like the group shots in the schoolyard, carefully composed and at times highly contrived, as in a sequence where a skirted girl

Casselton, North Dakota
(1941). Arthur J. Higgins
Collection; courtesy of the
author.

watches askance, arms akimbo, while a man cranks a car to get it started. The stranger with the camera must surely have been more of a novelty than the man working at his car, yet the girl stares at the local man, a suggestion of a smirk on her face that delivers a familiar jape: the impatient, pretty girl waiting on the fumbling, incompetent male. Another man in work clothes drains a soda and lets out a satisfied gasp—the folks at Dr. Pepper could not ask for a better model.

The film is a richly textured document that in one sense captures people as they were in their natural element but also as they, or Higgins, felt was most photogenic and appropriate according to the filmic sensibility of the time. Many of the poses seem expressive of how people in the movies are supposed to look. This element of playacting may be seen at times as a version of mugging for the camera, but it is also in keeping with the Hollywood audition pretext that commonly accompanied itinerant film productions of the day. Researchers mining

the Higgins films for historical evidence would do better to examine the raw demographics of height and hem style than to conclude that games of leapfrog were a typical childhood pastime in the 1930s.

THE HIGGINS FILM DIASPORA

After examining the first shipment of films, I felt it was important to acquire as many Higgins reels as I could. I emphasized to the seller that the films he was selling were historically important and that I would be interested in buying all remaining reels at a price typical of those already sold, or, if the quantity of reels was beyond my resources, that I could extend an appeal to archives I felt certain would take an interest in the collection. The seller was reluctant to reveal how many films he had yet to sell, and it was clear that the occasional reel that had fetched an eighty dollar price made his father hesitant to sell them at any lower rate. Besides, he liked the idea of allowing people who lived in the locale of each film to have a chance at acquiring it—a sentiment with considerable validity, as any proponent of regional archives might agree. Auctioning the films separately gives them an opportunity to be "repatriated" to the locus of their creation, to be understood and appreciated by those most closely connected to the history they preserve. If one could trust that eBay's marketplace would deliver the many reels into the hands of individuals with a preservationist bent and a dedication to preserving local history, it might be best to let them "fly home." In practice, however, the fragmenting of the collection would likely find a majority of the reels sinking into permanent oblivion in various individuals' collections. The broad geographic scope of the films and the common pattern the Higginses brought to filming each community compelled me to unite as many as possible into a single collection, for each reel is illuminated by comparison with the rest. While a unified collection can be shared with regional archives, the films, once scattered, would have little chance of ever being understood as a whole.

Without knowing how many films were yet to be sold (dozens? hundreds?) and without unlimited personal funds to devote to acquisitions, I determined to purchase as many as I could and to make contact with as many other buyers as possible in the hope of creating as complete a record as possible of the Higginses' film production and the locations of the film-makers' original materials. Back in those days, it was relatively easy to contact other eBay bidders, and I sent a message to each Higgins film buyer inviting him or her to pool informa-tion about the films and open a door to future collaboration in preservation of the films as an integrated collection.[7] Some responded enthusiastically, others rudely, and others not at all. Regardless of response, I was able to compile a database record of the films, draw-ing on information about each film visible from the auction, the usernames of buyers, and any further contact or film information from those who responded cooperatively.

The auctioning of the films continued in waves and intervals for several weeks. I eventually persuaded the seller to sell me his remaining stock of approximately thirty reels, and along with them a master list of the reels, with town name and year for each (compiled not by Higgins but by the seller's father when he inventoried the films sometime in the 1980s). Adding the names of the reels I had missed see-ing on eBay, there had been a grand total of 234, of which I eventually managed to acquire 114.

Of the other 120 reels, approximately 70 had been purchased by the aforementioned rival buyer whose home movie auctions I had noted in the past. In a telephone conversation with him in February 2006, I learned he had an interest in creating some sort of documentary work with the films he was acquiring while fund-ing further film purchases by selling films of less interest to him. My efforts to engage him in the broader archival community—including urging him to attend the 2005 Orphans V Symposium that spring—came to nothing and, in fact, had a boomerang effect. To the dismay of several archivists whom I had alerted to the situation, or whom he had contacted himself in search of information on itinerant films, his new ad copy boasted, as a selling point, that major archives had expressed interest in the material. Because his auctions included images demonstrating the quality of the film and because he took the care to describe them thoroughly and list them in the most appropriate eBay categories,

he enjoyed selling prices in the seventy-five to two hundred dollar range. To my dismay, my efforts to alert certain Texas archivists about some reels of Texas towns being auctioned at prices beyond my resources to buy resulted in further interest in Higgins films that drove prices even higher, with a Farmer's Branch, Texas, reel selling for $316, 20 percent more than any previous reel had gained. After sell-ing twenty-two Higgins reels in this fashion, he appears to have sold the remainder to a single buyer. When the dust settled, the Hig-gins collection had been distributed into the hands of approximately forty different collectors scattered all over the map, a kind of itinerant film diaspora.

THE PRACTICE BEHIND THE FILMS

Plotting the location for all 234 reels of film on a Google Map and color coding the pins according to year—as noted in pen on the original box, or otherwise according to postal date stamp or inferred from the film expiration date—yields a tantalizing picture of a prolific film practice following a remarkably expansive itinerary.[8] The Higgins team ranged all the way from northern Minnesota to southern Texas. A small cluster of five towns filmed in California shot in Janu-ary and early February 1940 would seem to be an anomalous western jaunt, whereas a lone outlier from Jeffersonville, Georgia, dated 1936 on the master list is possibly a mistaken reading of the box address—the buyer of that reel has not replied to any of my inquiries.

Given the distribution of filming dates in the many towns in the five-year span repre-sented by the films, it seems unlikely that there could have been time for more extensive tours of California or other regions. The paucity of information available from the seller makes it impossible to say for sure, but there is reason to believe that Higgins may have shot more material than was eventually sold on eBay. There is also an unevenness of representation from town to town. One hundred twenty-five of the towns the Higgins filmed are represented by only a single reel of film; thirty-seven by two reels; four by three reels; and five by four reels. Is it likely that he could have visited so many towns where he shot so little footage? How does an itinerant showman parlay a paltry four minutes of entertainment (a one-hundred-foot reel projected at 16 fps) into a sufficient spectacle to warrant his participation in a screening event and a substantial enough portion of its proceeds? It is perfectly conceivable that the 234 surviving reels of film were those on the top shelves that survived a basement flood or some equally arbitrary culling process.

Efforts to locate contemporary newspaper accounts of the Higginses' work that would provide a context for the surviving footage have been nearly fruitless, despite efforts by a number of collectors in various states. The sole exception is a crucial discovery passed along to me by Stephen Calvert, a docent at the Swindler's Ridge Museum in Benton, Wisconsin. Stephen had sent me the one reel of film from Benton he had managed to acquire on eBay, after having it transferred to DVD. His work testifies to the value of returning orphan films to the communities whence they came. Calvert arranged community screenings of the Benton material and sold DVD copies to the public for a nominal fee.[9] He also created a shot list of the reel and succeeded in identifying a great many of the individuals captured in the Higginses' shots of the town. Unfortunately, although some elderly community members shown in their youth were still alive, they could recall neither the filming of their community nor any exhibition of such films. Calvert did, however, send me the text of an article he transcribed (with parenthetical commentary) from the *Benton Advocate,* dated Friday, March 22, 1940:

> *Benton in the Movies*
> Looks like the home folks will soon be Hollywood bound. Potential movie stars of Benton had their chance before the newsreel camera last Tuesday and Wednesday [either March 12 and 13 or 19 and 20, 1940] when Arthur Higgins, Victor newsreel representative was here making a movie of "Our Home Town." Over a 1000 feet was shot and you will want to see who the future Dorothy Lamour and Tyrone Power will be.
> Many of the scenes will lend comedy to the feature. Reverse and slow motion shots will enliven the scenes. This program will be shown in conjunction with a complete program of sound pictures; including a feature, novelty short, and news. Don't forget the date, Monday, March 25 at the Blende Theatre.
> An Action Movie

The revelation that Higgins shot one thousand feet in Benton (only two hundred feet of which made it onto eBay) is ample evidence that a great quantity of his work is yet to be accounted for. It is possible that the Higginses kept only the candid, unedited footage while leaving behind the longer feature for the town to keep. Indeed, most of the one-hundred-foot reels came with a small, six-inch length of white leader spliced at the head, perhaps suggesting they had been compiled into longer programs and then returned to their boxes afterward.

The attribution in the Benton article of Arthur Higgins as a "Victor Newsreel representative" seems a promising lead, but I have found no other reference to such an organization.[10] It might be a bit of a P. T. Barnum ploy, elevating a pair of independent photographers to the status of industry scouts. The Casselton, North Dakota, footage includes one clear view of a shop window advertisement for the film screening, featuring a bold *Home Town Movies* title with the image of a cameraman and the event information written into a space in the top. The poster has a generic but professional look to it, and if the "Higgins" name appears on it, it must be very small, suggesting either that they had a modest streak or that there *was* a Victor Newsreel organization that outfitted the Higginses with the tools of the trade. In some reels, children streaming from the schools can be seen grasping handbills advertising the show, with the word "Victor" visible under a loupe.

The various "trick shots" alluded to in the Benton article are wholly absent from the 115 reels on which I have performed simple conservation. As I shifted each reel from original reel to three-inch core, I took a cursory look at the contents of each reel and found them quite uniform in their simple approach to recording portraits of individuals and small groups of people. Whereas the surviving Higgins footage I have seen is very similar in style to some of

the school sequences and portraiture seen in H. Lee Waters's work, this article from the *Benton Advocate* suggests that yet-to-be-discovered Higgins work may share even more similarities with Waters's often playful technique.[11]

A pair of boys in Casselton, North Dakota (1941), walk past a *Home Town Movies* flyer. Such promotional material is visible in many of the Higgins films. Arthur J. Higgins Collection; courtesy of the author.

RETRACING THE HIGGINS ITINERARY

The short Benton article also provides some insight into the pace of the Higgins work process. While Calvert points out in his parenthetical note that "last" Tuesday and Wednesday is ambiguous, it would seem unlikely that Higgins could have sent the film off for developing late on a Wednesday and have it back and ready for projection the following Monday. An eleven-day shooting-to-exhibition cycle seems more likely, and the box information suggests that they shot several towns then consolidated their material in a larger nearby town before returning to screen the films. For instance, table 1 shows the information for the 1938 Texas stops, in a plausible order of itinerary based on box information and/or geographical proximity.

The filmed towns appear to be a convenient day-trip distance from the delivery towns. Looking at the full map, it is striking how widely the Higginses traveled each year, and it is dif-

ficult to discern any seasonal pattern to their itinerary. In the California cluster, they shot six towns in sixteen days, and six seems to be about the most they had delivered to one general delivery address in one stretch.

In January 2009, I took a few days to drive through a dozen of the Higgins towns in the San Antonio and Austin areas of Texas to see what remains of them and to try to turn up some reference to the Higginses' work in local libraries or museums. Unfortunately, few specimens of the small-town and county newspapers published during the time of the Higginses' travels in Texas appear to have survived, judging from the holdings at the San Antonio Public Library and the Lyndon Baines Johnson Library (LBJ) in Austin; a careful scanning of all the microfilmed issues of the *Atascosa County Monitor* from the late 1940s through all 1941 at the LBJ and the *Colorado County Citizen* from late 1937

Table 1. A likely itinerary of Higgins's activity in Texas in 1938, suggested by geography and film box information.

Town name	Date	Delivery*
Jourdenton/Charlotte	1938	San Antonio?
Charlotte	January 27, 1938	San Antonio
LaCoste	1938	San Antonio?
Lytle	1938	San Antonio
Poth	1938	San Antonio
Kingsbury	February 8, 1938	San Antonio
Fentress	February 17, 1938	Austin
Calallen	March 16, 1938	Alice
Pettus	March 18, 1938	Alice
Ingleside	March 1938	Alice
Agua Dulce	March 1938	Alice?
Howe	1938	McKinney
Prosper	December 12, 1938	McKinney

*A question mark indicates speculation.

through mid-1938 held at the Nesbitt Memorial Library in Columbus, Texas, yielded no mention of their passing.

The discovery of a catalog entry at the Campbellsport Historical Society for two reels of 16mm "Local Shots of Campbellsport" dated 1936 and 1938 that credit "Arthur J. Higgins of Fond du Lac, Wisconsin," along with the heavy concentration of Wisconsin towns represented in the films sold on eBay (92 of 234 reels) suggests that the Higginses may have resided in that state; they also appear to have had ties to Minnesota (where the eBay seller's family became acquainted with the Higginses) and Nebraska (where Mrs. Higgins gave the films to the seller's father).[12] My efforts to locate a death record, obituary, or any other concrete identification pertaining to Arthur J. Higgins or his wife have been inconclusive.

THE FUTURE OF THE HIGGINS COLLECTION

If my first imperative on discovering the eBay sales of the Higgins films was to reunite as many as possible; my second is that I would like for as many residents of the towns the Higginses filmed to see their local footage for themselves and to make all of the films readily available to the broader community of scholars and enthusiasts who might take an interest in them. I have only begun to think about how best to go about fulfilling these aims. Donation to an archive willing to commit to seeing the complete collection preserved and released on DVD is a possibility. Another is to pursue something like the homegrown approach of Stephen Calvert, securing transfers on my own and distributing them via regional organizations that can offer them to their communities at town halls and local events. Ideally these organizations could return information to me about the content of the films after screening them at town halls or schools. Among the many buyers of the Higgins films is a documentarian who holds forty-five of the reels, and we have hopes of collaborating on a project, pooling our material, and visiting some of the Higgins towns to shoot comparative footage of the communities and people then and now.

The copyright status of the Higgins films may prove an obstacle. The original exhibition of their films would not in itself constitute publication, and so these orphaned works would fall under the copyright protections for unpublished works, which last seventy years beyond the death of the author.[13] In the absence of clear legal guidelines that define due diligence for attempting to locate a surviving rights holder or adequate legal protections for an archive that might choose to distribute the Higgins films even in the absence of affirmative rights to the footage, many archives might balk at doing anything more than making the material available for on-site study by visiting scholars. I would be very hesitant to entomb the Higgins films in an environment with such limited prospects for popular viewing.

Thanks to the democratization of moving image editing and distribution technology (desktop editing suites, home-market DVD-burning hardware, inexpensive online marketplaces), some amateur film collectors sell homemade DVDs of found footage, often consolidating material on a theme of specialized interest (steamships, military aircraft, particular geographical locations) gleaned from a variety reels acquired at estate sales or on eBay. Other found-film aficionados post their findings on YouTube, where they can be accessed instantly by anyone who happens to search on a relevant key word term.[14] These enthusiast-entrepreneurs appear to be largely indifferent to (or perhaps ignorant of) the fact that they are violating the strict letter of copyright law. Or perhaps they are simply willing to accept the remote risk that some rights claimant or angry individuals appearing in the film who felt their privacy was being violated might object and that the consequence in such cases would be more severe than removing the material from circulation. Scrupulous archivists may find it impossible to give their blessing to this approach but at the same time might have to admit that most of these films—lacking documentation, permissions, or ready patrons to foot the bill for thorough examination and cataloging, let alone preservation funding— would simply languish in their vaults, occupying a dreary "someday when we get the time and resources" level of priority.

In a May 12, 2009, posting to the AMIA-L Listserv, Rick Prelinger suggested, in response to current threads of discussion criticizing the dominant storytelling mode of modern documentary production, that moving image archivists should become moviemakers themselves: "Let's put original, unedited archival material out in the world in such a way that it competes with documentaries."[15] In this regard, it may be that some of the amateur collector-enthusiasts are ahead of the curve, investing their own time and resources on behalf of orphaned materials in ways that established archives have not yet been doing, even with materials to which they have clear copyright. Looking forward, I hope to find the best means to make the entirety of the Higgins footage available to the public in a high-quality format, while also ensuring its preservation for posterity. I also look forward to someday just *seeing* it all in motion, from beginning to end.

Notes

My thanks go to Snowden Becker for hosting my visit to Austin and pointing my way to the most useful libraries and to Skip Elsheimer for providing the transfer of the Moore, Texas, film and uploading it to Archive.org. For their assistance with my research about the Higginses and their work, I am also grateful to Nancy Pfotenhauer at the Mineral Point Historical Society in Mineral Point, Wisconsin; Elias Savada of the Motion Picture Information Service; and New York University graduate student Martin Johnson.

1. An example of this sort of interest in buyer identity and motivation was an exchange on the AMIA-L Listserv, when someone inquired as to the real identity of an eBayer who had been buying large numbers of home movies,

often at great expense. When one respondent defended the right of the buyer to remain anonymous, several others (including me) argued that people who draw attention to themselves by "cornering a market" in any sort of rarity are liable to invite appropriate curiosity about their identity and interest in the material. See Rick Prelinger, "eBayers—Who Is ocbstore?" October 28, 2007, http://lsv.uky.edu/archives/amia-l.html.

2. I know of at least one archive that welcomed donations of films bought on their behalf by donors, who were recompensed in one way or another by the archive. I think it very likely that this sort of practice is common.

3. E-mail correspondence with the author, March 11, 2006.

4. Orphan Film Symposium, "Orphans 04: On Location—Place and Region in Forgotten Films," http://www.sc.edu/filmsymposium/archive/orphans2004/program.html.

5. In addition to an opening bid amount, a seller may place a higher "Buy It Now" (BIN) price at which a buyer may purchase the item outright. If a minimum bid is placed first, the BIN option is neutralized and the auction plays out to the closing date. Therefore items may sell for prices much higher than a BIN price.

6. Stephanie Elaine Stewart, "*Movies of Local People* and a Usable Past," *The Moving Image* 7, no. 1 (2007): 59.

7. Since then, eBay has incorporated measures that disguise the usernames of bidders on all auctions, making it far more difficult to identify and communicate with winners of auctions to which one was not a party. These measures were implemented to preclude the sorts of off-eBay negotiations that tend to cut eBay out of revenues, yet they also have made it difficult to contact winning bidders for purposes of honest collaboration.

8. View the map at http://tinyurl.com/cwb5de.

9. During the drafting of this article, I learned that Stephen Calvert passed away in March 2009. Owing to his foresight, DVD copies of the Benton Wisconsin Higgins films will continue to be available from the Swindler's Ridge Museum, 25 West Main Street, Benton, WI 53808, tel. (608) 759-5182.

10. An inquiry to the Special Collection and University Archives at the University of Iowa Libraries yielded no reference to Higgins in the company records or newsletters of the Victor Animatograph Company nor any reference to any "newsreel"-related activities within that company.

11. See, e.g., Tom Whiteside, *The Cameraman Has Visited Our Town* (1989), http://www.folkstreams.net/film,115.

12. Campbellsport Area Historical Society, "Finding Aid for the Holdings of the Campbellsport Area Historical Society," http://campbellsport.govoffice.com/index.asp?Type=B_BASIC&SEC={9D56D5BF-B57E-47E5-8600-838FA8E7D82A}.

13. "Copyright Term and the Public Domain in the United States," http://copyright.cornell.edu/resources/publicdomain.cfm.

14. E.g., http://www.youtube.com/watch?v=6HS2pgA5TQ8. Many further examples can be found by typing "found home movie" in the YouTube search field.

15. Rick Prelinger, "Beating a Dead Horse," May 12, 2009, http://lsv.uky.edu/archives/amia-l.html.

Itinerant Filmmaking in Knoxville in the 1920s

A Story Told through Unseen Movies

BRADLEY REEVES AND LOUISA TROTT

As film archivists, we like to brag about our latest discoveries. Occasionally, while describing the finer details of location, plot, and characters, we may have to remind ourselves that we have never actually seen the film we are talking about. The vivid moving image in our heads has often been created solely from references gleaned from newspapers, scrapbooks, and oral histories. The number of lost films, especially from the silent era, is vast; the survival rate for amateur and nonstudio system commercial films is likely far lower even than that for silent-era studio productions. Thanks to the efforts of regional film archives, special collections within universities, and historical societies in particular, awareness and knowledge of these films has steadily increased.

As a new regional film archive—the Tennessee Archive of Moving Image and Sound (TAMIS), founded in 2005—we have been surprised by the number of itinerant films we have been able to locate in the very small area we cover. Many of these are the your-town-in-the-movies type, usually commissioned by the local theater owner to portray his or her hometown and entice audiences to the theater to see themselves, their friends, and their town on the big screen. We classify these films as itinerant films because many of the same crew members traveled from town to town to work on each production. At TAMIS, we have two examples of your-town-in-the-movies films made by the John B. Rogers Company: *Athens, TN* (1940) and *Sweetwater, TN* (1937). However, we have been unable to find much information about either the man or his company. This is not unusual when it comes to itinerant filmmakers, who are often difficult to pin down. These two films, along with other examples of this type of film in our collection, provide unique portraits of towns across our region even if no circumstantial information about their makers is available. Such films not only capture the town's former

physical and commercial geography but also shed light on the world of itinerant filmmaking, primarily through the newspaper stories surrounding the films' production.

The earliest known examples of itinerant films made in Tennessee that we have been able to find are, unfortunately, no longer extant. The first reference we have located is to a one-reeler, made in Knoxville, titled *Aunt Sally Visits Knoxville* (December 1915).[1] The film was produced by an out-of-town firm, the Gullette and Harris Empire Amusement Company, based in New York, and made under the auspices of a now-demolished Knoxville movie house, the Gay Theatre. The film, shot entirely in Knoxville, featured many prominent members of Knoxville society, including local artist Hugh C. Tyler, uncle of Knoxville-born author James Agee. The film's production and release was covered by the *Knoxville Sentinel*. According to the *Sentinel,* Mr. Tyler himself took the lead role as Aunt Sally, a primitive old lady residing in the hills of the nearby Cumberland Mountains. When oil is discovered on her property, Aunt Sally suddenly becomes a fabulously wealthy woman and travels to the big city of Knoxville for a series of shopping sprees, with comical results.[2] The article lists some of the prominent names in the cast, along with some of the locations used in the movie, including a number of Knoxville's most prominent businesses. So it seems that even as early as 1915, the die had been cast for what would become a standard method of operation for many itinerant films: townspeople took lead roles, and location shooting took place at businesses that had paid to be advertised in the movie as well as at historic homes and landmarks about town (in this case, the stately mansion of Colonel L. D. Tyson). The film premiered in late December 1915 at the Gay Theatre, home base for the films produced by Triangle and Fox Film Studios. It was included on a bill with *Stolen Magic,* a Mabel Normand comedy, and *Matrimony,* directed by film pioneer Thomas Ince. The film was a hit: "Several thousand people saw the Triangle program, including the Knoxville Picture, 'Aunt Sally Visits Knoxville,' yesterday and last night, but they were unable to accommodate all that came, as they were forced to turn away at least a thousand last night."[3] The film was held over for an entire week so that as many Knoxvillians as possible would have a chance to view what was dramatically described as "Absolutely the Best Motion Picture Ever Made in Knoxville!"[4]

As thrilling as it is to discover extant itinerant rarities, the films that remain lost can often be the most tantalizing. In what follows, we will focus on two films—*A Knoxville Romance* (1925) and *Too Much Flapper* (1928)—that we have never actually seen, and probably never will, as both are considered lost. They are the only two examples of itinerant films in 1920s Knoxville of which we know. We have spoken with local historians, old projectionists, and people connected with the theaters in Knoxville, yet no one remembers anything about these films. Even without viewing the films, the stories surrounding them can contribute much to the rich history of itinerant filmmaking during the early part of the last century. As both films were big news in the city of Knoxville, in addition to being produced under the auspices of the local newspapers, any progress or pitfalls were usually reported in some detail on a daily basis, thus providing us with a well-documented (if somewhat biased) account of the project. The stories and events surrounding the production of these films reach far beyond the actual making of the movies themselves, shedding light on both itinerant filmmaking methods and the cultural climate of a moderate-sized southern city during the early twentieth century.

SLIM BROLUND'S ROMANCE FILMS

During the 1920s, Knoxville, Tennessee, was a thriving city with a distinct southern flavor. The textile industry was at its peak, providing gainful employment to those traveling from the surrounding rural areas and mountain towns. In this pre-Depression era, there was a feeling of optimism in the air. The city was growing and had just about everything a larger city could offer: plenty of restaurants, department stores, hardware stores, an opera house, a university, and several vaudeville and movie theaters scattered about the large downtown area. It was an ideal environment for an itinerant filmmaker such as J. B. "Slim" Brolund.

Brolund was unknown to us at TAMIS until an acquaintance, who was researching an entirely unrelated subject, spotted a mention of Brolund and the film he planned to make and brought it to our attention.[5] Fortunately, Brolund was a master at the publicity game. Before even reaching town, Brolund contacted the newspapers to inform them that he was just finishing up a production in a nearby town and would soon be arriving in Knoxville to begin work on a new motion picture production, a tactic he apparently repeated with each new production. He even included publicity photos of himself. One could easily mistake him for screen actor Slim Summerville, a lanky comedian who had gained popularity as one of Mack Sennett's players. Brolund certainly looks the part of the silent movie clown. Standing six feet tall and weighing in at a whopping ninety-eight pounds, Brolund is all skin and bones. His tall, skeletal appearance is further accentuated by too-short flood pants, too-long workman's boots, the obligatory derby hat (stock-in-trade of the silent screen comedian), and a whimsical expression. This mistaken screen star identity is probably what Brolund was hoping to cash in on.

The first local mention of Slim Brolund appears in a *Knoxville Sentinel* newspaper article in early July 1925. A photo of the comical-looking Brolund is accompanied by the heading "'Slim' Brolund of the Movies." Underneath the large photo spread is a caption stating, "J.B. 'Slim' Brolund is coming to Knoxville with his complete movie outfit to make comedy-publicity picture for Knoxville. This picture will be of tremendous interest inasmuch as several of the leading people in the cast will be well known Knoxville citizens. Work on the picture will be started within a few days, and when the film is completed it will be shown three days at the Riviera Theatre and three days at the Strand Theatre."[6] This article was the first of many, with progress reports on the film running in the *Sentinel* every day through most of July and August.

So just who *was* Slim Brolund? The *Sentinel* bio for Brolund reads as follows: "Brolund has played for four and one half years with the Fox Company. Also with Mack Sennett and Universal before entering the business of a producer himself. He has also played upon the legitimate stage."[7] The article further states that Brolund could be seen in Universal's classic *Hunchback of Notre Dame* (1923) and Sennett's

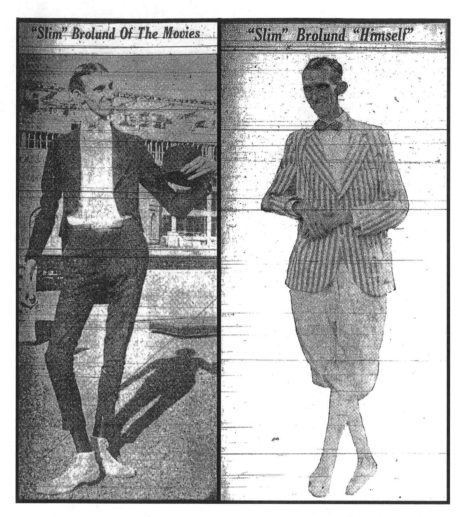

"Slim" Brolund Of The Movies   "Slim" Brolund "Himself"

Two publicity photographs
of "Slim" Brolund, 1925.
Knoxville Sentinel, July 6,
1925, 14, and July 12, 1925, 12.

production of *Flip Flops* (1923).[8] Brolund professed associations with silent film luminaries such as Ben Turpin, Al St. John, Clyde Cook, and others. The *Sentinel* proclaims that Brolund "is not only an actor and producer in the motion picture world, but has achieved considerable success as an artist, cartoonist, and caricaturist."[9] Indeed, Brolund's self-portrait caricature was incorporated into many of the sponsors' advertisements in the *Sentinel*. Brolund proved himself to be a master at celebrity endorsement: his caricature was used in newspaper advertisements promoting the film and hawking everything from homes to Frigidaire refrigerators, furniture, and even a local beauty shop!

Implying (or perhaps even inventing) connections to Hollywood was a practice that helped itinerant filmmakers secure the interest of the public and sponsors alike. Perhaps Brolund *had* managed to secure a number of minor parts in the silent film comedies of the day, but we have yet to find evidence to substantiate his claims. Brolund is mentioned, however, in "The Directory of Artists under Exclusive Management of the Edward Small Company."[10] This Hollywood trade book, dating from the early 1920s, featured a listing of actors then under contract to film producer Edward Small. Brolund is listed along with silent comedians Billy Bevan, Eddie Boland, Lloyd Hamilton, and many other supporting cast silent film comedians and actors, though we have found no other evidence of an acting career beyond this listing.

According to the *Sentinel*, Brolund was currently working on a film in Asheville, North Carolina. The "famous elongated film comedian" had secured the services of legendary North Carolina–based photographer and Pathé News cameraman George Masa.[11] Masa was an early supporter of the Great Smoky Mountains National Park and documented the mountains of western North Carolina with exquisite photography during the 1920s and 1930s.[12] The *Asheville Citizen* reports that Masa was working with Brolund on the production of *The Asheville Romance*, filmed in spring and early summer 1925, and that he intended to go on the road with Brolund to make Romance films in other towns.[13] The *Sentinel* underscores Masa's credentials by asserting that "he is the only motion picture photographer who has ever been allowed to 'shoot' a set in 'Biltmore,' the estate of Mrs. George K. Vanderbilt."[14] According to an article dated July 5, 1925, the *Asheville Citizen* reports that "Mr. Brolund goes next to Knoxville, Tennessee. From there he goes to Charlotte (North Carolina) and thence to Greeneville."[15]

Slim Brolund arrived in Knoxville the first week of July with the fanfare usually accorded a star. Brolund proclaimed the town "ideal" for location shooting.[16] He became an instant celebrity and man about town, entertaining local civic groups such as the Exchange and Shriners Clubs, where he "sang a number of comic and other songs with Ukulele accompaniment, and did a number of his famous comic stunts, to the great enjoyment of his audience."[17] Touting the film as a "comedy-publicity picture for the town," Brolund apparently made the right connections at these social affairs.[18] Replicating what appears to have been the production model of the Asheville production, several Knoxville business owners signed up to participate in the film, offering their premises as sets, various

Brolund's caricature is used to advertise the film sponsors' products, July 1925. *Knoxville Sentinel*, July 15, 1925, 18.

products for use as props, and financial support. The Henry G. Trent Furniture Company, East Tennessee Electric Company, Knoxville Gas Company, Akers Jewelry Company, and I. J. Cooper Rubber Company are just a few of the businesses listed in the newspaper.[19] Even the 117th Infantry Tennessee National Guard offered the use of their headquarters and some military personnel for extras.[20]

A citywide talent search began to find the perfect leading lady for the film. According to the *Sentinel*, "with the large list of talented Knoxville girls to draw from in his choice of leading lady for the film, [Brolund] sees no reason why the local picture should not rival anything ever done in Hollywood."[21] Two coupons were printed in the *Sentinel* each day, one for nominations and one for votes. This was a stroke of genius by the newspaper, as the votes were valid only when submitted on the coupon published in the *Sentinel!* The girl getting the largest number of votes would, of course, become Slim Brolund's lucky leading lady. Ballot boxes were placed in the lobbies of the Strand and Riviera theatres and in the Knoxville *Sentinel* business office. The call for a leading lady received a "hearty response."[22] In the end, the girl with the most votes was popular and talented society girl Mazie Huffaker, the daughter of a local doctor. Mazie's admirers credited her victory to "her most unusual qualities of vivacity, personal charm, and pleasing personality."[23] Brolund himself was reportedly pleased, stating that Huffaker was "full of pep, and has certain intellectual qualities absolutely essential to the screen star. Coupled with this, Miss Huffaker is just the proper physical type required by the pictures."[24] The newspaper also anticipated additional roles for many of Knoxville's other young wannabes: "Crowds on the streets and in the parks will also play an important part in the production of the film and a great many of Knoxville's 'sweet young things' will be given the chance to see themselves on the screen where they have probably spent many happy hours in wishing that some day they might get behind the footlights and in front of the spot light on the screen."[25]

Filming was set to begin in mid-July; however, it was delayed while the crew waited for newly ordered 35mm motion picture cameras to arrive. The *Sentinel* remarked, "Brolund is so enthused over the work in Knoxville, that he wishes to film only the best pictures. Therefore he is getting a Bell and Howell and a Universal camera, which will guarantee the perfect filming of the photoplay."[26] The newspaper comments on the proposed plot, in which Brolund plays Harry Beanpole, a poor laborer caught up in a love triangle: "A very interesting story has been written by Mr. Brolund to fit with the local conditions."[27] This mirrors the method used by other itinerant filmmakers such as Melton Barker and his Kidnappers Foil films.[28]

The *Sentinel* seems torn between wanting to foster people's interest in the movie with plot details and a fear of revealing too much of the story. In one article, the newspaper holds off on revealing too much. It reports that the poor laborer, Beanpole, gets involved in a spectacular thrill chase and is "seen floating down the Tennessee river clad in the proverbial barrel. He does, however, wear a smile. . . . Next—well, next happens many things. There is no need

THE ROMANCE OF KNOXVILLE

MOVING PICTURES

Will Be Made of the

28 & 30 E. MARKET SQUARE

HENRY G. TRENT FURNITURE CO

SATISFACTION GUARANTEED OR MONEY REFUNDED

28-30 MARKET SQUARE

TOMORROW, THURSDAY, AT 3:00 P. M.

The Public is Invited

GET IN THE PICTURE

THE ROMANCE OF KNOXVILLE

A local merchant invites the public to its premises for the next day's filming. *Knoxville Sentinel,* July 29, 1925, 15.

to spoil the show by giving a detailed account of it."[29] Yet a later article provides a detailed, scene-by-scene account of the film, and this time, the river scene is not mentioned (it is replaced instead with Slim ending up in a "rather unsightly condition" as a result of a backcountry chase and having to buy a whole new outfit).[30] By August 9, the plot had changed again, and the *Sentinel* apparently decided to ditch its concerns for revealing the storyline with the hope that the more it revealed about the locations and plot, the bigger the audience it might attract.

Despite many delays, location shooting for *A Knoxville Romance* began on Monday, July 27.[31] Shooting times, dates, and locations were advertised in the newspaper, and businesses invited the public to come by their stores and watch Brolund and company in action on the set and, of course, to perhaps purchase a few goods while there.[32] The newspaper often published details of the day's shooting schedule to encourage crowds at each location. Throngs of onlookers appeared wherever the crew filmed, egged on, no doubt, by the newspaper's encouragement.[33]

The final synopsis of the film, as described by the *Sentinel,* is an incomprehensible and dizzying series of visits by our hero and leading lady to jewelry and furniture stores, real estate offices, automobile lots, and other business locations, all squeezed into a two-reeler (approximately twenty minutes in length). Amid the convoluted details of the plot, a new twist to the real-life production story quietly slipped in. The chosen contest winner, leading lady Mazie Huffaker, had been mysteriously dropped from the film and replaced by another local girl, Miss Elizabeth Burkes.[34] No explanation was given. Curiously, no mention of the leading lady's name had appeared since the winner was announced on July 19. The first mention of the new leading lady's name appears on August 9, with no information regarding a change of actress. Perhaps Huffaker had never officially accepted the role or was overruled by cautious parents. Or had she begun the project and dropped out after some time? Whatever the explanation, it was Burkes who ended up as Brolund's competent lead: "Miss Elizabeth Burkes, a Knoxville girl, who performs most interestingly and plays in the pictures in a manner that Mr. Brolund and his artists declare is exceptionally clever and capable for one who has never before posed for the movies."[35] Intriguingly, newspaper reports concerning the filming of the movie focus on Brolund himself and not on the locals chosen to play the leads. This is of particular significance to the history of itinerant filmmakers. Most of the itinerant filmmakers known to us place the local stars at the center of the movie; here Brolund is the star. He is producer, director, and leading man.

Production work for the much-anticipated *A Knoxville Romance* was finally completed in early August. A *Sentinel* article dated August 9, 1925, mentions that "the film is now being 'cut' and printed, and the sub-titles inserted. This work [is] being done in Mr. Brolund's studios in New York City. 'Slim' will reach Knoxville next Saturday personally bringing the film, and he will be present at the 'preview' of the picture at the Riviera, preliminary to its offering to the public on Monday following."[36] The premiere of the film was set to take place on August 17 at the Riviera, and "Mr. Brolund is promising the Knoxville public a most entertaining picture in which many will see their friends and perhaps themselves as they were caught by the ever ready filmmaker. . . . All of Knoxville will want to see *A Knoxville Romance.*"[37]

The final article before the film's premiere appeared a few days later. The *Sentinel*'s excitement for, and promotion of, *A Knoxville Romance* continued with announcement of the imminent arrival of the film in Knoxville: "A message from Mr. Brolund received by the Sentinel yesterday, stated that the film is completed, at that time en route to Knoxville, and that it would be both surprising and pleasing to the thousands of Knoxvillians who will witness it throughout the week."[38] Yet no further reports appeared over the next week—there were no reviews or follow-up articles, no reports of the gala premiere. There was only a single line in a Riviera Theatre advertisement in the August 16 edition of competing newspaper the *Knoxville Journal:* "Added Attraction: *Romance of Knoxville.*"[39] The movie was scheduled to play along with the main feature, *Introduce Me,* starring Douglas MacLean.

The lack of reporting surrounding the film's premiere made us wonder: had the city of Knoxville, with movie stardust in its eyes, been had? Many of those within the community would have had more than ample reason to be embarrassed had they been duped by a charming out-of-towner claiming Hollywood connections. Theater owners, local merchants who paid to be advertised in the film, prominent Knoxville citizens appearing in the alleged production, and most of all, the *Knoxville Sentinel* stood to be humiliated had J. B. 'Slim' Brolund taken them for a ride.

Had the film actually been made at all? Was there film stock in Brolund's cameras, or was this all a ruse to get easy money out of local merchants? Brolund had plastered his name and face all over the newspapers and town, which would make such behavior seem unlikely or at least extraordinarily risky. Another possibility was that Brolund had produced a film so unbelievably amateurish and unwatchable that theater management (and/or he himself) refused to show it. Or had there been a technical or processing disaster? Or had the film been lost in transit? Whatever happened, there was no explanation in either Knoxville newspaper. Surely, if there had been an accident of some sort, the *Sentinel* would have published something about it, and the *Journal* would have reveled in its rival's misfortune and splashed a scandalous explanation all over its front cover.

The lack of fanfare and follow-up reviews led us to investigate the Asheville production further. Had *An Asheville Romance* premiered over the state border in North Carolina, or had the film's completion met with the same lackadaisical response? If so, did we have an itinerant con man on our hands? Our starting point was to contact Paul Bonesteel, a filmmaker who recently made a documentary about the photographer George Masa, who was reportedly the cameraman on Brolund's Asheville (and Knoxville?) film. Surely he would know if Masa had been involved in such a production. Unfortunately, he did not know. However, he copied his e-mail reply to a reference librarian in Asheville who pulled a subject file on the Ashville Motion Pictures Corporation and found a reference to George Masa's involvement in *An Asheville Romance*.[40] The *Asheville Citizen* had covered its town's story as extensively as the *Knoxville Sentinel* had covered its brush with local filmmaking. The *Citizen* even included a photograph of Brolund with some of the cast. Most important, in Asheville, the story concluded with a rave review of the final production, albeit from the newspaper that presumably had a stake in the film's production. Indeed, the *Asheville Citizen* headlines ran, "Largest Crowd This Year with the Exception of July Fourth Witnesses Presentation of 'An Asheville Romance.'"[41] According to the manager of the Imperial Theatre, the film was "well received," and "there were many hearty laughs and applause."[42] Brolund was, it seems, at least capable of completing a town movie of this sort.

We later learned that Brolund continued his work as an itinerant producer in other states. We have since discovered two other locations where Brolund produced a version of this same movie: St. Petersburg, Florida, in April 1926 and Chicago, Illinois, later that same year. These examples have only recently come to light, so we have not yet conducted comprehensive newspaper research, nor have we determined whether the films are extant. In fact, we hope that the publication of this essay will yield further information on "Slim" and his movies from other archives. It also seems possible that Brolund may have made more than one movie in St. Petersburg. An advertisement for the Capitol Theatre in the *St. Petersburg Times* states that Brolund "has just finished a story called 'A St. Petersburg Romance'" and that he was about to start work on a new production, *Sunshine Slim*.[43] Another article in the same edition states that "[he] had just organized the J.B. Brolund Motion Picture Company, with headquarters at the Capitol Theatre on First Street North, and plans to make a series of two-reel comedies with St. Petersburg as the locale."[44]

What is revealed through these local newspaper articles is that the same formula was used to entice participants into starring in or contributing to the productions. Referring to Brolund's proposed second film, the *St. Petersburg Times* emphasizes (to potential sponsors) the publicity aspect of the movies with the headline "Movies Used as Ad Medium—St. Petersburg Gains Publicity by Scenes on Silver Sheet."[45] A cash incentive of two hundred dollars is offered for the leading lady, who, again, will be chosen by popular vote.[46] An interesting addition to the St. Petersburg story is that Brolund included a philanthropic aspect to the movie's production. The article introducing the *St. Petersburg Romance* states that "the proceeds [will go] to the Forty and Eight society for community work during the coming year."[47] In his second St. Petersburg production, Brolund proposes that "5 per cent of the profits from 'Sunshine Slim' will be donated to various charities in St. Petersburg."[48]

In Chicago, according to newspaper reports, Brolund obtained support of some magnitude: "White City, in association with the National Theaters corporation, operating the Capitol, Stratford, Jeffrey and Chatham, will conduct a four weeks' search for five prize-winning beauties who will appear in a motion picture to be made in Chicago under the direction of the famous director-comedian, J. B. 'Slim' Brolund."[49] The auditions were to be held over the next four Wednesday evenings at the White City Ballroom and Casino "and will be adjudged from screen tests to be made at the time of the preliminaries of the leading candidates."[50] The newspaper explained that "photographs taken on Wednesday at White City will be shown the following week in the houses controlled by the National Theaters corporations" and "will be featured in the motion picture palaces all over the country."[51]

As if starring alongside "Slim" Brolund in a movie was not enough, candidates were offered further incentive: "Upon [Brolund's] return to Hollywood, he will take with him the best of the stars he finds in this motion picture and she will be given an opportunity to be featured in Universal Pictures."[52] A later article reiterates this: "Valuable prizes are being given the winners including an all-expense paid trip to Universal City, Calif., with a movie contract with the Universal Film company, an excellent short time vacation. All the features of the offer are unique in that the lucky girls will be feted in Hollywood by Slim Brolund and his gang which includes everyone who counts in film-land."[53] Whether any of this was true remains to be seen. However, from the newspaper accounts that we have so far, it does seem that this was to be a larger-scale production than previous ones. Given the size of the city and that four theaters were involved, it was to be expected. Additionally, it was reported that this was to be a three-reel production (as opposed to other towns' two-reelers).[54]

Having discovered these new locations, we decided to go back and search the microfilms of the Knoxville newspapers to see if we could find out what had happened to the Knoxville film. Exactly one week after the film had been scheduled to premiere, the *Sentinel* carried an article on the front page announcing, "'Slim' Brolund Refilming 'Romance'; Original Movie Is Lost in Transit."[55] The article describes how the large package containing the film had been lost in transit between New York and Asheville.[56] Brolund engaged the help of post office officials and employees of the *Knoxville Sentinel* in his attempt to locate the film, but without success. So "in order that Knoxville shall not be disappointed, Mr. Brolund reached Knoxville yesterday afternoon, accompanied by his director Mr. George Massa *[sic]*, and bright and early this morning the re-filming of the 'Romance' was commenced."[57] Brolund hoped to have the

filming finished by the end of the week, the film sent to New York to be "finished," and on its return to Knoxville, to have it "shown at the Riviera and Strand theatres, three days and nights at each, as had been originally planned."[58] The *Sentinel* expressed regret over the inconvenience and disappointment caused by the mix-up. An apology appeared at the end of the article, along with a long list of participating "business interests" who had invested in the film's production and were expecting press and screen coverage. By way of reassurance, the article concludes that "in making the second picture, Mr. Brolund promises an even better picture than the first, if possible . . . for the reason that the local participants likely will appear to better advantage by reason of their training in the first picture, which naturally stands them in good stead in this instance."[59]

No further reporting of the refilming appears in the newspaper. Indeed, the film is not mentioned again until September 11, eighteen days later! But this time it is good news: "'Slim' Brolund's Moving Picture to Be Exhibited Here Next Week."[60] The newspaper reports that "the film has reached Knoxville and has been previewed, with the result that it has won commendation and high praise."[61] Two days later, in the Sunday edition of the paper, a fairly lengthy piece provides a full description of the film's plot and its locations. The leading lady even gets a mention in the headline, albeit with her name misspelled: "'Slim' Brolund and Eliabeth *[sic]* Burkes in the Sentinel's Local Movie Film to Be Seen on Screen All This Week."[62] We also learn that this "second" film is an incredible thirty-minute epic: "Fully thirty minutes are required to exhibit 'A Knoxville Romance.'" It will be the big feature at the Riviera the first half of the week and at the Strand the last half."[63] Probably as a gesture of goodwill to those businesses who had invested in the film, the *Sentinel* printed a prominent advertisement for the film listing all the contributing businesses' names.

So the film had been made after all and, according to those at the preview, had been a success.[64] Perhaps most interesting to us, as film archivists, was learning that there were two prints of the film made and that one had possibly been sent to Asheville, where it got lost and where it could well still be waiting to be discovered.

KNOXVILLE IN THE JAZZ AGE:
TOO MUCH FLAPPER

Just a few years after Brolund passed through Knoxville, another itinerant filmmaker proclaiming Hollywood connections would come to town. Knoxville was a swinging town in the late 1920s. Yet the town also possessed a strong undercurrent of conservatism, which would be the cause of much grief for the next itinerant filmmaker who rolled into town. The production of *Too Much Flapper* was fairly routine for an itinerant film; however, the events that unfolded when production wrapped make this particular example of itinerant production worth exploring.

"Here's Your Chance to Act in Movie of 'Journal and Riviera'" heralded the headline on the front page of Knoxville's morning daily, the *Knoxville Journal*.[65] The issue, dated May 16, 1928, features an intriguing photograph of itinerant filmmaker James Baret and two children, described as "two of his Hollywood Kiddies." The girl in the picture, Little Peggie Hames, is said to be "one of [Baret's] most recent discoveries for the silver sheet . . . little leading lady of the *Our Gang* comedies."[66] By 1928, there had been two Peggys in the Our Gang comedies, neither one, however, with the surname Hames. The first was Peggy Cartwright, who appeared in the earliest Our Gang shorts; then, between 1924 and 1927, Peggy Ahern took over the role. We have found no sources indicating that a Peggie Hames appeared in any Our Gang productions. Was Baret using implied, or even invented, Hollywood connections to win over his audience and sponsors? Or perhaps it was a newspaper error?

Regardless, three years after Slim Brolund's moviemaking in Knoxville, the downtown Riviera Theatre was ready to take a chance on another itinerant filmmaker, this time in partnership with the *Knoxville Journal*, the rival paper of the (recently merged) *Knoxville News-Sentinel*. Again, a call for local talent was put out in the newspaper, asking for young hopefuls interested in appearing in Mr. Baret's comic two-reeler to drop off "a good, clear kodak picture" of themselves at the offices of either the theater

The final advertisement for *A Knoxville Romance*. *Knoxville Sentinel*, September 13, 1925, 1.

or the *Journal*.[67] The newspaper hailed Baret as a professional director and photographer of motion pictures, having had experience with many of Hollywood's greatest stars, including Marion Davies, Mary Pickford, Douglas Fairbanks, Norma Talmadge, and Billie Dove.[68] Baret's *Journal* résumé goes on to state that he spent a decade working for the Famous Players-Lasky Corporation and spent time as a newsreel photographer with Pathé News. With credentials such as these, what could go wrong?

Baret set about searching for his leads, mainly focusing on students attending Boyd Junior High School and Knoxville High School. He and his assistant, Mrs. Leona Hazlett, concocted a script revolving around those business merchants contributing funding or merchandise for the film. According to the plot synopsis offered by the *Knoxville Journal*, the basic premise of the script involved a stubborn uncle refusing to purchase a long-promised Studebaker for an errant niece.[69] The forsaken niece then persuades the local vamp to romantically entice the uncle to change his mind. Along the way, much supposed hilarity and high jinks—along

He Directs It

James Baret, director of
Too Much Flapper (1928).
Knoxville Journal, May 16,
1928, 1.

with plugs for local businesses—ensues. In the end, the niece gets her wish and drives away with a carload of friends in her brand-new Studebaker. After a long week of anticipation, the final casting decisions were announced from the stage of the Riviera in front of a large and excited audience.

The leading role in *Too Much Flapper* went to "attractive Knoxville High School student Mary Daly."[70] According to Baret, "Mary Daly makes a splendid photographic subject. She's the Clara Bow type. Unspoiled—one of the cleverest amateur actresses I have seen."[71] Joyce Burnett was "the perfect vamp." As Baret explains, "Miss Burnett is a wonderful photographic type. In this regard, I think she surpasses Billie Dove, generally recognized by screen experts as having admirable photographic qualities."[72] Others cast in the film were also students, including young Jackie Comer (who, in later years, ran as Independent candidate for governor of Tennessee); Grace McNutt, daughter of a local florist; Edward Pearce; and twelve-year-old Boyd Junior High School student Pinkie Lee Koehn. As a consolation to all the disappointed aspirants hoping to be in the film, Baret let it be known that they could serve as extras in the crowd scenes to ensure

that nobody would be excluded as a potential ticket buyer.

Baret made the usual rounds of civic groups and business luncheons, giving speeches about life in Hollywood and attempting to round up paying sponsorships and endorsements from local business owners. Like Brolund before him, Baret must have been a persuasive fellow as several of Knoxville's most prominent merchants jumped on board. Sanitary Laundry and Dry Cleaning Company, East Tennessee National Bank, Hall's Clothing Store, Knoxville Business College, and the local Studebaker dealer Cherokee Motor Company all agreed to provide services and goods for the production of the film. Prominent advertisements for these companies were taken out in the *Journal,* linking their services and products with the upcoming film.[73]

Location shooting took place primarily around downtown starting on May 20 and attracted as much attention as Brolund's movie had several years prior: "Knoxville yielded to the glamour of winking cameras and turned out eagerly yesterday afternoon to see a movie being made in its own backyard."[74] The *Journal*'s daily reports reassured the town of the film's progress, and the paper even included a cartoon sketch featuring the movie. Heavy rainstorms frequently delayed the location shooting but failed to dampen the enthusiasm of the local stars, and neither did the intense work schedule, which was apparently far from glamorous: "The tiresome drilling required for some of the scenes, the incessant grinding of the cameras and the many demands made upon the principals of the cast have in no way dampened the enthusiasm of the boys and girls."[75] Director Baret screened occasional daily rushes for audiences at the Riviera Theatre. On viewing this raw footage, the *Journal* declared that "Baret knows his celluloid."[76]

Production work on *Too Much Flapper* finally wrapped on June 6, 1928. As a reward for their acting labors, the entire cast was treated to a fancy dinner party and talent show at the exclusive Whittle Springs Hotel. The day before the show was due to open (Monday, June 18), the *Journal* ran a double-page spread under the headline "See Knoxville's Boys & Girls—'Too Much Flapper'—in Knoxville's Own Movie."[77] The spread consisted primarily of advertisements for the businesses that had contributed to appear in the film. All the ads referenced the movie and detailed the roles the businesses had played in it, using phrases such as "'On Location' at Halls" or "That's why Uncle Ben and the Little Flapper selected this half-century old bank for their financial headquarters. See them in the movies." Most of the ads featured a few film frames depicting their scenes in the movie.

Tuesday morning's newspaper, however, did not bring the rave reviews for which everyone had been waiting. In fact, it brought no reviews at all. Instead, there was a story detailing the program's delay because of the loss of the film: "'Too Much Flapper' Program Delayed. Loss of Film Holds Up Program; Show on Today."[78] The article explains that "several hundred feet of positive film necessary to making the subtitles were found missing when the director and his assistant began putting the finishing touches to the two-reel comedy."[79] Much disappointment resulted among the audience, many of whom had come to see themselves and friends on the screen. By way of compensation, the theater management offered free passes for the following day's program. The report ends by assuring all that Mr. Baret "would work far into the night" to have the film ready for the next day.[80]

True to his word, Mr. Baret finished the postproduction, and the long-anticipated *Too Much Flapper* officially opened at the Riviera on Tuesday, June 19, 1928. Advertised as "Knoxville's own Movie, with Knoxville's own Movie Stars," the short movie appeared on a bill with the now-lost Paramount feature *The Street of Sin* (1928), starring Emil Jannings and a young Fay Wray. Also included in the program were vaudeville performers Hutchins and Holloway with their Harmonious Harmonicas. The *Journal* reported that "a large house greeted the first performance of the Journal-Riviera comedy when it was thrown on the screen at 3:10 o'clock. It won immediate laughter and applause."[81] Baret had scored a hit, and the Riviera could boast of another successful itinerant film.

Too Much Flapper continued playing at

A cartoonist's impression of the local movie. *Knoxville Journal,* May 22, 1928, 6.

the Riviera for the rest of the week, and the newspaper coverage surrounding the picture died down. But just as the film ended its run at the Riviera, it was announced in the paper that Pinkie Lee Koehn, a twelve-year-old girl who had appeared in *Too Much Flapper,* had vanished from her home the previous Saturday.[82] Mrs. Koehn, Pinkie Lee's mother, said that "all efforts made to locate her have proved fruitless."[83] There had been a possible sighting of the girl: one source reported that she was last seen entering the Farragut Hotel in downtown Knoxville, possibly with a group of much older girls. Both newspapers carried daily headlines about Koehn for weeks, and her parents pleaded for her return. A cash reward was offered to anyone who could locate her.[84]

Pinkie Lee's friends from Boyd Junior High later told the newspaper that "Pinkie Lee was a good girl. She didn't wear fancy socks, never cared for boys—didn't even use powder and paint. She read a lot—mostly books of adventure, never love stories. She even wrote stories, some of which were published."[85] A reporter for the *News-Sentinel* wrote that "her friends believe she may have been stricken by the glamor of a movie career. She called herself 'June Windsor' and may be known by that name

THE FLAPPER in
TOO MUCH FLAPPER

TURNED THE TOWN UPSIDE DOWN TO GET A

STUDEBAKER

True, a Studebaker is worth going to a lot of trouble for, but you do not
have to sacrifice to own a Studebaker.

TRAD'IN CLAUD

Makes it possible for anyone to own a Studebaker. Just bring in your
old car, jewelry, live stock, etc.—You are sure to get a trade and the
terms will be right.

CHEROKEE MOTOR CO.

HEMLOCK 3208   318 STATE STREET   MAIN 3208

now."[86] Indeed, Pinkie Lee fancied herself a writer, sometimes using the name June Windsor as a pseudonym. She also wrote a regular column in the Sunday edition of the *Knoxville Journal* reporting news and events about her school. Rumors circulated that Pinkie Lee had been star-struck after appearing in the local film and had run away to Hollywood. The *News-Sentinel* proliferated these rumors; under the headline "Still Lost—Movies Lured Girl from Home, Says Mother," the paper reports her mother as saying that "Pinkie Lee Koehn, 13, always loved her home until the click of the camera and the glare of the Kleig lights dazed her."[87] With statements like these, director James Baret began to arouse more and more suspicion among the citizens of Knoxville, including Pinkie Lee's parents.

Like Brolund before him, Baret had breezed into town proclaiming a multitude of Hollywood connections. But was James A. Baret who he said he was? Our research to date has yielded no information on Baret's Hollywood career. An article in the *Knoxville Journal,* dated Wednesday, June 7, states that "Baret was author of the story, and did all the title work for *For the Love of Mike* (1927) a First National feature production exhibited in Knoxville several months ago."[88] However, we can only find reference to the now-lost Frank Capra production of the same year with authorship credits to J. Clarkson Miller and John A. Moroso. Additionally, as discussed earlier,

Detail from a double-page spread of advertisements and an article announcing the premiere of *Too Much Flapper. Knoxville Journal,* June 17, 1928, 4-A, 5-A.

no information could be found for Little Peggie Hames, Baret's alleged Our Gang discovery. According to the *Journal*'s initial introduction, "Mr. Baret has been in the moving picture business for the past 20 years, working for 10 years with Famous Players Lasky Corp., with Pathé News and, during the World War, motion picture photographer, first with the Canadian Royal Air Force and later, the American Air Force."[89]

Private detective M. J. Elliot was hired by the Koehn family to assist in locating their daughter and to track down the whereabouts of Baret and his assistant, Leona Hazlett, who had apparently left town after completing the movie.[90] Elliot began his search by investigating Baret. Only then did Baret's claims begin to unravel. Detective Ellison stated that Baret "gave the names of several well known studios as references but was known at none of them."[91] It was then reported by the *News-Sentinel* that while in Knoxville, Baret had been posing as the ex-husband of popular screen actress Billie Dove. Under the headline "Baret Posed as Ex-Spouse of Miss Dove," the paper quotes two of the young female cast members claiming that Baret had told several members of the cast that he had been married to the actress and had a little daughter with her.[92] One of the young female cast members also claimed that "Baret did say that if I'd come to Hollywood and he had a film he could use me in he'd be glad to. He even asked my mother if I could go and she gave him evasive answers."[93]

This was all the Knoxville newspapers, city leaders, and local law enforcement officials needed to hear. There was no doubt in the minds of many Knoxville citizens that itinerant filmmakers James Baret and Leona Hazlett were directly responsible for the disappearance of Pinkie Lee Koehn. An intensive three-month search for the couple was initiated by Knoxville attorney Frank P. Bowen, who traced the pair over more than a thousand miles through six states. The trail led them through Illinois; Erie, Pennsylvania; and New York City. Acting on a tip from Baret's wife in Cleveland, Ohio, Bowen finally caught up with Baret and Hazlett in Buffalo, New York, in late August 1928.[94]

The two filmmakers were arrested in Buffalo, jailed without bond, and charged with the abduction of Pinkie Lee Koehn. Attorney Bowen sought extradition papers from the governor of New York to bring both Baret and Hazlett back to Knoxville to stand trial. Both parties denied any wrongdoing or knowledge of Koehn's whereabouts.[95] Baret and Hazlett were eventually extradited to Knoxville and spent two weeks in the local jail before being cleared and set free by the Knox County grand jury.[96]

Meanwhile, as Baret and Hazlett attempted to prove their innocence, Pinkie Lee was still missing. Even a local clairvoyant, Gene Dennis, got in on the act. Dennis, advertised as the schoolgirl marvel, answered questions and gave advice from the stage of the Tennessee Theatre. "Your little girl is dead," Dennis told Pinkie's mother. "I can see her body near a great fall. A mist is around this fall and the mist from a rainbow."[97] These statements fanned the flames of rumors that Pinkie had been murdered and that her body was buried next to Rainbow Falls at Mt. LeConte in the nearby Smoky Mountains.

A break in the Pinkie Lee Koehn case finally came in late October 1928, at which point Pinkie Lee had been missing almost five months. Newspaper coverage of the story had petered out, until the *Knoxville News-Sentinel,* cooperating with a committee formed by the

The Picture That Found Pinkie

PINKIE LEE KOEHN

The photograph circulated by the *Knoxville News-Sentinel* that eventually helped locate the missing girl. *Knoxville News-Sentinel,* October 25, 1928, 1.

Knoxville Parent-Teacher Association, revived the case by sending her photograph for nationwide publication in its sister newspapers. The strategy worked. On October 25, Koehn was identified and located in Asheville, North Carolina, by *News-Sentinel* reporter Bayard Yadon.[98]

But where had Pinkie Lee been, and what had she been doing all these months? Pinkie Lee's explanations and reasons for leaving seemed somewhat implausible. However, contrary to the popular consensus, her running away had *nothing* to do with wanting to be in the movies. According to Pinkie, she had caught a train alone from Knoxville to Chattanooga on the evening of June 16, spent the night in a rented room, and traveled on by bus to

Cincinnati, Ohio, the following day (she does not give an explanation why she chose Chattanooga or Cincinnati). Once in Cincinnati, Koehn "came down with rheumatism" so spent some time at a local hospital, where she purportedly had her tonsils taken out. It was at this same hospital that two nurses befriended her, eventually getting her a job at a restaurant frequented by the hospital's medical staff.[99] After a while, Koehn moved on to Asheville, North Carolina (again, no explanation offered), staying in cheap boarding rooms and working at local diners as a means of supporting herself. It was during her time in Asheville that a local young man, James Plemmendon, befriended her and took her to live with his grandmother. Several years later, it would be revealed that thirteen-year-old Koehn had been briefly married to Plemmendon while in Asheville, divorcing him after her return to Knoxville.[100]

The nurses who had assisted her in the Cincinnati hospital were able to identify Koehn from the *News-Sentinel*'s nationally published photo. The family of James Plemmendon also recognized Pinkie Lee from the photo published in the Asheville paper. Both parties contacted the Knoxville authorities, resulting in *Knoxville News-Sentinel* reporter Bayard Yadon traveling to the North Carolina town and driving Pinkie Lee back to her home in Knoxville.[101]

The reunion at the Koehn home was, by all newspaper accounts, a touching one. The *News-Sentinel* published a front-page photograph of Pinkie Lee and her mother reunited.[102] Pinkie Lee told stories of a hard life of wandering, homesickness, illness, and strange men who wanted to get to know her better. She also exonerated James Baret and Leona Hazlett, claiming they had nothing to do with her disappearance: "I've had a pretty hard time. But no one is to blame but myself. No one induced me to leave. James Baret and Mrs. Leona Hazlett, who produced a movie in which I took part just before leaving, had nothing whatever to do with my going."[103] Indeed, she was "amazed that any one should think James Baret had anything to do with her leaving. She said she had made up her mind to leave long before Baret came [to Knoxville]."[104] When asked why she left, Koehn simply claimed she ran away to gather material for her book, *When Girls Leave Home*.[105] Pinkie Lee's father, Fred Koehn, a bricklayer, filed for

bankruptcy on October 25, 1928.[106] He had spent his life savings to finance the search for his missing daughter. James Baret and Leona Hazlett each filed lawsuits of fifty thousand dollars, seeking damages for false arrest in conjunction with Pinkie Lee's disappearance.[107] Pinkie Lee's final word on the matter: "I'll never leave home again."[108]

After several years' absence, Knoxville's favorite bad girl once again made the front page of the local newspaper. An article in the Saturday evening edition of the *Knoxville News-Sentinel,* dated August 18, 1934, ran a story under the heading "Pinkie Lee Koehn Reported Arrested with I.C. King Jr. Girl Who 'Disappeared' Six Years Ago and Son of Former U.S. Marshal Allegedly Held in Arizona on Car Charge."[109] Pinkie Lee, by now about nineteen years of age, had taken off in a rental car with the seventeen-year-old son of one of Knoxville's most prominent citizens, I. C. King Sr. The two renegades were stopped by the Arizona Highway Patrol on a minor traffic violation, when it was discovered that the couple did not have a bill of sale for the automobile. Both were held in Duncan, Arizona, on a charge of taking a rented car out of the state without permission of the owner, the Hertz Drivurself System in downtown Knoxville. It was left to young King's uncle, deputy sheriff Ethel King, to make the trip to Duncan and retrieve both the car and the runaway youngsters.

This last mention in the *Knoxville News-Sentinel* seemed to mark the end of the line in our research regarding both the Pinkie Lee Koehn and *Too Much Flapper* sagas. Not so. While scouring a 1970s microfilm on an unrelated research project, we made a chance discovery of the obituary for I. C. King Jr. in the *Knoxville News-Sentinel* dated December 10, 1978. The obituary mentions that King, a member of a prominent south Knoxville political family, had passed away in his home at the age of sixty-one.[110] He left behind a daughter, several grandchildren, and a widow, June Ward King. Remembering that Pinkie Lee had previously used the pseudonym June, we took a chance, knocked on some doors, made some phone calls, and eventually reached June King's caregiver.

After comparing notes and information, we discovered that the ninety-four-year-old

June Ward King was indeed the former Pinkie Lee Koehn, and she was now residing in a north Knoxville nursing home. Koehn had indeed long ago assumed a new identity and life as the wife of the prominent south Knoxville businessman I. C. King Jr. After some deliberation, the caregiver (who was also June's friend and confidant) asked June about her former name and participation in *Too Much Flapper* during those heady spring months of 1928. June, understandably surprised, confessed everything, even relating several anecdotes about the filming of the movie. When asked if she would be willing to meet us and discuss the film, her only comment was that "perhaps bygones should be bygones."[111]

But that is not quite the end of the story. We were invited to a birthday celebration for June (aka Pinkie Lee), held at the nursing home in December 2007. There was, however, one condition given to us by the caregiver: we were not to mention the long-ago itinerant film or June's previous life. We attended the party, sitting next to and conversing with June, while remembering stories to ourselves about the Pinkie Lee Koehn of long ago. It was odd: sitting next to our subject of several years' research, someone who we had admired for her bravery, spunk, and rebelliousness, and possibly the only surviving cast member of *Too Much Flapper,* yet we were unable to ask her the questions we so desperately wanted to ask. We honored her desire not to discuss her past. So close, yet so far.

CONCLUSION

The films *A Knoxville Romance* and *Too Much Flapper* remain lost. The chances of their survival and discovery are slim to none. The original Riviera Theatre in Knoxville burned down in 1963 in what might have been a nitrate fire, and although the theater was rebuilt, it was later demolished in the late 1980s. Consequently, the likelihood of a print surviving is very low. Additionally, it would have been very unlikely that this type of film would have been shown (or stored) anywhere other than at the theater involved in its production. We have asked former projectionists and others with connections to the theaters, but so far, we have not had any luck.

Despite never having seen the films themselves, the full newspaper coverage has helped us build a vivid picture of how an itinerant filmmaker worked. The newspapers' daily reports have given us insight not only into the daily events of the filmmaking but also into the itinerant filmmakers' world. The documentation relating to these films contributes to the broader picture of itinerant filmmaking in a way that viewing the films alone could not do. If we had had the films but not the documentation, we might not have learned so much about those involved in the productions. Even though the films are missing, the newspaper coverage offers an invaluable sociocultural snapshot. The reports bring to life the character of the filmmakers, especially as they publicized themselves and their productions. They highlight the promotional nature of the films and how businesses were keen to associate their names and invest their money in these productions. We also get a glimpse of an often movie-mad public, eager to buy into the Hollywood dream.

Locating and documenting itinerant films like these—whether the actual films themselves are extant—is an important part of a regional film archive's mission. The films or accounts of their production provide a significant source of information about a town's past. Many of the businesses that contributed to the films discussed here are no longer around. Indeed, many downtown areas barely exist in the same way they did before the advent of the suburban malls.[112]

In a broader context, the documentation relating to the production of these films alone can contribute to the emerging literature on the practices of itinerant filmmakers and their work. With so few regional film archives across the country, this type of film should be considered among the rarest and most endangered. With more and more old theaters falling into disuse (these being the most likely places to find itinerant films), the chances of discovering extant films becomes slimmer each day. As the heyday of itinerant filmmaking predates television, many itinerant films are likely to be on nitrate stock and so are at even greater risk of deterioration.

Yet there is still hope. While completing the final edit on this essay, TAMIS discovered two reels of nitrate motion picture film at the

Paramount Theatre in Bristol, Tennessee. Its contents? A previously undiscovered edition of a Melton Barker Kidnappers Foil production (ca. 1948). The search for the newspaper articles is on.

Notes

1. *Aunt Sally Visits Knoxville* is considered a lost film. Newspaper articles relating to the film are held at the Tennessee Archive of Moving Image and Sound.

2. "Aunt Sally Is at the Gay Theatre All This Week," *Knoxville Sentinel,* December 20, 1915, 20.

3. "It's a Rotten Shame," *Knoxville Journal and Tribune*, December 21, 1915, 7. Interestingly, the short piece from which this quotation is taken has the abbreviation "—Adv." at the end of it, suggesting that it was a paid advertisement and not an actual report.

4. Advertisement for the Gay Theatre, *Knoxville Journal and Tribune*, December 19, 1915, 5-A.

5. Our thanks to Danette Welch of Knox County Public Library, Tennessee, who first brought this story to our attention. Coincidentally, Danette also has a familial connection to the protagonist of our next case study, Pinkie Lee Koehn.

6. "'Slim' Brolund of the Movies," *Knoxville Sentinel*, July 6, 1925, 14.

7. "'Slim' Brolund, Elongated Comedian, Frolics Merrily with the Shriners," *Knoxville Sentinel*, July 8, 1925, 7.

8. Ibid. Brolund's name does not appear in the credits of these films. It is most likely that he appeared as an extra in crowd scenes (if indeed he does appear at all), and given the enormity of the crowd scenes in *Hunchback of Notre Dame*, it may be some time before we spot him!

9. Ibid.

10. Edward Small Company, *The Directory of Artists under Exclusive Management of the Edward Small Company* (E. Small, 1920). Accessed via Google books.

11. Another example of Pathé cameramen working as itinerant filmmakers can be found in Dan Strieble's essay about itinerant filmmakers in North Carolina. He mentions that the two filmmakers working on a "homemade Our Gang" in Anderson, North Carolina—Sammy Fox and R. R. Beatty—were also "representatives of Pathé News." Dan Streible, "Itinerant Filmmakers and

Amateur Casts: A Homemade 'Our Gang,' 1926," *Film History* 15, no. 2 (2003): 177–92.

12. Masa's photographic work is now fairly well documented. A documentary movie was made by Paul Bonesteel and released on DVD in 2004: *The Mystery of George Masa*.

13. "Local Picture Is Considered Good," *Asheville Citizen*, July 5, 1925, 36. As yet, we have found no evidence that Masa did go on the road with Brolund.

14. "Miss Maizie Huffaker Is Selected as Leading Lady in Knoxville Film Featuring 'Slim' Brolund, Comedian," *Knoxville Sentinel*, July 19, 1925, E-2.

15. We have not had the opportunity to research the local papers for evidence of Brolund's trips to these other towns.

16. "Knoxville Is Ideal Location for Filming Comedy Says 'Slim' Brolund," *Knoxville Sentinel*, July 11, 1925, 6.

17. "'Slim' Brolund, Elongated Comedian."

18. "'Slim' Brolund of the Movies."

19. "Initial Scenes of Knoxville's First Movie Will Be Made Monday," *Knoxville Sentinel*, July 25, 1925, 8. It is worth noting the claim regarding "Knoxville's First Movie." Had *Aunt Sally Visits Knoxville* already been forgotten, just ten years after it had been made?

20. "Initial Scenes of Knoxville's First Movie Will Be Made Monday."

21. "Knoxville Is Ideal Location for Filming Comedy."

22. "Contest to Select Leading Lady for Brolund Closes; Announced Sunday," *Knoxville Sentinel*, July 15, 1925, 1.

23. "Miss Maizie Huffaker Is Selected as Leading Lady."

24. Ibid.

25. "Contest to Select Leading Lady for Brolund Closes."

26. Ibid.

27. "Initial Scenes of Knoxville's First Movie Will Be Made Monday."

28. Caroline Frick and Dwight Swanson have created a Web site dedicated to providing and gathering information about Melton Barker and his Kidnappers Foil films: http://www.meltonbarker.com/. Readers should also refer to Caroline Frick's essay on Melton Barker in this issue.

29. "Miss Mazie Huffaker Is Selected as Leading Lady."

30. "Initial Scenes of Knoxville's First Movie Will Be Made Monday."

31. "First Scenes of Film Shot," *Knoxville Sentinel*, July 27, 1925, 10.

32. "More Scenes in Movie Romance," *Knoxville Sentinel*, July 29, 1925, and advertisements for Henry G. Trent Furniture Co. and I. J. Cooper Rubber Co., *Knoxville Sentinel*, July 29, 1925, 15.

33. "Filming of 'Knoxville Romance' Attracting Throng of Onlookers," *Knoxville Sentinel*, July 30, 1925, 13.

34. "'Slim' Brolund's Local 'Romance' to Be Shown Here Week of Aug. 17," *Knoxville Sentinel*, August 9, 1925, B-10.

35. Ibid.

36. Ibid.

37. Ibid.

38. "'A Knoxville Romance' with 'Slim' and Knoxville Movie Stars Will Be at Riviera and Strand This Week," *Knoxville Sentinel*, August 16, 1925, 10.

39. Advertisement for the Riviera Theatre, *Knoxville Journal*, August 16, 1925, B-5.

40. Our thanks to Zoe Rhine at Buncombe County Library, North Carolina.

41. "Asheville Comedy Is Well Received," *Asheville Citizen*, July 8, 1925, 1.

42. Ibid.

43. "Movie Contest at Capitol Theatre," *St. Petersburg Times*, April 6, 1926, section 2, 8.

44. "Movies Used as Ad Medium," *St. Petersburg Times*, April 6, 1926, section 3, 7.

45. Ibid.

46. Ibid.

47. "Technician Here to Help Brolund in Legion Film," *St. Petersburg Times*, January 30, 1926, 7.

48. "Movies Used as Ad Medium."

49. "Beauty Winners Will Appear in Movies to Be Made in Chicago," *Englewood Times*, July 9, 1926, 1–2. White City was built in 1905 and became one of the South Side's most popular entertainment venues. It had almost completely closed down by 1934, its demise due in part to a large fire in the late 1920s.

50. Ibid.

51. Ibid.

52. Ibid.

53. "Winners in White City Beauty Contest to Be Selected on August 2," *Englewood Times*, July 30, 1926, 5.

54. "Ten More Beauties for White City Film Contest," *Englewood Times*, July 23, 1926, 1.

55. "'Slim' Brolund Refilming 'Romance'; Original Movie Is Lost in Transit," *Knoxville Sentinel*, August 24, 1925, 1.

56. There is no explanation as to why the film would have been sent to Asheville.

57. "'Slim' Brolund Refilming 'Romance,'" *Knoxville Sentinel*, August 24, 1925, 1.

58. Ibid.

59. Ibid.

60. "'Slim' Brolund's Moving Pictures to Be Exhibited Here Next Week," *Knoxville Sentinel*, September 11, 1925, 1, 13.

61. Ibid.

62. "'Slim' Brolund and Eliabeth [sic] Burkes in the Sentinel's Local Movie Film to Be Seen on Screen All This Week," *Knoxville Sentinel*, September 13, 1925, 1.

63. Ibid.

64. "'Slim' Brolund's Moving Pictures to Be Exhibited Here Next Week."

65. "Here's Your Chance to Act in Movie of Journal and Riviera," *Knoxville Journal*, May 16, 1928, 1.

66. Ibid.

67. Ibid.

68. Ibid.

69. "Ready? Action! Camera! To Resound at Caswell Park," *Knoxville Journal*, May 20, 1928, 1–2.

70. Ibid.

71. "Knoxville Yields to Glamor of Movies and Flocks to 'Location,'" *Knoxville Journal*, May 21, 1928, 1–2.

72. "Work on 'Too Much Flapper' Moves Despite Too Much Rain," *Knoxville Journal*, May 23, 1928, 1.

73. "See Knoxville's Boys & Girls—'Too Much Flapper'—In Knoxville's Own Movie," *Knoxville Journal*, June 17, 1928, 4-A–5-A.

74. "Knoxville Yields to Glamor of Movies."

75. "Work on 'Too Much Flapper' Moves."

76. "K.H.S. Furnishes Background for Scenes in Local Movie," *Knoxville Journal*, May 22, 1928, 1.

77. "See Knoxville's Boys & Girls."

78. "'Too Much Flapper' Program Delayed," *Knoxville Journal*, June 19, 1928, 13.

79. Ibid.

80. Ibid.

81. "'Too Much Flapper' Opens at the Riviera," *Knoxville Journal*, June 20, 1928, 4.

82. "Pinkie Lee Koehn Remains Missing Despite Search," *Knoxville Journal*, June 22, 1928, 4.

83. Ibid.

84. "Parents Offer Reward of $50 for Pinkie Lee," *Knoxville Journal*, June 27, 1928, 3.

85. "Revive Search for Pinkie Lee," *Knoxville News-Sentinel*, October 19, 1928, 1.

86. Ibid.

87. "Still Lost. Movies Lured Girl from Home, Says Mother," *Knoxville News-Sentinel*, August 30, 1928, 1.

88. "Art Work 'Too Much Flapper' Starts," *Knoxville Journal*, June 7, 1928, 1.

89. "Here's Your Chance to Act in Movie of Journal and Riviera," *Knoxville Journal*, May 16, 1928, 1.

90. One report describes Baret's departure as hasty: "His suspiciously hurried departure from Knoxville was attributed by Baret to the fact that his funds had run low, according to a United Press dispatch from Buffalo." However, no further evidence is offered to back this up. "Two Arrested as Abductors of Pinkie Lee," *Knoxville News-Sentinel*, August 29, 1928, 1. Another report states that Pinkie Lee "disappeared a few days before Baret and Mrs. Hazlett left Knoxville." "Baret Papers to AL," *Knoxville News-Sentinel*, September 15, 1928.

91. "No Bond for Baret," *Knoxville News-Sentinel*, August 31, 1928, 14.

92. "Baret Posed as Ex-Spouse of Miss Dove," *Knoxville News-Sentinel*, August 30, 1928, 1.

93. Ibid.

94. "Two Arrested as Abductors of Pinkie Lee," *Knoxville News-Sentinel*, August 29, 1928, 1.

95. "No Bond for Baret."

96. "Pinkie Lee Says She Ran Away to Secure Material for Book," *Knoxville Journal*, October 26, 1928, 1.

97. "And Gene Dennis Said Pinkie Lee Was Dead," *Knoxville News-Sentinel*, October 26, 1928, 1.

98. "Pinkie Lee Koehn Is Located in Asheville, N.C.," *Knoxville Journal*, October 25, 1928, 1, and "Pinkie Lee Koehn, Located as Result of Pictures Sent Out by N-S, Is On Way Home" and "The Picture That Found Pinkie," *Knoxville News-Sentinel*, October 25, 1928, 1.

99. "Pinkie Lee Tells Story of Hard Life Wandering," *Knoxville News-Sentinel*, October 26, 1928, 1.

100. "Pinkie Lee Koehn Reported Arrested with I.C. King Jr.," *Knoxville News-Sentinel*, August 18, 1934, 11.

101. "Pinkie Lee Tells Story of Hard Life Wandering," 1.

102. "When Pinkie Came Home," *Knoxville News-Sentinel*, October 26, 1928, 1.

103. "Pinkie Lee Koehn, Located as Result of Pictures Sent Out by N-S, Is On Way Home," *Knoxville News-Sentinel*, October 25, 1928, 1.

104. "Pinkie Lee Says She Ran Away to Secure Material for Book," *Knoxville Journal*, October 26, 1928, 1.

105. Ibid.

106. "Koehn Files Plea in Bankruptcy," *Knoxville Journal*, October 25, 1928, 4.

107. Ibid.

108. "Pinkie Lee Koehn Reported Arrested with I.C. King Jr."

109. Ibid.

110. "I.C. King Jr., of Widely-Known Knox Family, Dies," *Knoxville News-Sentinel*, December 10, 1978, B-12.

111. June Ward King and her caregiver, conversation with the authors, October 2007.

112. Knoxville does currently have a thriving downtown area and even has a new Riviera Theatre at the same location as its predecessor, where *A Knoxville Romance* and *Too Much Flapper* were shown.

The *Huntingdon's Hero* Story

NATHAN WAGONER

During the bicentennial celebration of Huntingdon, Pennsylvania, in 1966, the manager of the Clifton movie theater showed a film that had been made in Huntingdon in 1934 but that had not been shown in thirty-two years. Those who remembered it were excited at the chance to see it again. Those who had only heard of it looked forward to seeing what they had heard so many of their friends and neighbors talk about. Many of the local cast who starred in the film were still alive and living in the area. People who were there remember that the theater was full and the audience seemed to enjoy the movie very much, laughing all the way through, pointing out their friends, family, and familiar landmarks. After the showings, the film was put away and again forgotten.

In the early 1970s, a professor at Juniata College named Bruce Davis heard about the film and was curious enough to make inquiries. Although hired to teach English, Davis was very interested in film. He taught courses on film history and criticism and had volunteered to be the assistant manager of the Clifton, hoping to save it from the doom and destruction threatening most small-town movie theaters at that time. Naturally, Davis asked the manager of the Clifton, the same manager who had arranged to show the film a few years before, about the movie.

The manager claimed to have no knowledge of the film's whereabouts. Davis approached the local historical society, but they also knew nothing about the movie. Articles were written in the local newspaper, employees and former employees of the theater were interrogated, but the movie never turned up. *Huntingdon's Hero* became mythic—the lost film of Huntingdon. There were rumors that particular people might have hidden the film away. The hypothetical reasons varied: family feuds, small-town class warfare, dreams of making a fortune with the movie. Davis eventually gave up his management of the Clifton and left Juniata, moving to Los Angeles to become the executive director of the Academy of Motion Picture Arts and Sciences. As time passed, and

those who remembered *Huntingdon's Hero* died or forgot the film, the movie faded into local legend.

In December 2000, I was hired by the Teaching Learning Technology Center (TLT) at Juniata. The TLT was charged with a broad mission, which included being a testing ground for new educational technologies. One of these was the newly emerging technology of digital video, which quickly became my area of expertise. Although there were no courses and no formal structure to its study, a number of students took on the task of producing quality video for the campus and for various faculty projects. I supported and guided that work as best I could. As the students worked longer with the technology, they began to have more creative ideas and decided, eventually, to begin an independent project of their own.

The students chose to make a documentary on the history of the Clifton Theater. The Clifton had stood since the 1920s and would serve not only as an interesting subject in its own right but also as a lens through which to look at the history of the community. Obviously, an interview with the retired manager was a good place to start. I spoke with him and arranged for him to come to campus. He was then in his eighties but had a good memory of his time at the theater and was eager to talk about it. I helped the students set up the lights and microphones, but I was not in the room while the students taped their interview.

I watched the footage with the students a few days later, taking notes and looking for areas that might be fruitful for further investigation. We left with a few questions, and because I often saw our interview subject at his part-time retirement job, I offered to go over the questions with him. The next morning I caught up with him and we chatted about the interview and our follow-up questions. When we were finished, I was about to leave when he suddenly said, "There is one more thing you might be interested in. I have the only copy of an old movie that was made here way back in the 1930s."

I was mildly stunned. I did not know the entire history of that movie, but I had heard it discussed often enough to know it was missing. I asked him for more details: the name of the film was *Huntingdon's Hero,* it was a 35mm

THE DAILY NEWS
presents
"HUNTINGDON'S
HERO"
Produced By
The Consolidated Film Producers
of California

Frame from *Huntingdon's Hero* (1934).

sound film last shown during the bicentennial celebration, and it was in good shape. He volunteered that he had kept it in his closet all those years. I asked if I might be able to borrow it to ascertain the condition and perhaps get some advice on if it was safe to show the movie. Surprisingly, he agreed. A few days later, I met him again, and he handed me the can.

Although I had been a student of Davis's in the 1970s, I was not aware of his search for the film. I only knew that I knew someone in the preservation end of the film industry who might be able to give me some advice or point me to a resource that would help. I had no intention of trying to show the movie—I knew enough to know that old film could be fragile and perhaps even flammable. So I called Davis.

"That son of a bitch! He had it all along!" Davis exclaimed, laughing at the same time. Naturally, after all those years, he very much wanted to see it himself. We talked a little bit about what might be done, then he referred me to one of the Academy specialists in preservation for more detailed conversations. The guys in the lab asked very specific questions about the condition of the print (which was very good) and about any text that might be visible on the edge of the film.

There was text. It said "Nitrate"—apparently that complicated things. After the situation became clearer, I had more conversations with Davis, who offered the resources of the

Academy to restore the film and make a new exhibition print on safety stock, plus a digital copy for local use and distribution. Normally the Academy restricted itself to Hollywood productions, but in this case, they would make an exception. All I had to do was get the owner of the print to agree.

I went to see him the next morning and explained the situation. We did not dare project the movie, nor did we have the money to assume the costs of restoration and duplication. The treasure he had guarded all those years would quickly become worthless if we did not find some way to have it restored and copied. I told him that Davis—whom he remembered well—had offered to assume the cost, and to my astonishment, he readily agreed. I called the Academy, and we began to make plans to ship the movie.

Then things really got interesting. The Academy worked with a number of shipping companies that were both familiar with nitrate films and had the proper hazmat credentials to handle them, but none of them were anywhere near us. Chris Fedak, the Academy archivist with whom I worked, began calling the people he knew, hoping for a referral to a local company. I started on my end by talking to our chemistry department in the hope they would have a

APPLICATION BLANK

Name ....

Street......................... Phone.........

City .... Age.......

Height....... Weight...... Complexion........

NOTE:—Fill in this coupon with either your name or the name of some good looking girl and mail or bring to the Movie Editor of The Daily News. A photograph accompanies this application, to be called for if I desire its return, after the cast is selected.

Application for casting,
Huntingdon Daily News,
April 27, 1934.

shipping company familiar with hazardous materials, then by calling every local shipper I could find. I even spent an hour or so on the phone with environmental officials in Harrisburg, a town three hours away, all to no avail.

After nearly two weeks of looking, the Academy found a company that claimed it could move the film. The truck would pick up the film the next morning, take it to a shipping company near the airport in Pittsburgh, handle the packaging, and put the film on a flight to Los Angeles, where Fedak from the Academy of Motion Pictures would pick it up. Things were looking up.

At first, everything went according to plan. The truck arrived at eight o'clock, picked up the film can, gave me a receipt, and drove away. Then it all went bad. About 11:45, I got a call from the air freight company in Pittsburgh. According to them, the movie had been improperly shipped, without the proper packaging and, even worse, by a trucking company that lacked the proper credentials even to touch it. The film was therefore illegally on their loading dock, and they wanted nothing to do with it. Worse, they had to get it off their premises as soon as possible—if I did not get there by close of business, they were going to toss it into a public dumpster. It was November; it was snowing; and Pittsburgh airport was three

and a half hours away, on the other side of the mountains.

After half an hour of frantic calls—to Fedak at the Academy, my boss, my family—I was in my car headed west. By then, I was seriously considering simply driving all the way to Los Angeles as it was beginning to look like we would never get the film on a plane. I got about thirty miles when the Academy reached me on my cell phone. They had found a certified shipper in central Ohio who was already on his way to Pittsburgh airport and who would properly package the film on site and then drive it to the airport in Cleveland, where it would be flown to Los Angeles in the morning. The next afternoon, I got a call that the movie had arrived safely in Los Angeles and was in the hands of restoration experts. Work was delayed by Christmas holidays and then preparations for the Oscars, but a few months later, a new print and a DVD arrived—with no trouble in the shipping this time. The original nitrate print remains in the Academy vaults.

Huntingdon's Hero is one of a series of films produced by Donald Newland between the 1920s and the mid-1930s. An itinerant filmmaker, Newland traveled around the country,

GRAND

MONDAY
and
TUESDAY

On The Stage Daily At 3:00 And 9:00

SEE A MOVIE IN THE MAKING

"HUNTINGDON'S HERO"

With An Entire Cast of Huntingdon Favorites.
Something New — Hollywood Before Your Eyes

—ON THE SCREEN—
RICHARD
DIX in "ACE OF ACES"

Advertisement,
Huntingdon Daily News,
April 27, 1934.

going from one town to the next, casting local people and shooting what was essentially the same movie over and over. When Newland completed a film, it was shown in a local theater to the same people who had participated in its making. Then he and his crew would move on to the next town. Films by Newland were made as far north and west as Janesville, Wisconsin, and as far south as Americus, Georgia. As more newspaper archives come online, more Newland film sites are being discovered.

Newland worked under the name "Consolidated Film Producers, L.A. California," a credit that appears under many of the titles. I have not found any evidence that such a company actually existed or that Newland or any of his crew ever worked in California, despite his claims to the contrary. Newland often said that he worked for Warner Bros., Universal Pictures, and on Mack Sennett pictures. In many newspaper articles, he said that his cameraman, Howard Prager, had worked as a cameraman for "Eric von Stroheim, Hoot Gibson, Eva Novak, Alice Howell"; however, no evidence has surfaced to substantiate any of these claims.[1] Consolidated did, eventually, become attached to a real en-

tity. Either in late 1934 or 1935, Newland's wife, Opal, demanded that he settle down and make a home for their young family. According to his daughter, Newland started a company with a partner in Chicago, Ralph Phillips, called Consolidated Movie Studios, which made poster and picture frames as well as display cases for movie theater lobbies. Newland stayed with the company until he died in 1951.

In each town, Newland partnered with a local newspaper that "presented" the film, which meant financing and publicizing. Although I am not aware of any existing transaction or contractual records, the arrangements are fairly easy to derive from the evidence contained in the films themselves and the sequence of newspaper articles that appeared concurrently with each production.

In the *Huntingdon Daily News,* the first article connected to *Huntingdon's Hero* appeared on April 23, 1934. Like the first article that appeared in the Janesville, Wisconsin, *Gazette* on December 27, 1926, and in the Coshocton,

Frame from *Huntingdon's Hero* (1934).

Ohio, *Tribune* on August 19, 1927, and all the others I have seen, this article announced the upcoming production and encouraged local girls to apply for the leading role: "The secret ambition of nearly every girl, to star in a motion picture, is about to be realized in the near future by some Huntingdon young woman." The article then goes on to say that the film will be made entirely locally, with all local talent. It discusses the equipment and crew that would shortly be arriving in Huntingdon to make the movie, the extensive preparations involved, and the expectations of great success.

The leading role was not to be determined by a contest but through applications followed by interviews conducted by the editor: "The movie editor assures those interested that there is no contest attached to the selecting of the star, but personality and screen ability are the guiding points." The application was printed in the same issue of the *Daily News* and was to be delivered or mailed to the newspaper's offices.

The article in the following day's paper led with the headline "Movie Director Has Task Selecting Girl for Lead." Within one day, the office had received "scores" of applications. This second article also describes the production in greater detail, including the much-anticipated car crash scene. The descriptions served to build interest in the entire production. The public was encouraged to come to the loca-

tions and watch the movie being made. The newspaper kept them informed of the progress and the schedule.

On April 26, the third article on the production promises a "Hollywood Premiere" at the beginning of the production. Another article followed on April 27, giving more tantalizing details about the premiere and the prizes that would be awarded to the best movie star impersonators. Finally, on April 30, a week after the first article appeared in the paper, the headline read "Filming of Local Talking Picture Will Begin Tonight." The article announced the girl chosen to play the lead role and detailed plans for the scenes that would be shot on stage at the theater at the conclusion of the premiere. Daily articles followed through May 8, when it was reported that the first showings of the film had been a "great success."

The Hero films offer an intriguing window into the history and process of filmmaking. They are fascinating in part because of their small scale and the necessarily improvised nature of the productions. It is particularly interesting to observe Newland and his crews manage the transition from silent film to talkies, which required far more than simply mastering another technology on a limited budget. Comparing the silent *Janesville's Hero* (1927) with the talking *Huntingdon's Hero* (1934), for example, reveals how profoundly the transition to talking pictures changed his methods of storytelling and how difficult that transition must have been to master for a director working on this scale of production.

Each of these films also offers a window into the history of a particular small town. *Huntingdon's Hero* has been screened locally many times since it was restored. The local paper—the same *Huntingdon Daily News* that produced the film in 1934—took an interest in the restoration of the film and ran several articles about the movie and its history in 2003 and 2004. These articles reached many residents of Huntingdon who remembered seeing the film being made or who attended the premiere. A woman who played one of the main characters in the movie, Katrinka, the "country flapper," was still alive in 2004, and we were privileged to be able to screen the film for her and her son. One local man saw his uncle—the car salesman—for the first time. His uncle had died before he was born, and though there were family pictures and stories, he had never seen him alive and did not think he ever would; the film gave him a sense of having seen him in the flesh that he could not have experienced any other way.

The rediscovery and restoration of *Huntingdon's Hero* became an opportunity for many people to revisit a period of local history, to remember local figures and vanished landmarks, and also to celebrate the history of a small town that has not, in many ways, changed all that much since 1934. The street scenes do not look that different in the film than they do now. For Juniata College, which coordinated the restoration and the screenings, it has been a welcome opportunity to offer institutional resources for the sake of local and regional communities. For me, personally, it has been a rewarding chance to preserve a unique treasure and share in the rediscovery of both the film and its history.

NOTE

1. "Who'll Be Lucky Girl to Star in Janesville Movie?" *Janesville Gazette,* December 28, 1926.

REVIEWS

Books

*Cupboards of Curiosity:
Women, Recollection,
and Film History*
BY AMELIE HASTIE
DUKE UNIVERSITY PRESS, 2007

Sarah Resnick

In *Cupboards of Curiosity,* Amelie Hastie posits a complex and innovative reimagining of historical film scholarship. At stake are the lost histories—both popular and scholarly—of cinema's female contributors, particularly those of the early silent era. Hastie mines unconventional sites and spaces to emerge with works seemingly tangential to traditional historical scholarship: scrapbooks, memoirs, marginalia, how-to manuals, cookbooks, and other ephemera wherein women directors and stars inscribed critical knowledge, ranging from reflections on their private lives to the film industry at large.

Yet, having resurfaced, these forgotten texts provide more than evidence for the integration of marginalized figures into recognized historical narratives. For Hastie, these works question relationships between a text, its subject, its author, and the historian who studies them. To clarify and evaluate these various interrelations, Hastie organizes her study into four chapters—"The Collector," "The Historian," "The Critic," and "The Expert." She casts Colleen Moore, Alice Guy-Blaché, and Louise Brooks as case studies in the first three roles, respectively, whereas the final rubric surveys an array of celebrities and moves the discussion into contemporary times.

With her panoply of scrapbooks, photographs, souvenirs, and miniatures, Colleen Moore as collector "anticipates both the loss of her history and the eventual retrieval of it" (67); it is here that Hastie lays the groundwork for her exploration. Most adventurous—and ultimately most remarkable—is her reading of Moore's "Fairy Castle," a dollhouse filled with tiny jeweled furniture, paintings, tapestries, and a library of one-inch, first- or unique-edition books and on which she spent more than seven years and four hundred thousand dollars building. Once completed, Moore's dollhouse traveled to various department stores throughout the United States and Canada to raise money for charities and now resides on display at the Chicago Museum of Science and Industry, where it was acquired in 1949. Approaching the dollhouse as an invitation from Moore to reconsider what is present, Hastie examines its history; its connection to the narrative structures of autobiography, fairy tales, and fantastical storytelling; and its relation to film culture to reveal essential aspects of both Moore's career and private life and the broader history of 1920s Hollywood.

To introduce complex questions of authorship and their relationship to historiographic practices, Hastie surveys the celebrity scrapbooks of Mary Pickford, Claire Windsor, Colleen Moore, and Louella Parsons. Long overlooked in traditional film scholarship, these fragmented histories comprising news clippings and photographs seem undeniably to hold as their subject the star herself. Hastie, however, asks whether the author—often a fan, a family member, or an assistant—might not also be the subject, as in the scrapbooks of Pickford, where some more markedly narrate the fascination of the fan with the celebrity. And do they not, she asks, also make historians out of their authors? Hastie asserts that these roles are unfixed, interchangeable, and ever shifting.

Chapters 2 and 3 consider women whose own authorship is responsible for what we know of them today: director Alice Guy-Blaché, as historian, authors her own lost image, while as critic, Louise Brooks recasts hers. Having recognized that her work as cinema's first woman filmmaker and founder of the Solax Company had been practically erased from film history, Guy-Blaché took to authoring her memoirs. These, along with a number of interviews, have become central resources for any scholarly work that treats her in depth. And thus, as Hastie emphasizes, Guy-Blaché is mostly known through her own work of remembrance and recollection.

Similarly, in her perceptive analysis of the essays, interviews, and marginalia of Louise Brooks—revealing an educated, snarky, and contemplative critic—Hastie demonstrates how Brooks, too, is an active and self-conscious participant in the production of her own history. Moreover, Brooks is at least partially responsible for the discourse that circulates around her history, including even the overshadowing of her intelligence by her sexual exploits. In both cases, Hastie celebrates authority through authorship and yet identifies hazards in the simple recirculation of ideas produced by and about a subject within a critical historical discourse. Here she astutely acknowledges the collaboration between scholar and subject in the production and authoring of history; historians, too, must maintain self-awareness of their role.

In her final analysis, Hastie turns to the expert celebrity advice found in how-to manuals, cookbooks, and exercise videos to revisit discussions of authority and the complex temporal framework within which the scholar engages with the object and/or subject of study. Works such as Pickford's *Why Not Try God?* (1934), Moore's *How Women Can Make Money in the Stock Market* (1969), and Marlene Dietrich's *ABC* (1961) presume future moments of production and consumption, in which the reader will engage with and even embody their knowledge. And by venturing into contemporary times with her discussion of model Christy Turlington and Isabella Rossellini, Hastie reminds us that "these histories and these futures are always in the present making" (158).

Though sometimes dense, overall, *Cupboards of Curiosity* is enjoyable to read. The author skillfully navigates the concerns of heavyweights Jean Baudrillard, Walter Benjamin, and Gaston Bachelard to yield a generous interweaving of critical theory and anecdote, fact and narrative, history and historiography. In writing a book about film history in which the films themselves move to the background, Hastie broadens the scope of the historical archive and offers cinema's lost women renewed consideration. And in her most compelling argument, she offers these women their due credit, making explicit how the production of knowledge, indeed the authoring of history, is always the work of collaboration across time—past, present, and future.

Inherent Vice: Bootleg Histories of Videotape and Copyright
BY LUCAS HILDERBRAND
DUKE UNIVERSITY PRESS, 2009

Jimi Jones

A few years ago, a popular internet T-shirt company released a shirt with the words "Analog Is Warmer" emblazoned on the front. Though the shirt features an image of an audiocassette instead of a VHS tape, the sentiment of the shirt nevertheless perfectly describes *Inherent Vice,* a new book by Lucas Hilderbrand, assistant professor of Film and Media Studies at the University of California, Irvine. *Inherent*

Vice is on the surface a history of analog video and its relation to U.S. copyright law at the end of the twentieth century and the beginning of the twenty-first. It is when the reader really spends some time with the book that the spirit of *Inherent Vice* becomes apparent: the book is a paean to analog video and its heyday. Even though Hilderbrand spends much of the book in scholarly discussion of how video informed and changed (and was changed by) U.S. copyright law, he still peppers his discourse with anecdotes (sometimes personal) about his interactions with home videotape and fond reminiscences of the predigital video era. *Inherent Vice* also contains, in Hilderbrand's words, an "implicit call for policy reform" (243) with regard to copyright in the twenty-first century.

Inherent Vice is not just a history of the labyrinth that is audiovisual copyright in the United States. It is an exploration of the tension between the top-down control of cultural products by their corporate producers and the (at times arguably) fair-use consumption and dissemination of these products. Hilderbrand uses case studies of bootlegged and/or home-produced videos to explore the "self-appointed archivists"—those people who take it on themselves to copy and disseminate video copies of television broadcasts, pornography, and rare films (25). Hilderbrand, in the course of his exploration of this copy-of-a-copy-of-a-copy videotape trading, introduces a key concept to *Inherent Vice,* which he calls the "aesthetics of access" (163). Hilderbrand uses this term to describe the look and feel of the video noise of generational decay (the diminution of image quality inherent in a many-generation analog video copy). This fuzziness and distortion of image is to Hilderbrand more than just an unfortunate defect in the process of copying a copy of a video—it is actually a part of the fun of the bootleg. In the first chapter, Hilderbrand discusses the bootleg homemade pornography of stars like Rob Lowe and Tommy Lee and Pamela Anderson. According to Hilderbrand, part of the enjoyment of watching these bootlegged videos is found in the poor image quality. The image defects inherent in the analog-to-analog copying of these bootlegs obscure certain key body parts, forcing the viewer to peer closer at the image and use his or her imagination to fill in what the generational decay hides. In these examples, analog video's aesthetics of access create more of a tease than crisp, impeccable digital video can.

Chapter 1 gives us a history of analog video and its entrance into the American home. This chapter is, like much of the book, written in a colloquial style that is loose and rarely laden with scholar-speak. (I was stunned to find very few references to Foucault or Derrida in the entire book.) It is surprising to find a scholarly work that contains both the words *lacuna* and *pussy*. This mixture of tones feels at times like a collision but ultimately gives the impression that Hilderbrand is a human being first and a scholar second. When Hilderbrand does delve into scholar-speak, he almost seems to do it with a sigh, as if he knows it's expected of him and he must oblige. Furthermore, Hilderbrand's history of analog home video reads more like reminiscence than a dry history. Readers who grew up during the rise of home video in the 1970s and 1980s will find parts of this chapter a charming walk down memory lane. There is, however, enough serious history and discussion in the chapter to elevate it well above the content of the average VHS fan site.

Chapter 2 slows down the pace a bit with a lengthy discussion of home video and its relation to U.S. copyright. This chapter is a bit drier than the previous, but considering it's about the byzantine nature of copyright, how could it not be? The chapter plods through a lengthy but necessary discussion of the *Sony v. Universal* case and how it changed the face of home video. This landmark case, sometimes called the Betamax case, allowed Americans to copy legally broadcast television and have greater agency in how they interact with TV. In the age of TiVo, TV-on-DVD, online streams, and YouTube, it can be hard to remember a time when viewers had no control over how they interacted with broadcast television beyond changing the channel or turning off the TV. With this chapter, Hilderbrand charts how home video influenced (and was influenced by) copyright legislation. This chapter is more than just a history—Hilderbrand uses its final pages to discuss how *Sony v. Universal* influenced the rulings in recent peer-to-peer (P2P) file-sharing lawsuits. Hilderbrand uses the lawsuit

against the P2P Web site Grokster to show how the *Sony* case has been used recently as an (ineffective) argument for the legality of P2P networks. One of the key components in the ruling in favor of Sony is the court's decision that Sony could legally sell the home video recorder because the onus would fall on the user to decide whether the machine is used for copyright-infringing purposes, not on the manufacturer of the machine. Grokster used this argument for its P2P Web site and, for a brief time, was allowed to operate, until the Supreme Court overturned the circuit court ruling and shut Grokster down. That the Supreme Court did not allow Grokster to use the Betamax precedent as defense was a key shift between the analog and digital worlds.

Chapter 3 moves *Inherent Vice* into its second section, which consists of case studies of people and organizations pushing back against, interpreting, and influencing copyright law with respect to video. The first case study is the Vanderbilt Television News Archive (VTNA). In the late 1960s, Paul Simpson started the VTNA, which is still a thriving collection today, at Vanderbilt University to catalog and preserve television news broadcasts and make them accessible to the public. CBS pushed back against the VTNA in a court case, which helped lead to the 1976 expansion of copyright to include the protection of off-air videotaping with some restrictions. This expansion caused CBS to request that its lawsuit against the VTNA be dismissed and paved the way for other collections such as the University of Georgia's Peabody Awards Collection. This chapter, again somewhat dry, is nevertheless a heartening read as it shows the power of archives sometimes to move mountains in the name of increasing access. Hilderbrand wisely connects this case study to the Digital Millennium Copyright Act and its implications for diminished access to digitally produced materials.

It is in chapter 4 where *Inherent Vice* really soars. This chapter consists of Hilderbrand's discussion of the bootleg circulation of *Superstar,* Todd Haynes's indie biopic about the life and career of Karen Carpenter. Haynes used Barbie dolls to tell Carpenter's life story in an attempt to bring her battles with her body image to the fore. Sadly Haynes did not have the rights to use the Carpenters' music in the film, and the film was driven underground, where it was usually circulated on bootleg VHS tape copies. In this chapter, the basic concepts of the book—copyright, the "aesthetics of access," and "self-appointed archivists"—come together to explore Haynes's film and its illicit circulation. Hilderbrand points out that every transfer of *Superstar* has an effect on the image quality of the copy made, thereby stamping each analog video generation of the movie with a unique look and feel. Hilderbrand argues that with analog video (and *Superstar* copies specifically), the viewer can enjoy the artifacts of generational decay themselves by choosing either to peer through the distortion or focus on it (181). This distortion, according to Hilderbrand, actually helps to further the thesis of *Superstar* in that "videotape duplication of the work formally changes the text, so that its thematic concerns—distorted mass media and their relations to subjective and bodily breakdown—become rendered on the surface" (163). Hilderbrand's analysis of *Superstar* shows us an example of a film whose theme is enhanced by the qualities—the inherent vices—of analog videotape and its bootleg circulation. Showing the film on a pristine print in a theater may not have the same effect on the viewer. This chapter is a tour de force that synthesizes all the previous discussions in the book and contains some beautiful screen captures from VHS copies of *Superstar*. These images are at times nearly inscrutable but are always haunting. Chapter 4 also includes interviews with people who have (and have circulated) video copies of *Superstar* and their reminiscences about these copies of the film. This section is so enjoyable that it's a shame that it's only a few pages—it really could be expanded into a stand-alone work about the glory days of analog home video, perhaps in the same vein as Thurston Moore's book *Mix Tape: The Art of Cassette Culture* from a few years ago.

Chapter 5 is a history and analysis of video chain letters—videotaped diaries that are passed from person to person. The center of the discussion is Miranda July's Joanie 4 Jackie video community. This open-ended video-by-mail project has been a way for many young women to express themselves with home video

equipment and predates YouTube by about a decade. Hilderbrand's analysis of the gender and self within this gift economy is spirited and compelling, but it seems at times to drag a bit as he spends perhaps too much time discussing the history and themes of these videos and not very much time on the connection to copyright, ownership, and the other themes of the book. This section, while undeniably interesting, seems a bit out of place within the book and feels somewhat like a stand-alone essay that was later shoehorned in. It also seems a bit odd that this chapter (or the larger book) doesn't include a mention of Sadie Benning's Pixelvision diaries, which also use the defects of analog video to discuss gender and identity to very poignant effect.

The book concludes with a discussion of YouTube's "culture of the clip" and how it relates to, and is influenced by, the analog video era. Hilderbrand delves into a little bit of old-fogyism here when he talks about his irritations with YouTube: its automatic play feature, its tendency to stall out in the middle of the video stream, and its lousy image quality, among other factors. Perhaps we will one day consider these the "aesthetics of digital access." Hilderbrand also discusses how YouTube has changed his (and presumably his students') attention span: "Suddenly three minutes can seem like a life-sucking eternity, and I, for one, am prone to skipping ahead or moving on before a clip finishes if it's the least bit tedious" (228). This chapter isn't just a jeremiad against the newfangled digital—he takes some time at the end to bring it all home and discuss how the Betamax case and the analog video era have affected and infected the YouTube era. This is made particularly clear when he mentions the remediation of home video often found within YouTube: "The homemade status of many television clips [on YouTube] is marked by . . . , in the cases of older recording, VHS artifacts such as rainbows of discoloration and signal dropout. Such artifacts and alterations signal the videos' sources and demonstrate bootleg aesthetics" (233). Hilderbrand then ends the book on a somewhat (understandably) dour note with a mention of the Digital Millennium Copyright Act and how it has the potential to trump fair use with regard to digital audiovisual materials.

Inherent Vice makes it clear that though the champions of access to audiovisual information have made many strides forward in the analog era, those champions must once more step up to the plate in the digital era.

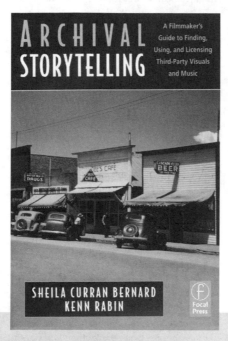

*Archival Storytelling:
A Filmmaker's Guide
to Finding, Using, and
Licensing Third-Party
Visuals and Music*
BY SHEILA CURRAN BERNARD AND KENN RABIN
FOCAL PRESS, 2009

Snowden Becker

S. R. Ranganathan's Third Law of Library Science declares, "Every book its reader." Some interpret this to mean that a book's reader is predetermined, either by the author who writes it for a specific audience or by the publisher who defines for it a specific market. The rule allows, though, for an unused book to be exposed via the library shelves to *all* readers, and through that exposure to find *its* reader: the person who finds the book of value, use, or interest.

The new book *Archival Storytelling* is aimed at the storytellers, for its cover declares it "a filmmaker's guide" and its contents indicate that it is meant for those who do (or could) work with existing footage; nevertheless, an archivist, too, could find much to intrigue and inform here. *Archival Storytelling* effectively conveys what experienced footage researchers and film producers feel everyone working in their field should know about working with archival media. Archivists who work with those same footage researchers and film producers can get from the book a better sense of what expectations, assumptions, and needs storytellers bring with them to the archive. Finally, and perhaps most important, it illustrates how broadly (and sometimes contradictorily) archives are defined by an influential community of users.

Authors Sheila Curran Bernard and Kenn Rabin both worked on the fourteen-hour *Eyes on the Prize* documentary series, which incorporated hundreds of archival film and audio clips from dozens of repositories and private collections—and which has been notoriously hampered by copyright clearance issues since its original release. With this credit alone, Bernard and Rabin's bona fides as field-tested guides to the complex process of researching and licensing archival media might be well established, but they each have other qualifications to recommend them: Emmy and Peabody awards in Bernard's case, and in Rabin's, archival researcher credits on many of the recent Hollywood features praised by critics for their use of vintage footage (*Milk, The Good German,* and *Good Night, and Good Luck,* among others).

Bernard and Rabin define *archival materials* broadly, as ranging from home movies and snapshots owned by their creators to commercially produced and owned materials such as wire service photos, news footage, music, and radio broadcasts. They define *archives* broadly, too, but often indirectly and in a contradictory way. Early on, they answer the question of "who owns archival materials" with "everybody, from you and your family . . . to some of the wealthiest individuals, institutions, and corporations in the world" (4). Elsewhere in the book, when Bernard and Rabin refer to an "archive," they mean either a commercial stock-image entity or a major public institution like the Library of Congress or National Archives and Records Administration; on the other hand, they may also be referring to a smaller site such as a university library's special collections department or a small-town historical society.

This undifferentiated use of the *A* word is, admittedly, in keeping with the general tendency to describe any collection of stuff that is not in one's current issue, episode, or inbox as being "in the archive." Here, as elsewhere, this casual usage has the potential to confuse and mislead, as when the authors assert that "most archives now have online databases" (35). That sentence opens the section on commercial still and moving image providers, but it is not made clear that commercial archives are really the only ones to whom the statement applies. Anyone working in one of the smaller historical societies or special collections that are mentioned later in the book has known the frustration of trying to deal with the average researcher's already-present expectation that *all* holdings in *any* collection will be available for browsing online and will probably be dismayed to see that expectation reinforced here. The authors' interpretation of the "archival" part of *Archival Storytelling* nods to the idea of a community of archives that are large and small, but their bias throughout is toward the big players, not the little ones. This conveys something about how archives in general are understood and defined, but it also reflects the archive community's diversity of self-definition and professional practice and the degree to which the major entities exist apart from smaller institutions.

The book addresses each of three facets of archival storytelling—discovery of material, determining what material to use and how to use it, and licensing issues—in a separate section. The section on licensing is the longest and most detailed, including chapters that define the public domain and fair use and discuss how the legal boundaries of copyright specifically affect filmmakers. The sections on discovery and use of archival materials, though shorter, are by no means thin. Chapter 8 ("Creative Considerations") offers examples of the rich variety of uses to which archival footage has been put and advocates creativity and thoughtful experimentation over more clichéd uses for vintage clips. Chapter 10, "Ethical Considerations," tackles a topic one might call archival-use literacy through a roundtable discussion of documentary ethics, filmmaking practice, and artistic interpretation. Chapter 6 focuses on production work flow. Archivists without a production background will find this section especially enlightening as it helps illustrate how filmmakers' ways of working differ from the (often slower paced or less flexible) practice of an archive.

Also of value in *Archival Storytelling* is chapter 5, "A Global Perspective: Conversations with Image Researchers," which reproduces conversations between the authors and consultants who work with producers to find motion pictures, audio, and still images in the United States, Canada, Russia, and Australia. The consultants' anecdotes are fascinating; their advice to other filmmakers is made more compelling by the weight of their expertise and experience; and in at least once instance, they will endear themselves to hardworking film preservationists by speaking plainly about the visual quality of archival materials:

> *So on some of the lower-budget history programs, when the footage looks pretty dreadful, it's possible someone is airing their dub of a screener?*
> BONNIE ROWAN: "Old film looks old." That's a lie; you can find old film from 1900 that just sparkles. Cheap filmmaking looks like that, not old footage.

Though some of these consultants discuss the issue of obsolete or changing moving image technologies and their impact on access to desirable materials, there is little mention anywhere in *Archival Storytelling* of other technical considerations that crop up frequently when archival footage is used in new productions. Aspect ratios, frame rates, the advent of high-definition and digital broadcast standards, the need for and expense of film-to-video transfer—these matters are significantly absent and left for the individual archivist to address with his or her clients.

The book repeatedly refers readers to its

companion Web site (http://www.archivalsto-rytelling.com/) for additional resources and information, including a list of archives and professional organizations referred to in the book—little of which information was yet in evidence on the site at the time of this writing. Although the "Sources and Notes" section of the book did contain quite a few of the URLs that one presumes would be offered on the Web site, there were no pointers to any actual directories of audiovisual archives such as the International Federation of Film Archives member database or the Moving Image Collections directory. A selected filmography in the appendices lists only films that were worked on, or mentioned, by the authors or those they interviewed; it does not include any other films that might be considered noteworthy for their practice of archival storytelling. An expanded—and, perhaps, annotated—list of feature films, documentaries, and television programs making use of archival footage could never be truly comprehensive but would offer a fuller sense of how many new productions rely on archival materials for their visual style, historical context, or basic subject matter. As the authors note, such films could help researchers find new sources for similar footage. The filmography, strangely, does not include release or production dates, which are often customary in citing moving images and which might be a significant help to a reader trying to track down viewing copies of a specific film or program.

Regardless of these minor shortcomings, and despite its focus on large archives and for-profit institutions, *Archival Storytelling*'s intended readers will receive from it a wealth of information that may improve their dealings with archives of all kinds. For unintended readers like archivists, this may still be "their" book for at least two reasons: through it, they may better know their licensees and researchers, what they are looking for, and how they want to use it; and archivists may be in the very best position to recommend this book to their clients, the storytellers for whom it was originally intended.

DVDs

My Grandmother (Chemi bebia) (1929)
DIRECTED BY KOTE MIKABERIDZE
BC8, 2005

Denise J. Youngblood

In 1929, a Soviet Georgian actor-turned-director, Kote (aka Konstantin) Mikaberidze (1896–1973), made his first film, *My Grandmother* (*Chemi bebia,* Georgian/*Moia babushka*, Russian), a cutting satire of Soviet bureaucracy. Stalin's Cultural Revolution (1928–1932) was well under way. This Cultural Revolution had two major components: the social and the artistic. In social terms, Soviet society was dedicated to ridding itself finally of the remnants of the old regime: people, practices, and ideas. An important part of the attack on antiquated practices was the campaign against bureaucracy, which had been the bane of tsarist as well as Soviet Russia. Mikaberidze had every reason to believe, therefore, that he was making a "politically correct film." He was wrong. The film was banned, not to be screened again until the Georgian film studio restored it in 1976 because, according to the introduction to the restored film, "even today, it will be able to combat certain shameful practices still present in our society." Composer and musician Beth Custer has added a lively musical sound track and an English-language narration of the Russian intertitles to this crisply restored version from a copy held by the Pacific Film Archive, who commissioned her to write the score with the support of an National Endowment for the Arts grant.

The plot of *My Grandmother* is simple. The executives of the "TORK" trust laze about all day, shuffling papers, smoking and eating, playing with toy trucks, and shooting paper airplanes. The business manager, who commits suicide when a typist (with fashionably bobbed hair) refuses his love, is replaced by another unnamed man. The new business manager (Alexander Takaishvili) strongly resembles his predecessor, both physically and in terms of his complete uselessness. When a worker (Akaki Khorava) appears at the offices of the trust bearing a request for fifty rubles to restore production, the executives and staff are temporarily shaken out of their torpor. But all they produce is a new sheaf of papers, signed and countersigned—no money. In a rage, the worker's inspection singles out the new business manager as a scapegoat, and he is fired as well as lampooned in a newspaper caricature. With a wife (Bella Chernova) and daughter to support, the ex-business manager is desperate to get his job back, especially because his wife is a well-groomed shopaholic who buys from the expensive black market. He considers suicide. Oddly enough (since he had the job in the first place), he doesn't seem to know that the key to securing another plum position is to find a "grandmother," an influential individual, to serve as his patron. When he thinks he has found one, to his horror, he learns that the letter of recommendation he pestered from his "grandmother" is in fact another denunciation. He is ejected once again. "Death to the bureaucrats" is scrawled on a wall outside the trust building.

On the surface, this sounds like exactly what the Communist Party had ordered: a black-and-white diatribe against the hated administrators and fat cats, in favor of the proletariat. Because of the film's style, however, it is any-

thing but. Even if its social message might have passed muster, its artistic style could not. The artistic component of the Cultural Revolution was waged against the avant-garde, who were condemned for the dreaded sin of formalism, an emphasis on form over content, directed at the few rather than the masses. This threat was real. The years 1928–1932 were an era of avant-garde masterpieces such as Alexander Dovzhenko's *Earth,* Fridrikh Ermler's *Fragment of an Empire,* Sergei Eisenstein's *The Old and the New,* and Grigory Kozintsev and Leonid Trauberg's *The New Babylon.* Mikaberidze was clearly influenced by these great directors, especially by the Workshop of the Eccentric Actor of Kozintsev and Trauberg (oddly referred to in the scant DVD notes as "a group of young Jewish artists from the provinces"). Even for viewers with no interest in the history and politics of the film, *My Grandmother* is a wonderful example of eccentrism and a catalog of the avant-garde's film techniques during Soviet cinema's golden age.

These techniques include a heavy reliance on quick cutting (known then as American montage), canted angles, stop-motion, out-of-focus camera, traveling camera, extreme close-ups, animation, superimposition, and various fantastical elements. The offices of the trust are minimally constructed with a large oval table with freestanding doors (no walls). The camera travels around and around to zoom in on the (in)action at any station. When the first business manager commits a cartoonish suicide, the focus blurs as he is dying, followed by a crane shot of his body being dragged away. (He raises his legs to help the filthy "doorman" [E. Ovanov] cart him off.) To indicate that time is passing, the stern worker is superimposed over a day calendar with pages magically turning. As the bureaucrat's wife dances with joy over her black-market purchases, the cutting becomes increasingly frenetic, with extreme close-ups of her dancing high heels. When the enraged worker shouts, "Bureaucrats! Bureaucrats!" time stops, as does all motion in the picture. Animated toys dance around the room as the new business manager contemplates his unemployed state and decides to practice committing suicide. As the business manager attempts to present his petition to the trust director, the director keeps disappearing, replaced by another and another, and so on. It's all a bit too much: the viewer is exhausted by film's end after watching sixty-five minutes of this barrage of bizarre images.

That said, the film's formal properties accentuate its message about the sorry state of Soviet society. Criticism of bureaucrats was certainly allowable, but Mikaberidze got carried away with his enthusiasm. Where are the positive role models? There is only one worker—strong, sweaty, tall—to serve as counterpoint to the bureaucrats and their hangers-on. Piles of crumpled paper, mounds of cigarette butts, and crumbs of discarded food litter the floor. People spit on the floor as well (there was a campaign against public spitting). Executives play with paper airplanes as the line of petitioners increases. Crude signs are everywhere: "Don't interrupt. Busy man at work"; "When your business is finished, leave." The bureaucrat's apartment is filled with bourgeois knickknacks. His wife, with her long, manicured fingernails and perky, short plaid skirt, is the picture of bourgeois womanhood, with her obsession for material goods and the perks of her husband's former position ("No car! No free tickets!" she shrieks disconsolately). The image of Soviet life is a grim one—and all too true.

What Mikaberidze forgot or ignored was that film during the Cultural Revolution not only needed to be critical but also needed to point to positive outcomes. True, the business manager loses his job, and his "grandmother" betrays him, but there are no healthy role models or images of what the new, truly revolutionary way of life would look like. Apart from the worker, a somewhat frightening character with his stern gaze, there is also a menacing shot of a Young Communist (Komsomol) member launching a gigantic fountain pen as a deadly weapon. Not only was the film formalist and inaccessible to the masses but it was also too negative to be acceptable regardless. *My Grandmother* well illustrates the difficult balancing act for directors at this perilous time.

Beth Custer's music, played by a small band, is delightful and perfectly suited to the action of the film. Nils Frykdahl's narration of the intertitles is amusingly ironic. The occasional addition of a "Georgian voice" (Edisher

Dabrundashvili) to the sound tracks adds to the overall strangeness of the film. The DVD would have benefited from more extensive notes or an extra feature that placed the film within a critical and historical context for uninitiated viewers.

The Joy of Sex Education
BFI, 2009

Leo Enticknap

"I suggest that in your next film, you show yourself being buggered by a long-haired hippy. That will make them sit up." Such was the reaction of one correspondent to Martin Cole, a hitherto unknown biology lecturer at an obscure British university, elicited by the storm of controversy generated by the release of *Growing Up* in 1971. The explicitness with which Cole's 16mm classroom film portrayed the facts of life has, it seems, actually gained some power to shock since: its inclusion in the BFI's DVD compilation *The Joy of Sex Education* is, according to an explanatory note on the sleeve, the sole reason for the entire set carrying an 18-certificate. Ironically, therefore, most of the age group for whom the film was originally intended cannot now, thirty-eight years later, legally buy a copy.

This sort of temporal anomaly characterizes the entire selection of sex "education" (the noun implies the ideologically neutral communication of knowledge and ideas, something that certainly does not happen in many of the films presented here) films, all but one British, produced between 1917 and 1973. The genre seems to have oscillated between conservative and liberal in approach. At one end of the story, we have *Whatsoever a Man Soweth* (1917), aptly characterized by Bryony Dixon's sleeve essay as a "straight sermon" on the consequences of venereal disease (the protagonist of which is aptly named Dick). At the other, *'Ave You Got a Male Assistant Please Miss?* (1973) closes with a similarly stark warning about the consequences of unwanted pregnancy. In between, less judgmental approaches can be found in *How to Tell* (1931), which urges parents to educate their children on the facts of life, and in *Learning to Live* (1964), which, while still condemning extramarital sex, does not portray sex itself as exclusively negative—hardly (no pun intended—honest!) surprising given that the film was sponsored by a condom manufacturer.

The films fall conveniently into three broad categories: morality tales about venereal disease, morality tales about unwanted pregnancy, and films explaining the biological nuts (oh, drat, another pun) and bolts, with varying degrees of moralistic spin attached thereto. A distinct pattern emerges in the conservative–liberal split: the "prophecy of doom" subgenre is most noticeable at times of conflict and political instability, whereas the films that do not start from the default position that sex per se should be considered undesirable tended to be made at times of comparative prosperity and in the absence of international conflict. Examples from both world wars advising service personnel stationed abroad to refrain from knocking up the natives feature prominently, notably *Whatsoever a Man Soweth, Love on Leave* (1940), and the gloriously politically incorrect Halas and Bachelor animation *Six Little Jungle Boys* (1945), which would make *Coal Black and De Sebben Dwarfs* look like a training film for equality and diversity officers. The less judgmental strand is represented primarily by *How to Tell* (released significantly before

the effects of the Great Depression were felt among the wider British population), which argues that full-scale sex education, delivered by parents to their children, is essential for them to develop into mature adults capable of sustaining their own marital relationships, and by what possibly remains the most infamous and most controversial classroom film ever made in Britain, *Growing Up*. Its infamy derives from the inclusion of actual, unsimulated intercourse and masturbation scenes in lieu of visual euphemisms involving farm animals à la *The Mystery of Marriage* (1932) or the animated diagrams used to convey the bulk of the factual information in *Growing Girls* (1949). Though the film's underlying moral message—that sex should ideally take place within a monogamous and committed relationship—is essentially similar to that of its predecessors (it also includes a warning of the consequences of unplanned pregnancy), the explicit scenes unleashed a wave of protest. *Growing Up* generated extensive media coverage: one city council banned the film from use in its schools citing the Obscene Publications Act, its female "star" was sacked from her job as a teacher, and Cole received hate mail from the public, a selection of which is reproduced in the booklet accompanying the DVDs (e.g., "I hope someone castrates you, you perverted bastard").

An intriguing curiosity is found in the only non-British contribution to the collection. *Her Name Was Ellie, His Name Was Lyle* (1967) was licensed for distribution by the Concord Film Council, originally a religious charity that, by the late 1960s, specialized in releasing foreign-made educational, political, and sponsored films on 16mm to U.K. schools and community groups. Though a relatively conventional cautionary tale about the spread of syphilis, the film is notable for its gritty, monochrome mise-en-scène; New York locations; and the future careers of the two teenage protagonists, whose "hit-and-run contact" is the origin of a syphilis epidemic: John Pleshette, who later became a mainstream Hollywood director, and Amy Taubin, the critic, feminist, and avant-garde filmmaker who, according to Jez Stewart's accompanying essay, has regretted her role in the film ever since.

The selection and curation of these films embodies the strengths and weaknesses of the BFI's prolific video publishing program in recent years. Following the precedent set by their British Transport Films and Documentary Movement DVDs, this set marks a welcome attempt to represent the broader range of the National Film and Television Archive's holdings in its publishing activity and not just a restricted range of iconic feature films. The accompanying thirty-seven-page booklet contains four extensive essays introducing the topic of sex education and public health and shorter introductory notes for each film, most of them by members of the BFI's curatorial staff. These pieces offer concise and well-focused introductions to the films themselves, though it would have been interesting to read a little more on the way they were distributed and shown and, in particular, their target audiences. The DVD-and-booklet package is a preferable way of presenting contextualizing material to commentaries and other multimedia extras on the DVD itself as the latter can be read before or after viewing the content and without the need for playback equipment.

The technical presentation of the films themselves is a real mixed bag. Most of the earlier titles appear to have been transferred from preservation elements, but the material from the 1960s and 1970s seems to derive from heavily worn 16mm release prints. Dirt, scratching, jump cuts, and dye fading are noticeable throughout most of the later films. The warts-and-all approach has been taken in previous BFI DVDs, notably the Documentary Movement set, and one could justify it on the curatorial grounds that such presentation is probably an accurate reflection of how most audiences would have experienced these films in a nontheatrical setting. In this case, however, some of the source elements are so worn out as to be seriously distracting, notably *Learning to Live* and *Don't Be Like Brenda* (1973).

The bit rate drops to as low as three to four megabits per second in many of the films, with the result that digital artifacts are clearly visible when the DVDs are viewed on anything larger than a typical computer monitor. And though it makes logical sense to encode mono sound tracks as a Dolby 1.0 audio channel, many 5.1 channel home theater systems are not capable of reproducing the center channel in isolation at a sufficient volume to be comfortably audible, hence the reason the vast majority of commercial DVD publishers duplicate mono tracks as a left and right, 2.0 audio stream. The use of 1.0 audio combined with a relatively low audio signal level on these discs is, in the opinion of this reviewer, a significant defect. Furthermore, that the musical accompaniments for the silent titles are presented as a 2.0 mix necessitates frequent volume adjustments.

Though I suspect that the choice of subject matter for these DVDs was chosen with popular appeal primarily in mind (in the same vein, the choice of *Salò o le 120 giornate di Sodoma* for the BFI's inaugural Blu-ray release resulted in one of their highest sales figures for a retail video title—the purchasers possibly having been persuaded to part with their cash by a morbid curiosity as to what that infamous chocolate sponge cake looks like in 1080p high definition), I hope that *The Joy of Sex Education* will provide the springboard for further explorations of educational films in the National Film and Television Archive. Some significant research and curatorship has taken place in relation to these genres in the United States in recent years, from Ken Smith's book,[1] Rick Prelinger's online collection, and critical documentaries such as *Hell's Highway* (2003, directed by Bret Wood). Despite them also having been an integral part of British film history and culture, from Gaumont-British Instructional in the 1930s to Boulton-Hawker in the 1970s, educational films in Britain remain largely forgotten by historians and curators, except to a limited extent within the regional film archive movement. Though *The Joy of Sex Education* does not match the standard of technical presentation of some of the BFI's other recent DVD publications, it represents a significant curatorial achievement, one that I hope will encourage further exploration of and research into educational films in the United Kingdom.

NOTE

1. Ken Smith, *Mental Hygiene: Classroom Films, 1947–1970* (Jackson, Tenn.: Blast Books, 1999).

Film

Storm under the Sun
(Hongri fengbao)

DIRECTED BY XIAOLIAN PENG
AND S. LOUISA WEI
BLUE QUEEN CULTURAL
COMMUNICATION, 2009

Michael Berry

A few days before sitting down to write this review, I received news of the August 18 passing of Shu Wu (1922–2009), noted writer, critic, and a major cultural figure of Mao's China. Shu Wu, who was eighty-seven years old at his death, makes a cameo of sorts toward the end of Peng Xiaolian and S. Louisa Wei's *Storm under the Sun*. It is, rather, an anticameo, as Shu's voice is heard on speaker phone refusing to be interviewed for the film he is effectively now in. Shu Wu is an important key to understanding the events depicted because in a film imbued with compassion and a strong humanistic spirit, he is one of the few characters on whom the filmmakers project a degree of moral culpability.

In 1955, years before the Anti-Rightist Movement and more than a decade before the Great Proletariat Cultural Revolution, Mao

Zedong unleashed an unprecedented attack on a group of writers and intellectuals collectively known as the Hu Feng Counterrevolutionary Clique. The incident centered around Hu Feng (1902–1985), a literary critic, poet, translator, and founder of the Leftist periodicals *July (Qi-yue)* and *Hope (Xiwang)*, who had advocated a form of realism in art that was seen as a direct challenge to the directions laid out by Mao in his 1942 Yan'an Forum on Art and Literature, a series of talks that would effectively dictate all artistic production in China for the next several decades. The attack on Hu was not an isolated political purge but rather a massive national movement that led to ninety-two arrests (seventy-eight were eventually labeled members of the Hu Feng Clique), and more than twenty-one hundred others were implicated in the ensuing political witch hunt. Victims suffered imprisonment and long sentences to labor camps, and many were persecuted to death. Only after 1980 was the case officially reversed. The political maelstrom was first ignited by a May 13, 1955, article printed in the *Peoples' Daily* titled "Some Information about the Anti-Communist Party Hu Feng Clique"—the author was Shu Wu (albeit also used as a political pawn in a larger ideological game in which the filmmakers seem to hint the real villains were Zhou Yang, literary theorist and vice director of the Department of Propaganda, and, of course, Mao himself).

Among those persecuted were some of the best and brightest of New China's literary scene such as writer Lu Ling, poet and theoretician Ah Long, and literary critic Jia Zhifang. Many of these writers and critics were seen to be carrying on the spirit of Lu Xun, the father of modern Chinese literature—Hu Feng was often considered his torchbearer. But though Mao praised Lu Xun, this group of Lu Xun's Leftist protégées would suffer unimaginable trials. As the film progresses, we are introduced not only to victims such as Lu Ling, Ah Long, and Jia Zhifang but also to their families. In one sequence, the son of Ah Long fights back tears as he describes refusing to visit his dying father because he had already cut him off for political reasons. Codirector Peng Xiaolian was just two years old when her father, Peng Boshan, was arrested in 1955 as part of the crackdown on the Hu Feng Clique—his persecution would not end until he was beaten to death by Red Guards in 1968. *Storm under the Sun* can be seen as Peng Xiaolian's personal attempt to come to terms with the violent history that shattered her family and an attempt to understand her lost father. At the same time, the film also serves as a powerful testament to a page in modern Chinese history that has been long overlooked. There have, of course, been several Chinese-language books about the Hu Feng Clique, but never has this important page in modern Chinese intellectual history been given such thorough and loving treatment in film. Peng and Wei's painstaking research resulted in the tracking down and interviewing of dozens of victims, family members, and scholars from China, Japan, and the United States (more than thirty-four additional interviews did not make the final cut). At the same time, far from being a detached documentary that aims for pseudo-objectivity, Peng Xiaolian's own personal story not only frames the film and carries us through but serves as a powerful counterpoint to the long segments highlighting macrohistorical changes. For Peng, who previously directed more than half a dozen feature films, including *Shanghai Women,* this is perhaps her most personal work to date, not only because of the subject matter's connection with her own family but also because of the multitude of roles she played in the film's production—coproducer, cowriter, codirector, narrator, cinematographer, she even contributed the oil paintings used to divide the film's chapters.

Although she never received the notoriety of her Fifth Generation classmates Zhang Yimou, Chen Kaige, and Tian Zhuangzhuang, with *Storm under the Sun,* Peng Xiaolian demonstrates admirable skills as a documentary filmmaker. Featuring a mix of stock newsreel footage; new interview footage; old audio interviews with an elderly Hu Feng; and images of political cartoons, photographs, archival documents, oil paintings, vintage woodblock prints from the 1930s and 1940s, and simple animation, the film presents an eclectic visual canvas against which to tell its story. The quick editing and panning with which (often text based) images appear does occasionally challenge the viewer when appearing in concert with voice-over narration or audio from interviews, requiring viewers to attempt to read two sets of text—subtitles and the other cartoon, essay, or alternate text-based image—on-screen simultaneously. Similarly, some of the simple animation—such as making a portrait of Chairman Mao mechanically wave his arm, an apparently sarcastic gesture meant to undercut the authority of the "great leader"—seemed to call too much attention to itself and felt out of tone with the rest of the film. These, however, are far outweighed by the rewards this 137-minute documentary presents to viewers. Although this year marks the thirtieth anniversary of the Reform Era, and it has been almost as long since the historical verdict on the victims of the campaign against the Hu Feng Clique has been reversed, there remain few opportunities for filmmakers to address frankly the missteps of the Chinese Communist Party such as the Anti-Rightist Campaign, the Cultural Revolution, and, of course, the attack on Hu Feng. Recent documentary films that attempt to address these moments, such as Hu Jie's stunning look at one man's memories of the Cultural Revolution in *Though I Am Gone* (2006) and Peng Xiaolian and S. Louisa Wei's *Storm under the Sun,* help to fill the gaps in the historical amnesia that has afflicted public commemoration of many of these events.

With Shu Wu's passing, his (guilt ridden?) perspective on this dark page will be forever lost to history; his silence in some sense echoes the relative silence the entire Hu Feng affair has garnered from official media outlets in China. At the same time, we are reminded of the great contribution *Storm under the Sun* makes by preserving the faces, names, and stories of so many victims of China's modern literary inquisition. Wei and Peng's film also helps us better understand the even more pervasive forms of political violence that would follow. In this sense, like Tian Zhuangzhuang's masterful meditation on the first seventeen years of Communist rule, *The Blue Kite* (1993), *Storm under the Sun* can also be read as a tour through the anatomy of political persecution that would plague China for many years into the future, from the Anti-Rightist Campaign to the Cultural Revolution and from Tiananmen to Tibet. This is a rare film that conveys the perseverance of the human spirit amid the relentless drive of a machine that demands subordinance to the party and the state.

Conference

Northeast Historic Film: "The Whole World Is Watching!"

Regina Longo

No, it was not the 1968 Democratic National Convention, and no, a riot did not break out in Bucksport, Maine, sometime between July 24 and July 25, 2009, but the phrase "the whole world is watching!" came to mind as I sat down to write about yet another stimulating year at the annual Northeast Historic Film (NHF) Summer Symposium. The year 2009 was, aptly, the ninth annual gathering of the tribes, and much of the conversation outside and inside the theater made note that we were quickly coming up on a decade of symposia. The study of amateur, regional, and noncommercial films has come of age, and NHF has had a great hand in encouraging, promoting, and supporting this scholarship. If I may stretch the comparison to Chicago 1968 a bit further, several months before the 1968 convention, activists had decided that this would be the place to confront the "system," demanding an end to the war in Vietnam. Like the dreamers and doers at NHF, who put out an open call for conference participants each year, encouraging them to think beyond the confines of commercial moving images, these activists were thinking big: they invited over one hundred thousand people to come and take part in this planned confrontation. The numbers they expected did not show. The official statistics report that only a few thousand people participated in the demonstrations, and most of them were locals who had been swept up into the fray by their sheer proximity to the events rather than by intention or personal political convictions. These protests would have remained small and inconsequential had they not been captured by TV cameras and subsequently transmitted to living rooms across the nation and the world. The whole world *was* watching. And as we know, thanks to the preservation efforts of the National Film Preservation Foundation, in addition to the commercial cameras present at these events, locals and amateurs, such as the Chicago Film Group (*People's Right to Know: Police vs. Reporters,* 1968) and the Youth International Party (*Yippie!,* 1968), also documented and reflected on these activities.

But why on earth am I going on some nostalgia trip about 1968? Well, thematically, it does tie in to NHF's opening presentation this year by Heather Norris Nicholson, "Purposeful Pleasures," which examined social awareness and film practice in Britain from 1927 to 1977. Indeed Britain's amateur cinema movement had been documenting not only leisure-time activities but also societal problems long before 1968. Nicholson's talk centered on research that she began in 2005 when she first started to work with the collections of the Northwest Film Archive in Manchester, United Kingdom, but that became more focused in 2007 as she was working with the Sam Hanna collection. We had the opportunity to screen some of Hanna's work from a career that began in the throes of World War II, along with the work of another schoolteacher turned headmaster. Though Hanna's principal career was that of a woodworking teacher at a school called Townley in the borough of Burnley in Lancashire, and though his early films often featured his students' projects, Hanna soon began to exhibit his films in venues that took him beyond the show-and-tell or how-to classroom act. In fact, by the 1950s, Hanna and his wife, Edith, were visiting local prisons to screen his films as well as other fiction films from his personal collection. Many of Hanna's films documented artisans and workers and the conditions of workers. They were eventually screened throughout England, giving his so-called simple films a larger reach and providing his audiences with a subtle yet effective means to think beyond their own identity and reflect on their place in a larger social framework. Nicholson demonstrated this larger social context by pointedly ending on a film shot by another Manchester school headmaster in the late 1960s that featured a protest and political rally.

Leaving the cottage industry of regional filmmakers in the United Kingdom, we then jumped back in time to Philadelphia circa 1907. Caitlin McGrath encouraged us to enter "This Splendid Temple" as she discussed the beginnings of her research into the exhibition and production of films by John Wanamaker in his flagship department store. Wanamaker's Grand Depot first opened in Philadelphia in 1876, and a large New York City store followed at the beginning of the twentieth century. Though Wanamaker was a businessman, he would have most likely considered himself more of an educator and philanthropist. In fact, the Philadelphia store featured a rooftop school for its employees, who would study by night and peddle Wanamaker's wares by day. In addition to the well-appointed classrooms featured in some of the still photos that were part of McGrath's presentation, there was a most impressive image of a gymnasium and track on the rooftop.

McGrath's research thus far has taken her to the Philadelphia Historical Society, which holds Wanamaker's collection of personal papers. There she unearthed many letters discussing expeditionary trips funded in conjunction with the U.S. War Department and the East India Company, collaborations with J. K. Dixon of the East India Company, programs of daily screenings that took place at the Philadelphia store, and letters that earnestly discussed Wanamaker's Christian values and his commitment to literacy among Native American peoples. In fact, in 1911, Wanamaker self-published his *Golden Book of the Wanamaker Stores,* a multivolume set that begins with the following epigraph: "Let those who follow me continue to build with the plumb of Honor, the level of Truth, and the square of Integrity, Education, Courtesy and Mutuality." The grandeur of Wanamaker's vision certainly matched that of the stills we saw of his department store's extravagant auditorium, which rivaled contemporary images of Carnegie Hall (which was actually built in 1891, fifteen years after the Grand Depot had opened its doors). It is important to note that Wanamaker is best known in film circles for his funding of the 1908 fictional film *Song of Hiawatha* and also *The Last Great Indian Council* (1909), both of which used Native Americans as actors. J. K. Dixon and Wanamaker's son Rodman worked together on these productions, which were funded in part by Wanamaker and in part by the U.S. War Department and the Smithsonian Institution. J. K. Dickson published a book that same year titled *The Vanishing Race: A Record in Picture and Story of the Last Great Indian Council.* Though McGrath's research has yet

to reveal whether these films were screened in Wanamaker's stores, she did locate some program records that listed shorter, lighter film fare as part of the store's daily screening schedule.

As the NHF audience screened Edwin S. Porter's 1907 biograph one-reeler *The Teddy Bears,* I could not help but wonder what might have been had Porter's film been followed by *The Last Great Indian Council.* Would a 1909 audience connect Goldilocks's invasion of the three bears' home with the U.S. government's invasion and annexation of Native American territories? For as we moved light-years ahead to 2009 and the work of DJ Spooky's collage remix, Kurt Lancaster demonstrated through sounds and images that DJ Spooky randomly assembles with his database generator, and through an interview with DJ Spooky himself, that a political ethos is almost always present. In fact, in his ghostly mixes and rhythms, DJ Spooky, "That Subliminal Kid" (Paul Miller), had deliberately chosen to reuse the title and some of the music from *Sinfonia Antarctica.* This symphony was originally conceived in 1947 by Vaughn Williams as the score for the film *Scott of the Antarctic* (1948), which traces the failed 1910–1912 expedition of Robert Falcon Scott, who wanted to be the first to the South Pole. After the release of the 1948 film, Williams continued to elaborate on his piece, which he deemed complete in 1952. DJ Spooky notes that Williams's piece is a strong commentary on the end of empire (particularly the British Empire) and the search for a new hero. Miller, however, is not seeking a new hero. In an interview clip that Lancaster screened during his presentation, Miller stated that his "Terra Nova" and "Manifesto for a People's Republic of Antarctica" (2008) projects both use found footage, print design, and propaganda to show how exploration at the edge of the world is a prism to view how nations look at one another and how art itself is a highly politicized medium. This film and score followed up his 2005 "Rebirth of a Nation," which remixed D. W. Griffith's *Birth of a Nation* (1915). Lancaster appropriately picked up the manifesto-type theme of Miller's recent works and provided us with the traces of a genealogy that reference the work of F. T. Marinetti and the Futurists from their 1909 "Futurist Manifesto." By comparing Miller's random generation of sound in his collages to the noncausal use of words employed by Marinetti, we are left to ponder the effect that is then produced by such violent rupture. What might DJ Spooky do with *Song of Hiawatha?*

Moving from the South Pole and the space of the concert hall, after a short recess, we reentered the formal space of the classroom, where Jennifer Peterson challenged the notion of the docile student of early educational films. Whereas the producers and distributors of the Eastman Teaching Films conducted studies and published their research findings lauding the success of their films in the classroom, Peterson posed the question of resistance. Resistance can take many forms, and Peterson suggested that anyone who has ever been a student can find myriad ways to resist an instructor's message, all while seated quietly at his or her desk, maintaining the calm, cool exterior of a docile body. Yet because of the nature of the educational film industry and the commercial imperatives of the Eastman Kodak Company, very little literature exists to corroborate this hunch. Even in teaching journals of the 1920s, such as the well-known and still readily available *Educational Screen,* the majority of the articles focus on the positive benefits of using audiovisual materials in a classroom setting. Peterson's research is ongoing, and her provocative questions will require a creative approach that goes beyond primary source research into journals of the time period. As we screened segments of Eastman classroom films, symposia participants began to suggest other avenues for Peterson to explore, such as oral histories. In fact, one of the audience members even recalled her time in a Catholic all-girl school in the 1940s, where the weekly educational film screening was more a social event than an instructive opportunity.

Coincidentally, Kirsten Ostherr's presentation also addressed the curious dichotomy between educational and social screenings. The year, 1929, and the film producer, Eastman Teaching Films, were the same, but the subject matter and the audience were decidedly different. Screening *Acute Appendicitis (Lay Public)* and *Acute Appendicitis (Professional)* back to back (or should I say side to side?), Ostherr demonstrated how the same subject matter—in two very similar films—could receive distinct

treatment and appeal to distinct audiences, one being the general public and the other being medical professionals, most likely members of the American College of Surgeons (ACS), who, along with Eastman, were the films' coproducers. Ostherr suggested that this practice of audience segmentation also produced distinct ways of seeing the body, an arrangement that benefited both sides of this partnership. In fact, we learned that Will Hays spoke at the annual ACS meeting in 1929. In a moment when Hollywood was just beginning actively and willingly to censor images of the body in its films, the U.S. medical community joined forces with Hays to achieve a somewhat different objective. The ACS saw this as an opportunity to further establish the medical profession, to promote the advancement of the medical establishment, and most important, to promote the scientific management of movement and the body. Ostherr demonstrated that in this particular historical instance, the lay and the professional spectator switched roles. Through the use of the popular medium of film, the lay public was being conditioned to view their own bodies as instruments of science, whereas the ACS audience was being conditioned to view surgical problems as spectacle. This shift was reinforced with anecdotal evidence that Ostherr found in the documents of the ACS that points to the increasing popularity of the film screenings at the ACS annual meetings throughout the 1940s, 1950s, and 1960s, culminating with awards not only for outstanding surgeons but also for outstanding surgical films.

Shifting gears from the realm of the professional to that of the amateur, Ryan Shand examined the "Role of Award Ceremonies within Leisure Activity." Shand's current work focuses on a series of oral histories that he has been conducting with members of the Merseyside filmmakers club regarding their participation in the annual *Amateur CineWorld* "Ten Best" competitions. The most striking aspect of this presentation was the ease with which Shand conducted these interviews, ingratiating himself to his subject and the viewer. The results are poignant and personal interviews that not only reveal a variety of motivations and characters but that also recognize that any attempt to generalize the motives and desires of the amateur filmmaker will not yield productive conclusions. Though the filmmakers are part of a larger community, Shand's work in establishing more specific and equally legitimate observations is what distinguishes this type of oral history. What has become clear in this ongoing project is that the central role of contests and awards in amateur film circles mimics the rise of contests and award ceremonies across many leisure-time pursuits. Whereas these activities may have initially been established for their potential to foster community among cineclub members, the end result seems to be a stronger commodification and stratification of a once communal culture.

The second day of presentations initially saw a shift away from the examination of the public spaces of communal exhibition to the private space of the home as experienced by the researcher as sole viewer. Cecilia Morner worked with private film collections from the 1960s and 1970s, housed since 2003 in the Swedish government-run archive in the town of Grängesberg. In 2005, Morner had the opportunity to be part of a team documenting several of these collections that arrived in the archive with no written documentation. Screening for the symposia participants several reels of home movies of one particular family whom she had studied at length, Morner outlined her speculative approach as a cultural historian, seeking clues in the gestures, activities, clothing, and outer trappings of the subjects. Though determining the basic facts, such as the date and location of the films, turned out to be a relatively simple task, nothing else about this research would be. Morner had established several scenarios in her mind to explain the actions she was watching on screen. In summer 2008, she decided to interview some of the film donors to compare her initial findings to their own interpretations and recollections. In many instances, Morner's hypotheses regarding the personal relationships depicted in the films were not on target. They were certainly plausible, but they were not the actual stories of the subjects. Yet when Morner asked her subjects if she should change the archival record to reflect these facts, the subjects themselves seemed nonplussed.

Morner recorded her own observations and interpretations before, during, and after her interviews with the subjects and used French historian Pierre Nora's idea of realms of memory versus sites of memory to elaborate further on her experience with these films. Whereas Nora's work poses grand questions about the very public constructs of the nation, nationalism, and national identity, Morner mapped these concepts to the very private realm of the nuclear family, interpersonal relationships, and individual identity within the closed group. Morner's thoughts unfolded simultaneously alongside the projection of the family films, evocatively demonstrating Nora's theories of a nonlinear historical narrative of multiple voices in perpetual reuse and misuse that constitute successive presents, eschewing the notion of tradition to concentrate on the manner in which traditions are passed on.

And so we traveled from Sweden in the 1970s to 2005 Norway, "Through Trondheim in a Time Machine," with Bjorn Sorenssen as our genial guide. Sorenssen discussed his encounters over a period of several years, beginning in the 1970s, when he was first working at Verdensteatret, one of Trondheim's four municipal film theaters, dating back to 1911, and discovered a large stash of 35mm nitrate film featuring scenes of daily life in and around Trondheim. Eventually these 250 reels of film ended up in the collection of the Norwegian Film Institute, and off and on through the years, Sorenssen continued his research into the collection. It was not until the news and scholarship of the Mitchell and Kenyon films began to circulate at film symposia and among a wider public that Sorenssen was able to link some cameramen and production details of this Trondheim collection to the Mitchell and Kenyon films. Several of the reels have now been preserved, and they were part of a very successful public screening during the 2005 Trondheim Film Festival, at which these films were projected onto walls and buildings that now stand in the locations where the films were originally recorded in the early 1900s. Again, we may borrow from Nora's sites and realms of memory to think about how the use and reuse of these images opens up new modes of exhibition while simultaneously exposing new threads that link the film production histories of two nations (Norway and the United Kingdom) divided by the North Sea. Sorenssen's time machine remains none other than the cinematic apparatus.

Obeying Newton's first law, the law of inertia, a body in motion must remain in motion. And in our cinematic apparatus cum time machine that was the NHF theater, the participants enthusiastically traveled, with Kimberly Tarr, "'Round the World and Back Again" with Adelaide Pearson from 1931 to 1940, as she and her partner, Laura Paddock, traveled the world documenting cultural practices in France, India, and North Africa. Pearson was a woman of means and a self-proclaimed amateur anthropologist and was therefore able to fund her own expeditions and determine her own agenda. Though she was inspired by the films of Burton Holmes and, like Holmes, shot motion pictures and still pictures, her hand and eye demonstrate a decidedly more personal—dare I say it—feminine touch. Her attention to ritual, costumes, and details is evident in much of her work and is particularly enhanced in her India footage by her use of color film stock. Though Pearson traveled far from her Boston home, it is unfortunate that she did not travel as far and wide with her lectures. We are left again to wonder what might have been had Pearson followed the lecture circuit as intensely as her cinematic vision.

In yet another reversal of fortune, Jennifer L. Jenkins's research into the work of Charles Herbert in "Western Ways Gone South" revealed a man with both vision and drive who also happened to be a poor judge of character. Though Herbert's imagination for Southwestern Motion Pictures and Television was as vast as the Arizona landscape he called home, the loss of one million dollars (head writer Tom Bailey ran off with the funds) put him out of business permanently. Jenkins examined both the paper records of the company and the short subjects and TV pilots that Herbert produced. Jenkins addressed yet another mode of watching when she discussed the use of these films as main exhibits in a court trial to recover the absconded funds. Once again, we can only imagine how these images might be viewed in the judge's chambers or the jury box.

Cristina Albu proposed that we examine another type of box in "From Introspection to Convivial Participation"—the black box of contemporary video art display. Though Albu's proposed typology demonstrated that many contemporary artists attempt to challenge the conventional modes of cinematic exhibition and spectatorship by deconstructing more traditional theatrical spaces to various ends, what remained in each unorthodox space was a very concrete and conventional notion of the screen. What will it take for the screen to be removed, replaced, reimagined? Even in the absence of the screen, some sort of frame remains, something that holds and fixes the spectator. What is it in the human psyche that seeks a fixed structure or form?

Sharon Thompson's discussion "Our Cameras, Our Lives: Lesbian Home Movies ca. 1935–1999" urged the audience to consider this question again. Moving from the public space of the museum or art gallery featured in Albu's typology, we returned to the very private place of the home movie. We were able to peek into the private lives of lesbian communities in New England and beyond, sharing poignant and intimate moments with women, their lovers, their friends, their children, and their extended families. Though three distinct collections spanning three different time periods were screened, the Ruth Storm Collection (1930s–1960s) and the Caren McCourtney Collection (1970–1990) were significant for the way in which behaviors and gestures, even in the very intimate milieu of the home movie, were coded (and framed). The specter of being outed still remained. It was not simply a matter of being caught in the act in a public place; rather, once that act was committed, and committed to film, it became a permanent record and something that could be used in a very real way against the filmmaker or the subjects.

Fortunately for all of us, in 2009, in Bucksport, Maine, women walk the streets freely hand in hand. And those of us present for the symposium were fortunate to share this final screening of the afternoon with the lesbian community way down East that came out in large numbers to fill the theater and to support Sharon Thompson. Sitting in the back row, I counted every seat in the theater filled. Suddenly, the whole world was watching. And as they watched, they called out the names of their friends—some living, some dead—who flashed before us on screen. They laughed at how young they had once been, how there seemed to be a moment in 1974 when every lesbian on earth was sporting coveralls, and in one final tribute and show of pride, members of the Shira Chorus featured in the third collection of poor-quality VHS videotapes from the 1990s hopped onto stage and remastered the faded audio track right on the spot. The whole world was not only watching—they were now listening. For a moment, it seemed as if we were on our way to removing the frame.

That evening, rather than screening home movies in a public theater, we were treated to a screening of a mishmash of shorts in the private home of Sharon Thompson. As locals and symposiasts arrived on the doorstep of Thompson's Victorian Greek revival home complete with whitewashed Doric columns holding up the facade and a croquet pitch and gazebo out back, Liz Coffey, film conservator at the Harvard Film Archive, was busy threading three different gauges of projectors with films from the Howard E. Burr Collection that had recently been donated to the archive. Burr was a dentist by day and a film enthusiast by night, but it seems that there were moments when his worlds collided as Coffey informed us that he even screened films in his dental office. Coffey selected a variety of gems from the collection that reframed the theme of women and film that was the focus of Thompson's earlier afternoon presentation at NHF. The screening began with a 16mm short featuring 1940s coeds frolicking in a canoe and ended with an extremely condensed 8mm version of Scorsese's *Taxi Driver* (1976) that reduced the film to a series of Jodie Foster's most memorable scenes. As women romped across the screen set up in Thompson's parlor room furnished with an elaborate chandelier and a mix of chairs and pillows dragged into the otherwise empty room from various corners of the house, the symposiasts transformed the traditionally staid bourgeois living room parlor into a space that felt more like a lively bordello.

Itinerant Filmography, North America

COMPILED AND EDITED BY CAROLINE FRICK

With an increased number of local newspapers available online, and with numerous regional library collections now searchable from locations all over the world, investigating itinerant-produced films proves a rich and, more than ever before, viable subject. The challenge of creating any kind of definitive filmography, however, serves as the flip side to the excitement of that research—whatever list we publish now will likely be out of date by the time it is being read. With that disclaimer firmly in place, what follows is the first attempt to create a filmography of itinerant filmmaking practice in North America. Although influential research has been undertaken on this subject in the United Kingdom as well as in Australia and New Zealand, attempts to do so in North America, and particularly in the United States, have been hampered by the lack of a formalized regional film archive network, by geographical difference, and by other issues endemic to a more pluralist cultural preservation policy. (For more information related to the network of U.K. film archives and repositories, see http://www.bufvc.ac.uk/faf/databases. htm).

Filmography data have been organized by filmmaker and/or production company as well as by geographical location. When possible, production dates and film titles (or approximations thereof) have been included. If all films listed within a series use the same title, then only the locations have been referenced in the body of the text. Extant film or video copies are listed in endnotes that appear after the filmography or within brackets. Please note that newsreel series produced by local production companies or purely local, one-off productions have been excluded from this list. We hope that this filmography will assist in uncovering new film and video copies of this kind of material as well as encourage the discovery of new locations, productions, filmmakers, and series. Many of the directors and producers referenced here claimed to have created hundreds on hundreds of films, and from the information unearthed thus far, there is no reason to doubt such claims. To contribute additional information or corrections, please e-mail Caroline Frick (cfrick@mail.utexas.edu).

Amateur Services Production: See Yourself and Your Town in the Movies Series (ca. 1930–1950)
United States: Illinois: Rossville (1939);[1] **Missouri:** Chillicothe (1939), Kirksville (1937),[2] Maryville (1940);[3] **New York:** Pulaski (1938), Jamestown (1938);[4] **Ohio:** Independence [film aka *Welcome*] (1935),[5] Lancaster (1937), St. Clairsville (1939–1940);[6] **Pennsylvania:** Aliquippa (1937),[7] Bellefonte (1941),[8] California (1935),[9] Gettysburg (1940–NOTE: The local Lions Club chapter canceled the contract with Amateur Services Production before the film's completion), Hamburg,[10] Hatboro (1939–1940),[11] Lansford (1939), New Holland (1939); **West Virginia:** Elkins (1938),[12] Charles Town (1941),[13] Whitesville (1937); **Wisconsin:** Reedsburg (1939),[14] Rhinelander (1939–1940),[15] Sauk City (1939),[16] Prairie du Sac (1939)[17]

Amateur Theater Guild: Movie Queen Films (1934–ca. 1940s)
Director(s)/Producer(s): Emilene Bouge, Madeline A. Chaffee, Margaret Cram/ Margaret (Cram) Showalter, Anne L. Lambert, Marilyn Lundy
United States: Indiana: Logansport (1938); **Maine:** Bar Harbor (1936),[18] Bath,[19] Belfast (1935), Bucksport (1935), Camden, Dexter, Eastport (1936), Lincoln (1936),[20] Lubec (1936),[21] Madison, Newport (1936),[22] Van Buren (1935); **Massachusetts:** Greenfield (1935), Groton (1939), Leominster (1935), Norwood (1934),[23] Reading,[24] Rockland/Abington (1938),[25] **Minnesota:** Brainerd (1937); **Montana:** Helena (1938); **North Carolina:** Burlington (1936), Wilmington (1938); **Ohio:** Zanesville (1936–?); **Pennsylvania:** Monessen (1941–?); **South Carolina:** Marion (1937); **South Dakota:** Huron (1938); **Tennessee:** Kingsport (1938–1939), Morristown (1939); **Texas:** Abilene (1938), Big Spring (1938); **Vermont:** Middlebury (1939);[26] **Wisconsin:** Appleton (1938–?)

Melton Barker Productions/Melton Barker Juvenile Productions (ca. 1932–1975)
Director/Producer: Melton Barker (NOTE: Some titles might have been
directed/produced by "Barker impersonator" George Sanderson. Such titles
are indicated by [GS].)
The Kidnappers Foil Series: **United States: Alabama:** Anniston (1938),
Birmingham, Opelika (ca. 1940s); **Arizona:** Tucson (1951); **Arkansas:**
Blytheville (1936, 1951, 1969, 1975), Camden (1937), Fayatteville (1969),
Fort Smith, Hope (1937), Little Rock, Pine Bluff (1952, 1969),[27] Texarkana;
California: Fresno (ca. 1950s), Long Beach (1961), San Diego (ca. 1950s);[28]
Florida: Miami; **Georgia:** Cedartown; **Iowa:** Council Bluffs (1949), Mason City
(1940), Muscatine (1939); **Illinois:** Alton (1950), Bloomington,[29] Carbondale
(1972), Galesburg, Mattoon (1951), Peoria (ca. 1940s), Robinson; **Indiana:**
Anderson (1953) [GS], Evansville, Loganport (1953) [GS]; **Kansas:** Atchison
(1939, ca. 1970s), Hutchinson (1939), Emporia (1938), Topeka (ca. 1950s);
Kentucky: Fulton (ca. 1960s), Owensboro (1938); **Louisiana:** Abbeville
(1940), Bastrop (ca. 1960s), Baton Rouge (1940), Lake Charles, Ruston (1940),
Shreveport (ca. 1940s); **Minnesota:** Brainerd (1940); **Missouri:** Carthage (1938),
Chillicothe (1939, 1949, 1970), Jefferson City (1950), Joplin (1949), Kansas
City (1950) [possibly five different theaters involved/versions shot during
Barker's visit], Moberly (1938), Saint Charles (1941),[30] Independence (1949);
Mississippi: Cleveland (1972), Greenville (1940–1941), Tupelo (ca. 1930s);
Nebraska: Columbus (1957), Fremont (1939), Grand Island,[31] Lincoln (1940),
Nebraska City, Norfolk; **New Mexico:** Albuquerque (1951), Clovis (1949),
Deming (1951), Las Cruces, Las Vegas (1951), Lovington (ca. 1940s), Portales,
Santa Fe (1951), Tucumcari (1946–1947); **North Carolina:** Burlington (1941,
1950), Gastonia (1941), Goldsboro (1941), Greenville, High Point (1941),
Lexington, Lumberton (1942), Reidsville (1947),[32] Statesville, Thomasville;[33]
Ohio: Marion; **Oklahoma:** Ada (1946), Anadarko, Guthrie,[34] Lawton (1947),
Oklahoma City, Pawhuska,[35] Shawnee;[36] **Pennsylvania:** Allentown; Upper
Darby [GS], Williamsport (1951) [GS]; **Rhode Island:** Newport (1952) [GS];
South Carolina: Aiken (1942, 1949), Florence (1949), Spartanburg (ca.
1940s); **Tennessee:** Elizabethton,[37] Kingsport (1938, 1949), Knoxville (1949),
Middleton;[38] **Texas:** Abilene (1937, 1946, 1952, 1960, 1961), Alice (1950/1),
Amarillo (1944, 1948), Andrews, Austin, Bay City (ca. 1940s), Big Spring
(1936, 1939, 1973), Brenham (ca. 1930s), Brownsville (1936, 1943, 1950),
Childress (1938, ca. 1940s),[39] Commerce (1967), Denton (1937, 1946, 1952), El
Paso (1937, 1949), Ennis, Floydada (ca. 1940s, ca. 1960s), Freeport (1970), Ft.
Worth (ca. 1940s), Galveston (1937, 1951, 1970), Gilmer, Greenville (1949),
Harlingen (1946), Honey Grove (ca. 1970s), Huntsville, Keller, Kerrville
(1965), Kingsport (1949), Kingsville (1951), La Mesa, Lockhart (1950), Lubbock
(1936, 1946, 1973), Marshall, Martin, McAllen, McKinney (1935, 1951, ca.
1960s), Memphis, Mineral Wells, Monahans, Mount Pleasant (ca. 1930s),
Munday, Nixon, Odessa (ca. 1940s), Paris (1937, 1952, 1975), Pflugerville
(ca. 1930s), Plainview (1936), Port Arthur (1946, 1947), Quanah, San Angelo

(ca. 1940s), San Antonio (1934, 1937, 1948), San Marcos (1943, ca. 1970s),[40] San Saba,[41] Terrell (1947), Tyler, Vernon (1939), Victoria (1970), Waco (ca. 1950s, 1960), Waxahachie;[42] **Utah:** Salt Lake City (1975); **Virginia:** Danville (1949); **Wisconsin:** Kenosha (1952) [GS], Madison (1952), Oshkosh (1952) [GS], Sheboygan (1941)

The Last Straw Series: **United States: Minnesota:** Duluth (1938);[43] **Texas:** Fort Worth (ca. 1930s)

The [City] Story Series: **United States: Illinois:** Jacksonville: *The Jacksonville Story*; **Missouri:** Cape Girardeau: *The Cape Girardeau Story*, Centralia: *The Centralia Story*; **South Dakota:** Rapid City: *The Rapid City Story* (1970); **Texas:** Commerce: *The Commerce Story* (1967), Port Lavaca: *The Port Lavaca Story* (1970); **Utah:** Salt Lake City: *The Utah Story of 1975* (1975)

Other Melton Barker Titles:

United States: Texas: Dallas, *Secrets of a Co-Ed* (1932) and *Carnival Days* (1932)

Blache Screen Service, Buy at Home Campaign Series (ca. 1930–1939)
Director/Producer: Mike Blache
United States: Idaho: Weiser (ca. 1930s);[44] **Montana:** Deer Lodge (1939); **Oregon:** Coquille (ca. 1930s), Enterprise (1935), Forest Grove (1934),[45] McMinnville (ca. 1930s), Prineville (1937); **Washington:** Tekoa (1938–1939)

J. B. "Slim" Brolund: A [City] Romance Series (ca. 1925–1926)
United States: Florida: St. Petersburg, *Untitled* (1926); **Illinois:** Edgewood, *Untitled* (1926); **North Carolina:** Asheville, *An Asheville Romance* (1925), Charlotte (ca. 1920s–?), Greenville (ca. 1920s–?); **Tennessee:** Knoxville, *A Knoxville Romance* (1925)

Arthur J. Higgins: Untitled Series (ca. 1936–1941)
(NOTE: The films included here were sold as individual one-hundred-foot reels on eBay in 2006 and currently reside with approximately forty different film collectors. This initial list was compiled by Albert Steg, who acquired over half the films at the time of their sale.)
United States: California: Bodega (1940), Geyserville (1940), Graton (1940), Pt. Reyes (1940), Tomales (1940); **Georgia:** Jeffersonville; **Illinois:** Butler (1936), Coffeen, Cowdon, Farmersville (1941–1942), Gays (1936), Hebron (1936), Marine (1936), Maryville, Odin (1937), Owaneco (1936), Raymond (1942), Richmond (1936), Riverton (1942), St. Jacob (1936), Strausberg (1936), Taylor Springs, Thayer (1942), Xenia; **Kansas:** Bayard (1939), Elsmore (1939), Fulton (1939), Kincaid (1937–1939), Mildred/Lone Oak (1939); **Michigan:** Crotian, Felch, Michigamme, Nadeau (1940), Powers (1939); **Minnesota:** Brooks, Campbell (1941), Center City (1940), Clitheral (1942), Dent, Erhard, Fisher, Flom (1941), Georgetown, Hendrum, Pelican Rapids (1942), Underwood, Willow River (1949–?); **Missouri:** Exeter (1936), Fairview, Midway, Rocky

Comfort (1936), Seligman (1936), Wheaton (1936); **Nebraska:** Avoca (1940), Bennington, Cedar Bluffs (1939), Colon, Craig, Elkhorn, Fort Calhoun (1939), Herman, Leshara/Weston (1939), Millard, Morse Bluffs, Murray (1940), Roslie (1939), Springfield (1939); **North Dakota:** Casselton (1941); **Texas:** Addison (1937), Agua Dulce (1938), Austin, Beasley (1939), Blessing (1939), Blue Ridge (1937), Brookston, Burlington (1937), Caddo Mills (1936), Calallen (1939), Celeste (1938), Charlotte (1938), Crandall (1936), Dodd City (1938), Ector (1937), Emory (1936), Farmers Branch, Fayetteville (1939), Fentress (1938), Friendship (1937), Caddo Mills (1936), Grapeville, Houston, Howe (1938), Hungerford (1939), Ingleside (1938), Jourdenton (1941), Katy (1939), Kingsbury (1938), La Coste (1941), Lytle (1938–1941), Manor (1937), Markham (1939), Moore (1941), Pecan Gap (1937–1938), Pettus (1938), Poth, Prosper (1938), Roxton, Rutersville (1939), Schertz (1938), Southmayde (1937), Thorndale (1937), Van Velck, Vickery (1936), Weimar; **Wisconsin:** Advance (1939), Arena, Argyle, Arnott, Arpin (1941), Balsam Lake, Belmont, Benton (1940), Bloomington, Boyceville (1940), Casco (1938), Cecil (1939), Champion, Clayton, Cochrane, Crivitz, Danbury, Downsville, Eden, Elmwood (1941), Fountain City (1937), Franken (1940), Gotham (1937), Hancock (1941), Hilbert (1938–1941), Hortonville, Kellnersville (1938), Kewaskum, Knapp (1940), Lowell, Luck, Lyons (1936), Maiden Rock, Maplewood (1934), Mendoa, Meskoro-Neskoro, Milltown, Morrison, Moscoda (1940), Neosha (1936), Neshkora (1938), New Diggings, New Franken, Osceola, Pembine, Peshtigo, Plum City, Pound (1938), Ridgeway, Ryariere (1939), Scandinavia (1938), Shullsburg (1940), Spencer (1942), Stephensville, Steuben School, Taylor Falls (1941), Tish Mills (1938), Unity (1941), Valders (1938), Wausaukee, Wayside (1938), Wild Rose (1938–1941)

Hudris Film Company (ca. 1916–1921)
Director/Producer: Walter Steiner
A/The Romance of [City] Series:
United States: District of Columbia: *A Romance of Washington* (1921); **Indiana:** Kokomo: *The Romance of Kokomo* (1917); **Iowa:** Waterloo: *The Romance of Waterloo* (1920); **Maine:** Bangor: *A Romance of Bangor* (1917), Biddeford: *A Romance of Biddeford and Saco* (1916); **Maryland:** *A Romance of Frederick* (1916); **Montana:** Butte: *A Romance of Butte;* **North Carolina:** Asheville: *A Romance of Asheville* (1916); **Washington:** Seattle: *A Romance of Seattle* (1919); **Wisconsin:** Appleton: *A Romance of Appleton* (1920), La Crosse: *A Romance of La Crosse* (1922), Madison: *A Romance of Madison* (1920), Oshkosh: *A Romance of Oshkosh* (1920)
The Belle of [City] Series:
United States: Maine: Biddeford: *The Belle of Biddeford* (1917); **Wisconsin:** Kenosha: *The Belle of Kenosha* (1923)

Interstate Film Producers (ca. 1920–1930s)
Director/Producer: Don O. Newland
The [City] Hero Series:
United States: Georgia: Americus: *Americus' Hero* (1928), Fitzgerald: *Fitzgerald's Hero* (1929); **Indiana:** Logansport: *Logansport's Hero* (1924); **Maryland:** Cumberland: *My Hero* [aka *Cumberland's Hero*] (1931), Salisbury: *Salisbury's Hero* (1924); **North Carolina:** Durham, Wilmington: *Wilmington's Hero* (1925); **Ohio:** Coshocton: *Coshocton's Hero* (1927), Lima: *Lima's Hero* (1928); **Pennsylvania:** Huntingdon: *Huntingdon's Hero*,[46] Wellsboro: *Wellsboro's Hero* (1928); **Virginia:** Danville: *Danville's Hero* (1925); **West Virginia:** Staunton: *Staunton's Hero* (1929); **Wisconsin:** Janesville: *Janesville's Hero*[47]
[City] Adopts/Takes a Baby Series:
United States: Michigan: Marshall, *Marshall Adopts a Baby* (1919); **Ohio:** Elyria, *Eylria Takes a Baby* (1922); **Wisconsin:** Wisconsin Rapids, *Wisconsin Rapids Adopts a Baby* (1920)
Other Interstate Film Producers' Titles:
United States: California: Woodland, *Untitled* (1924); **North Carolina:** Wrightsville, *A Good Catch at Wrightsville Beach* (1925); **Pennsylvania:** Towanda, *Towanda's Queen* (1934), Wellsboro: *Wellsboro's Queen* (ca. 1920s)

Hugh Jamieson: Won from the Flames Series (ca. 1916–1917)
United States: Texas: Denton (1916), Victoria (1916)

Sol Landsman and Arthur Loevin, Our Home Town Series (ca. 1946–1947)
United States: Georgia: Americus, Augusta, Dublin, Fitzgerald, Savannah, Swainsboro, Thomasville, Waycross

Life Newsreels: Life in [City] Series (ca. 1940s)
Director/Producer: Kathleen McCarey
United States: Ohio: Findlay: *Life in Findlay*; **Oregon:** Ashland: *Life in Ashland* (1950); **Wisconsin:** Oshkosh: *Life in Oshkosh* (1940), Appleton: *Life in Appleton* (1940)

McHenry Film Company: The Manhaters Series (ca. 1919)
Director/Producer: Basil McHenry
United States: Indiana: Anderson (1919),[48] Muncie (1919); **Kentucky:** Lexington (1916)

Pacific Film Production Company/Imperial Film Corporation
(NOTE: The connection between these two production companies remains unclear.)
Director/Producer for Imperial Film Corporation (Arizona and California titles):
Funiss M. Tisdale

Director/Producer for Pacific Film Production Company (South Carolina titles): H. C. Kunkleman

Things You Ought to Know About [City] Series:

Canada: Ontario: Kirkland Lake (1932)[49]

United States: Arizona: Prescott (1929);[50] **California:** San Jose (1927–1928);[51] **Iowa:** Emmetsburg (1934), dir. William Ramsell; **Kentucky:** Middlesboro (1935), dir. E. L. Baker; **North Carolina:** Reidsville (1935);[52] **South Carolina:** Anderson (1935), Florence (1935), Orangeburg (1935, 1946)

Other Pacific Film Production Company/Imperial Film Corporation Titles:

United States: Georgia: Cordele, untitled (1936); **Illinois:** Galesburg, *Scenes on Film, 1912–1931*;[53] **New Jersey:** Bridgeton: *It Happened in Bridgeton* (1937)[54]

Paragon Feature Film Company (ca. 1914–1916)
Director/Producer: O. W. Lamb (?)
United States: Alabama: Mobile, Montgomery; **Iowa:** Waterloo: *Cedar Valley Romance* (1916); **Illinois:** Springfield: *The Mine Owner's Daughter* (1915); **Kansas:** Topeka; **Louisiana:** New Orleans; **Missouri:** Kansas City; **Texas:** Austin: *A Political Touchdown* (1915), Galveston; **Wisconsin:** Wasau: *The Lumberjack* (1914)

Park Motion Picture Productions, My Hometown Series (ca. 1940–1950s)
Director/Producer: Don Parisher and George S. Gullett
United States: Florida: Orlando (ca. 1940s); **New Jersey:** Freehold (1947), Lakewood (1947); **North Carolina:** Monroe (ca. 1940s),[55] Rutherfordton (ca. 1940s),[56] Statesville (1947), Wilkesboro (1948), Wilmington (1947); **Ohio:** Bedford (1940), Chardon (1941); **South Carolina:** Bennettsville (1946), Orangeburg (1946); **North Carolina:** Durham: *Negro Durham Marches On* (ca. 1950s)

Powers Picture Company (ca. 1913)
Director/Producer: C. T. Van Steenburg
United States: North Carolina: High Point: *Untitled Local Film* (1913), Mt. Airy: *Untitled Local Film* (1913), Statesville *Untitled Local Film* (1913)

Superior/Tinsley Film Company: Two Troublesome Tramps Series (ca. 1917–1930)
Director/Producer: C. D. Tinsley
United States: Iowa: Bedford (1919), Carroll (1917), Glenwood (1922), Hamburg (1921), Mason City (1930); **Missouri:** Jefferson (1926)

Texas News Trailers Company: Our Home Town Series (ca. 1946–1959)
Director/Producer: Shadrack "Shad" Graham
(NOTE: In addition to the locations listed via endnote, 35mm prints of some

titles are part of restricted holdings at the Center for American History at the University of Texas at Austin.)

United States: Arkansas: El Dorado, North Little Rock; **Colorado:** Pueblo Cortez; **Idaho:** Boise, Coeur D'Alene; **Louisiana:** Houma; **Montana:** Bozeman, Butte, Kalespell, Missoula; **New Mexico:** Alamogordo, Farmington, Hobbs, Roswell; **North Dakota:** Williston; **Pennsylvania:** Doylestown;[57] **Texas:** Brownfield, Killeen, LaMesa, Odessa, San Marcos,[58] Wichita Falls.

H. Lee Waters: Movies of Local People Series (ca. 1936–1942)
(NOTE: Extant films held at Duke University's Rare Book, Manuscript, and Special Collections Library [DU], North Carolina State Archives [NCSA], South Carolina Department of Archives and History [SCDAH], and the University of South Carolina Newsfilm Library [USC]. When possible, locations are denoted by acronym.)

United States: North Carolina: Albermarle (1940) [NCSA], Angier (1937, 1939) [NCSA], Apex (1941), Asheboro (1938, 1939, 1940, 1941) [DU], Avondale [DU], Belmont (1936), Benson (1937) [DU], Bessemer City (1942), Boone (1936), Burlington (1939, 1940, 1941, 1942) [NCSA], Caroleen [DU], Chapel Hill (1939) [DU and NCSA], Charlotte (1938), Cherryville (1938), China Grove (1937, 1938), Clayton (1937) [DU], Cliffside (1937, 1940) [DU], Concord (1936, 1937, 1939, 1941, 1942) [NCSA], Conover (1941, 1942), Cooleemee (1936, 1939, 1940, 1941), Cramerton (1938, 1939) [DU], Denton (1939, 1941) [DU], Draper (1937), Durham (1937, 1940) [NCSA], Elkin (1938, 1940, 1941), Erwin (1937, 1939) [DU], Forest City (1937) [DU], Fort Mill (1942), Fuquay Varina (1937) [DU], Gastonia (1937, 1938, 1939, 1940, 1941) [DU], Gibsonville (1939), Graham (1942), Granite Falls (1937, 1938, 1941, 1942) [DU], Greensboro (1939) [DU], Haw River (1942), Henderson (1936, 1938, 1939) [DU], Henrietta [DU], Hickory (1941), Hillsboro (1937, 1939) [NCSA], Jackson (1939) [DU], Kannapolis (1936, 1938, 1941) [DU], Kernersville (1936, 1937, 1939, 1940), Kings Mountain (1937, 1940, 1941), Leaksville (1937), Lenoir (1937) [DU], Lexington (1938, 1940) [DU], Liberty (1936, 1939) [DU], Lillington (1939) [DU], Louisburg (1937) [DU], Lumberton (1941) [NCSA], Madison (1939, 1941) [DU], Mayodan (1941) [DU], Mebane (1939) [DU], Mocksville (1938, 1940, 1941), Monroe (1941) [NCSA], Mooresville (1937, 1938, 1939) [DU], Mount Holly (1936), Mt. Airy (1941), Mt. Gilead (1938), Nashville (1939), Newton (1938, 1939), North Wilkesboro (1937, 1938, 1939, 1941) [DU], Norwood (1938), Oxford (1938, 1939, 1941) [DU], Pilot Mountain (1939) [DU], Pineville (1939), Pittsboro (1939, 1941, 1942), Raeford (1938) [DU], Red Springs (1938), Reidsville [DU], Rockingham (1938, 1939, 1941) [NCSA], Rockwell (1941, 1942), Roxboro (1936, 1937, 1938, 1939, 1940, 1941) [DU], Rutherfordton (1937) [DU], Salisbury (1940) [DU], Sanford (1936), Scotland Neck (1939) [DU], Selma (1937) [DU], Shelby (1937, 1938), Siler City (1936, 1937, 1939, 1941, 1942), Smithfield (1937) [DU], Spencer (1938, 1939,

1941, 1942), Spindale (1937, 1938) [DU], Spray (1937), Statesville (1940) [DU], Swannanoa (1938) [DU], Taylorsville (1939) [DU], Thomasville (1936, 1937, 1939, 1940) [DU], Troy (1936, 1938, 1939, 1940) [DU], Valdese (1941, 1942), Wadesboro (1938) [NCSA], Wake Forest (1939) [NCSA], Warrenton (1939, 1941), Winston-Salem (1938); **South Carolina:** Bishopville (1938), Blacksburg (1937), Camden (1938), Cheraw (1938), Chester (1937) [USC], Chesterfield (1938), Fort Mill (1937, 1939), Fountain Inn (1939), Gaffney (1937, 1938), Great Falls (1937, 1938) [USC], Hartsville (1938), Lancaster (1937), Lockhart (1937) [USC], Rock Hill (1937, 1938, 1939), Timmonsville (1938), Whitmire (1939) [DU], Winnsboro (1936), Woodruff (1939), York (1937); **Tennessee:** Mountain City (1940); **Virginia:** Bassett (1937, 1938, 1941), Damascus (1940) [DU], Dante (1940) [DU], Danville (1939) [DU], Fieldale (1937, 1941), Lebanon (1940) [DU], Martinsville (1937, 1938, 1939) [DU], Saltville (1940), Wytheville (1939) [DU]

Miscellaneous Local Gang Comedies (ca. 1925–1930)
Canada: Manitoba: Winnepeg, *Local Gang Comedy* (1930)
United States: Massachusetts: Boston: *School Daze* (ca. 1926–1929);[59] **New Mexico:** Albuquerque: *Our Local Gang Comedy* (1929); **New York:** Dunkirk: *Our Local Gang Comedy* (1928), Syracuse: *Our Gang Comedy* (1928); **North Carolina:** Reidsville: *Local Gang Comedy* (ca. 1930s); **Ohio:** Zanesville: *Our Gang Comedy* (1929); **Pennsylvania:** Oil City: *Our Gang Comedy* (1929), Uniontown: *Our Gang Comedy* (1928); **South Carolina:** Anderson: *Our Gang (aka A Free Ride)* (1925)[60]

Miscellaneous Local Films (Narrative)
United States: Alabama: Montgomery: *Present and Past in the Cradle of Dixie* (1914)[61]; **Illinois:** Alton: *Untitled Local Feature* (1915), dir. R. E. Norman, Chicago: *Who Is Sue?* (1914),[62] Springfield: *The Mine Owner's Daughter* (ca. 1910s); **Iowa:** Waterloo, *The Man at the Throttle* (1915); **Kentucky:** Lexington: *When the Tango Craze Hit Lexington* (1914); **Mississippi:** Picayune: *A Day in Hollywood* (1928), dir. Lem Kennedy; **Nebraska:** Chadron: *In the Days of '75 and '76* (1915),[63] Omaha: *Untitled Local Feature* (1916);[64] **North Dakota:** Casselton: Misc. local comedies (ca. 1920s), dir. Angela Miller, Grand Forks: *Grand Forks' Own Local Movies* (1934–1935);[65] **Ohio:** Dayton: *Untitled Local Feature* (1914);[66] **South Dakota:** Joyland: *It Happened in Joyland* (ca. 1910s);[67] **Tennessee:** Athens: *Untitled* (1940), prod. John B. Rogers Company, Kingston: *Untitled* (1939), Knoxville: *Aunt Sally Comes to Knoxville* (1915), *Too Much Flapper* (1928), dir. James Baret and Leona Hazlett, Sweetwater: *Untitled* (1937), prod. John B. Rogers Company; **Texas:** El Paso: *Untitled Local Feature* (1915), Galveston: *The Tangle* (1914), *Sky Eye* (1915), Greenville: *A Heart of the Hills* (1914), dir. Charles L. Hilger, *His Reward* (1920), dir. J. R. "Jack" Dugger, Lubbock: *Untitled Western* (1909), director listed as "A Man from California," San

Antonio: *Twin Stars* (1928), Victoria: *King Cowboy* (1934), dir. Josh Binney;
Wisconsin: Winona: *Untitled Local Feature* (ca. 1910s)[68]

Miscellaneous Local Films (Nonnarrative)
Canada: Alberta: Calgary, *Know Your Friends in Calgary* (1928)
United States: Arkansas: Fayatteville (1948), dir. Hal Parker; **Illinois:**
Highland, *Highland's Centennial* (1938); **Indiana:** Muncie: *Your Own Home
Town* (1936);[69] **Iowa:** Cedar Rapids (1913), prod. Advance Motion Picture
Company; **Michigan:** Rockford (1940),[70] Traverse City (1905); **North Carolina:**
Reidsville: *Reidsville on Parade* (1947),[71] Thomasville: *Thomasville on
Parade*;[72] **Pennsylvania:** Levittown: *Our Home Town*,[73] Waynesburg (ca.
1920); **South Dakota:** Britton, Untitled Series (1938–1939), dir. Ivan Besse;[74]
Tennessee: Athens, Erwin (1940), Harriman (1939), Livingstone (1940),
Rockwood (1951), Sweetwater; **Texas:** Commerce (1913), San Antonio (1913),
prod. Advance Motion Picture Company

NOTES

Thanks go to Margaret Compton, Karen Glynn, Martin L. Johnson, Bradley
Reeves, Karan Sheldon, Albert Steg, Dan Streible, Dwight Swanson, and
Louisa Trott for their contributions to the filmography.

1. Video located at the Rossville (IL) Historical Society.
2. Video located at Truman State University, Kirksville, Miss.
3. Video located at the Maryville Public Library, Miss.
4. Video located at the Fenton History Center, Jamestown, N.Y.
5. Video located at the Cuyahoga County Public Library, Ohio.
6. Video located at the St. Clairsville Public Library, Ohio.
7. Media related to this version located with private owner and Geneva
College Library, Beaver Falls, Pa.
8. Film located with private owner.
9. Video located at the California Historical Society, San Francisco.
10. Film and/or video possibly still located with local theater.
11. An 8mm film transfer (from original 16mm) with private owner.
12. Video located at the West Virginia State Archives, Charleston, W.V.
13. Ibid.
14. Film located at the Wisconsin Historical Society Archives, Madison,
Wisc.
15. Ibid.
16. Video located at the Sauk City Public Library, Wisc.
17. Video located at the Prairie Du Sac Public Library, Wisc.
18. Film and video located at Northeast Historic Film, Bucksport, Maine.
19. Video located at Northeast Historic Film, Bucksport, Maine.
20. Film and video located at Northeast Historic Film, Bucksport, Maine.
21. Ibid.

22. Film and video located at Northeast Historic Film, Bucksport, Maine.

23. Ibid.

24. Video located at the Reading Public Library, Mass.

25. Film located at Northeast Historic Film, Bucksport, Maine.

26. Ibid.

27. Video of the 1952 version located with private owner.

28. Film located at the Library of Congress's National Audiovisual Conservation Center, Culpeper, Va.

29. Film located with private owner.

30. Film and video located at the Saint Charles County Historical Society, Miss.

31. Film and video located at the Nebraska State Historical Society, Lincoln.

32. Media related to this version located with private owner as well as East Carolina State University, Greenville, N.C.

33. Video located at the Thomasville Public Library, N.C.

34. Film located at the Oklahoma Historical Society, Oklahoma City.

35. Video located at the Oklahoma Historical Society, Oklahoma City.

36. Film and video located at the Oklahoma Historical Society, Oklahoma City.

37. Film and video located at East Tennessee State University, Archives of Appalachia, Johnson City, Tenn.

38. Film located at the Library of Congress's National Audiovisual Conservation Center, Culpeper, Va.

39. Film and video located at the Texas Archive of the Moving Image. Also available online at http://www.texasarchive.org/library/index.php/ Collection_-_Melton_Barker_Juvenile_Productions.

40. Video of the 1943 version located at the Texas Archive of the Moving Image. Also available online at http://www.texasarchive.org/library/index. php/Collection_-_Melton_Barker_Juvenile_Productions.

41. Ibid.

42. Film located with private owner.

43. Film and video located at the Minnesota Historical Society, St. Paul.

44. Film and video located at the Oregon Historical Society, Portland.

45. Ibid.

46. Film and video located at Juniata College, Huntingdon, Pa.

47. Film and video located at the Wisconsin Historical Society Archives, Madison, Wisc.

48. Film and video located at Ball State University, Muncie, Ind. Also available online at http://libx.bsu.edu/collection. php?CISOROOT=%2Fmnhtrs.

49. Film located at Library and Archives Canada, Ottawa.

50. Film located at the Prescott County Library, Ariz.

51. Film located at the University of California, Los Angeles Film and Television Archive.

52. Media related to this version located with private owner as well as East Carolina State University, Greenville, N.C.

53. Video located at the Galesburg Public Library, Ill.

54. Film located at the Cumberland County Library, N.J.

55. Video located at the Monroe Public Library, N.C.

56. Film located with private owner.

57. Video located online at http://www.archive.org/details/OurHomeT1954.

58. Video located at the Texas Archive of the Moving Image. Also available online at http://www.texasarchive.org/library/index.php/Our_Home_Town.

59. Video located at Northeast Historic Film, Bucksport, Maine.

60. Film and video located at the University of South Carolina Newsfilm Library, Columbia.

61. Cited in Stephen Bottomore, "From the Factory Gate to the 'Home Talent' Drama: An International Overview of Local Films in the Silent Era," in *The Lost World of Mitchell and Kenyon: Edwardian Britain on Film*, ed. Vanessa Toulmin, Simon Popple, and Patrick Russell (London: BFI, 2004), 41.

62. Ibid.

63. Film located at the Nebraska State Historical Society, Lincoln.

64. Cited in Bottomore, "From the Factory Gate to the 'Home Talent' Drama," 41.

65. Film and video located at the State Historical Society of North Dakota, Bismarck.

66. Ibid.

67. Ibid.

68. Ibid.

69. Film and video located at the Muncie Public Library, Ind.

70. Video located at the Rockford Historical Society, Mich.

71. Media related to this version located with private owner as well as East Carolina State University, Greenville, N.C.

72. Video located at the Davidson County Historical Museum, N.C.

73. Video located online at http://www.archive.org/details/OurHomeT1954_2.

74. Video collection located online at http://www.archive.org/details/sIvanBes1938_10.

Contributors

Snowden Becker is a PhD candidate in the University of Texas at Austin's School of Information, studying how audiovisual materials are integrated into our larger cultural heritage. She is a cofounder of the international Home Movie Day event and the nonprofit Center for Home Movies.

Michael Berry is associate professor of contemporary Chinese cultural studies at the University of California, Santa Barbara. He is the author of *Speaking in Images: Interviews with Contemporary Chinese Filmmakers* (Columbia University Press, 2005; Rye Field, 2007; Guangxi Normal University Press, 2008), *A History of Pain: Trauma in Modern Chinese Literature and Film* (Columbia University Press, 2008), and *Jia Zhangke's* The Hometown Trilogy (BFI/Palgrave Macmillan, 2009; Guangxi Normal University Press, 2009). He is also the translator of several novels, including *The Song of Everlasting Sorrow* (with Susan Chan Egan; Columbia University Press, 2008), *To Live* (Anchor, 2004), *Nanjing 1937: A Love Story* (Columbia University Press, 2002; Anchor, 2004; Faber and Faber, 2004), and *Wild Kids: Two Novels about Growing Up* (Columbia University Press, 2000).

Margaret A. Compton received her MLIS from the University of Texas at Austin in 1997. She was assistant photo curator at the Academy of Motion Picture Arts and Sciences Library from 1998 through June 2001. Since July 2001, she has been the Media Archives Archivist for the University of Georgia Libraries' Walter J. Brown Media Archives and Peabody Awards Collection, preserving industrial films, campus films, three newsfilm archives, home movies, educational films, television kinescopes and videotapes, and audiotapes of radio programs and regional music. She is the recipient of five National Film Preservation Foundation grants to preserve home movies and one National Television and Videotape Preservation Foundation grant to preserve DuMont Television Network kinescopes. Her "Small Gauge and Amateur Film Bibliography" appeared in *Film History* 15, no. 2, in 2003, and her essay on television archiving and research use appeared in the spring 2007 issue of *Cinema Journal*.

Leo Enticknap is lecturer in cinema in the Louis Le Prince Centre for the Study of Cinema and Television, Institute of Communications Studies, University of Leeds, United Kingdom. He is also a member of the Association of Moving Image Archivists Board of Directors.

Caroline Frick is an assistant professor in the School of Information and the Department of Radio-TV-Film at the University of Texas at Austin. She is the founder and executive director of the Texas Archive of the Moving Image, an organization devoted to the discovery and preservation of media related to the state. Prior to her work in Texas, Dr. Frick worked in film preservation at Warner Bros., the Library of Congress, and the National Archives in Washington, D.C. Dr. Frick also programmed films for the American Movie Classics cable channel in New York and has served as a director of the board for the Association of Moving Image Archivists. Her book, *Saving Cinema*, is forthcoming from Oxford University Press.

Martin L. Johnson is a doctoral candidate in cinema studies at New York University. His research is on the production and theatrical exhibition of local films from the 1910s to the 1940s in the United States.

Jimi Jones is digital audiovisual formats specialist for the Office of Strategic Initiatives at the Library of Congress. Prior to working for the Library of Congress, Jimi served as project coordinator for the University of Illinois at Urbana-Champaign Library's Audiovisual Self-Assessment Program, an Institute of Museum and Library Services–funded project. He is a 2007 graduate of the University of Illinois at Urbana-Champaign's Graduate School of Library Science, where he continues to serve as adjunct professor for Audiovisual Materials in Libraries, Museums, and Archives. Prior to his master's work, he worked as an audiovisual archivist at the University of Utah's J. Willard Marriott Library. He spent two years developing the Marriott Library's Utah Independent Film Archive, a collection of film and video art made by Utah artists. Jimi has worked professionally as a videographer, cinematographer, and editor and, in 2003, received his bachelor's degree in film production at the University of Utah.

Regina Longo is a PhD candidate in the Department of Film and Media Studies at the University of California, Santa Barbara. She is currently writing her dissertation titled *Marshall Plan Films in Italy 1948–1955: A Project of Postwar Consensus Building.*

Devin Orgeron is associate professor and director of film studies at North Carolina State University. He is the author of *Road Movies* (Palgrave Macmillan, 2007), and his articles have appeared in such journals as *Cinema Journal, The Velvet Light Trap, Film Quarterly,* and *The Moving Image.* Devin is currently writing a book about contemporary American directors, such as Errol Morris and Spike Jonze, who also work in commercial advertising. He is the coeditor of *Learning with the Lights Off: A Reader in Educational Film* with Marsha Orgeron and Dan Streible (Oxford University Press, forthcoming).

Marsha Orgeron is associate professor of film studies at North Carolina State University. She is the author of *Hollywood Ambitions: Celebrity in the Movie Age* (Wesleyan University Press, 2008) and a dozen articles in books and journals such as *Film Quarterly, The Moving Image, Cinema Journal, Quarterly Review of Film and Video,* and *Historical Journal of Film, Radio, and Television.* She is currently at work on a book about director Sam Fuller's war films, beginning with the 16mm amateur footage he shot of the Falkenau concentration camp at the close of World War II. She is the coeditor of *Learning with the Lights Off: A Reader in Educational Film,* with Devin Orgeron and Dan Streible (Oxford University Press, 2011).

Bradley Reeves is a graduate of the L. Jeffrey Selznick School of Film Preservation and has worked on film collections at the National Archives, the Library of Congress, and the Archives of Appalachia, ranging from silent films made during Hollywood's first golden era in the 1920s to regional home movies. Reeves recently participated in preservation project reformatting and cataloging for portions of an extensive, fifty-year collection of 16mm newsfilm and obsolete video formats originating from Knoxville television station WBIR-TV. He is cofounder of the Tennessee Archive of Moving

Image and Sound in Knoxville and, along with Louisa Trott, has curated many archival film screenings throughout Knoxville and east Tennessee. The pair also present a weekly radio show featuring archival material and the other vinyl treasures they have discovered.

Sarah Resnick is a graduate of the program in moving image archiving and preservation at New York University. She has since worked on a project basis for several artists and filmmakers and institutions such as the Museum of Modern Art and the library at the International Center for Photography. She is also editor at large for the online publication *Triple Canopy.*

Karan Sheldon cofounded Northeast Historic Film. She served on the Association of Moving Image Archivists Board of Directors from 2007 through 2009 and as founding treasurer in 2001. In 2010, she has been engaged in "Intellectual Access to Moving Images of Work Life," a project describing fifty Northeast Historic Film collections online. The results may be found at http://www.oldfilm.org/. She enjoys making expressive timelines, three examples being Amateur Film Preservation in the Context of AMIA, a forty-foot theater mural, and a chronology of Northeast Historic Film.

Albert Steg is a freelance archivist, Filemaker Pro database developer, and film collector living in Cambridge, Massachusetts. He holds master's degrees in philosophy (Edinburgh University) and English (Boston University). In 2004, he left his position as head of the English Department at the Winsor School in Boston to pursue a career in moving image archiving. Since completing the Selznick School program at George Eastman House in 2005, he has reorganized the film collection of the Baseball Hall of Fame, joined the board of the Center for Home Movies, and provided Filemaker cataloging solutions for a number of moving image archives and art collections.

Dwight Swanson is an itinerant archivist who has worked at film archives in Alaska, Maine, Wisconsin, the District of Columbia, Kentucky, and Pennsylvania. He now lives in Baltimore, Maryland. He is a cofounder of the Center for Home Movies and Home Movie Day.

Vanessa Toulmin is director of the National Fairground Archive and chair in Early Film and Popular Entertainment at the University of Sheffield. She has published widely on all aspects of early cinema and tenth-century entertainment, including *Electric Edwardians: The Story of the Mitchell and Kenyon Collection, Visual Delights, Pleasurelands,* and other publications.

Louisa Trott is cofounder of the Tennessee Archive of Moving Image and Sound. She earned an MA in film archiving at the University of East Anglia, United Kingdom, in 2003. Prior to her MA, she worked as a film cataloger and researcher at the Imperial War Museum Film and Video Archive in London, primarily on the amateur material in the collection. After graduating, she worked as a cataloger and researcher on Screen Archive South East's online access project (University of Brighton, United Kingdom). She has presented papers on film preservation–related topics at the Orphan Film Symposium, the Society of Tennessee Archivists, universities and historical societies, and has curated many archival film screenings throughout Knoxville and east Tennessee. Along with Bradley Reeves, she presents a weekly radio show featuring archival material and the other vinyl treasures they have discovered.

Nathan Wagoner is an artist and filmmaker. He manages the Digital Media Studio, a student-staffed media production unit at Jumata College in Huntingdon, Pennsylvania.

Denise J. Youngblood is a professor of history at the University of Vermont and has written extensively on Russian cinema, most recently, *Cinematic Cold War: The American and Soviet Struggle for Hearts and Minds*.

EXPLORING FILM & ART

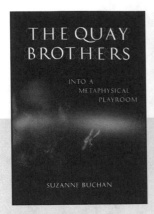

THE QUAY BROTHERS
INTO A METAPHYSICAL PLAYROOM
Suzanne Buchan

Known for their animation shorts that rely on puppetry, miniatures, and stop-motion techniques, the Quay Brothers's fiercely idiosyncratic films are fertile fields for Suzanne Buchan's engaging descriptions and provocative insights into their art—and into the art of independent puppet animation.

$25.00 paper • $75.00 cloth • 296 pages

JAPANESE COUNTERCULTURE
THE ANTIESTABLISHMENT ART OF TERAYAMA SHŪJI
Steven C. Ridgely

In this inventive and revealing study, Steven C. Ridgely examines Terayama Shūji's life and art to show that a conventional notion of him does not do full justice to the meaning and importance of his wide-ranging, often playful body of work.

$22.50 paper • $67.50 cloth • 264 pages

DREAM FACTORIES OF A FORMER COLONY
AMERICAN FANTASIES, PHILIPPINE CINEMA
José B. Capino

By tracking American fantasies in Philippine movies from the postindependence period to the present, José B. Capino offers an innovative account of cinema's cultural work in decolonization and globalization.

$25.00 paper • $75.00 cloth • 320 pages

YELLOW FUTURE
ORIENTAL STYLE IN HOLLYWOOD CINEMA
Jane Chi Hyun Park

In *Yellow Future*, Jane Chi Hyun Park examines the emergence and popularity of techno-oriental representations in Hollywood cinema since the 1980s, focusing on the collective fantasy of East Asia as the future.

$25.00 paper • $75.00 cloth • 272 pages

University of Minnesota Press • www.upress.umn.edu • 800-621-2736

BLACK CAMERA

IU Press, in partnership with the Indiana University Black Film Center/Archive, is now the publisher of *Black Camera*, The New Series, edited by Michael T. Martin.

Black Camera is devoted to the study of the black cinematic experience and is the only scholarly film journal of its kind in the United States. It features essays and interviews that engage film in social as well as political contexts and in relation to historical and economic forces that bear on the reception, distribution, and production of film in local, regional, national, and transnational settings and environments.

Published semiannually

eISSN 1947-4237 | pISSN 1536-3155

SUBSCRIPTIONS

Individuals: electronic $37.80; electronic & print $46.20; print $42.00
Institutions: electronic $76.50; electronic & print $119.00; print $85.00
Print Single Issues: general $26.00; thematic $29.00
Foreign first class postage: $10.50 | Foreign airmail postage: $18.00
Electronic Single Issues: general $22.50; thematic $24.50

SUBSCRIBE   800-842-6796 | 812-855-8817
http://inscribe.iupress.org
iuporder@indiana.edu
ADVERTISE   http://inscribe.iupress.org/page/advertising
CONTRIBUTE   Contact Mary Huesback, mhuelsbe@indiana.edu

INDIANA UNIVERSITY PRESS
INDIANA UNIVERSITY

IUP/*Journals*

601 North Morton Street, Bloomington, Indiana 47404-3797 USA

CANADIAN JOURNAL OF FILM STUDIES
REVUE CANADIENNE D'ÉTUDES CINÉMATOGRAPHIQUES

Scholarly articles in English and French on theory, history and criticism of film and media; book reviews; rare and archival research documents.

The journal is edited by Catherine Russell and Charles Acland at Concordia University. Submissions are welcome at cjfsedit@filmstudies.ca.

VOLUME 19 NO. 1   SPRING • PRINTEMPS 2010

SUBSCRIPTIONS

Individuals, $35 (CAD) in Canada; $35 (US) in all other countries.

Institutions, $45 (CAD) in Canada; $45 (US) in all other countries.

Payment to the **Canadian Journal of Film Studies** Department of Communication Studies Wilfrid Laurier University Waterloo, ON, Canada N2L 3C5 Fax: (613) 533-2063

E-mail: cjfs@post.queensu.ca Website: www.filmstudies.ca/journal

CJFS / RCEC is published biannually by the *Film Studies Association of Canada / Association canadienne d'études cinématographiques*

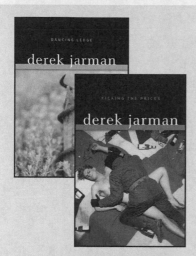